For Keith,

From one old fart to
another, to remind you of the
advertising life we enjoyed at
Dorland.

Tony.

1997.

Vet in Africa

Vet in Africa

Life on the Zambezi
1913-1933

Selected Letters
and Memoirs
of John Smith

Edited and with
commentary by
Tony Bagnall Smith

The Radcliffe Press
London • New York

Published in 1997 by
The Radcliffe Press
Victoria House
Bloomsbury Square
London
WC1B 4DZ

In the United States of America
and Canada, distributed by
St Martin's Press
175 Fifth Avenue
New York
NY 10010

A full CIP record of this book is available from
the British Library and the Library of Congress

ISBN 1 86064 132 6

Typeset and designed by Dexter Haven, London
Printed in Great Britain by WBC Ltd, Bridgend, Mid Glamorgan

For John Smith's daughter, Diana;
for his grandchildren, Jeremy, Sally, Sarah and Richard;
for his great-grandchildren, Clemmie, Patrick, Clare,
Freddie, Lucy, Archie, Henry and Fergus.

Contents

Foreword
Baroness Chalker of Wallasey

As one who has had the good fortune to visit Africa regularly since 1983, this remarkable diary has produced a perspective and filled in gaps in a delightful way. So many of the character pictures remain true today among the rural people of Zambia. The descriptions of animals, Victoria Falls and some travels immediately strike chords in harmony with my own experience up country.

In every way, John Smith was far more than 'a vet in Africa'. Time and time again, I stopped reading to recall my experiences of the modern challenge to improve life for local people. A sound colonial inheritance was too often undermined by the inadequacy of the immediate post-independence development programmes. In more recent years, concentrating on basic needs is helping to increase vital skills, but there is as great a need as ever for modern John Smiths in Africa. Such people deserve substantial donor support and local cooperation if the aspirations of today's Matapis, Sufus, Jakes and Masanges are ever to be realised.

Many of the descriptive passages, especially those about care of cattle and human beings, as well as of the rise and fall of copperbelt fortunes, bring home lessons that we have continued to relearn over the past 50 years. It is still true that if African nations are to prosper, there must be regular progress in agriculture and pastoral life. Funds generated by industrial prosperity still need to be ploughed back into basic health care and education for the ever burgeoning populations of African children.

I never met John Smith, but from these diaries I feel I knew a remarkable man of vision and tenacity. No wonder he was held in such high regard in Africa and in the UK.

Thank you Tony Bagnall Smith, his son, for reminding us of the lessons your father learnt and taught so many of us.

Acknowledgements

I am delighted to have the opportunity to thank all those who have helped me with this book. Very especially I want to thank three people. First, my dear Gordon McKenzie, who gave me tremendous encouragement from the outset and who went to very great trouble to introduce me, personally, to a number of his publisher friends. Then, Canon Denys Whitehead and his wife, Margaret, who were kindness itself when I visited Livingstone and who, through their fascinating *The Story of Livingstone, Tourist Capital of Zambia*, provided me with much detailed information. Thirdly, I am extremely grateful to Lynda Chalker, Baroness Chalker of Wallasey, for sparing the time to write the foreword when she leads such a hectic life.

Others helped me here and in Zambia and I hope they will forgive me for listing them alphabetically: they will each know how much they have contributed to the project. I could not have put this book together without their help. Nor would John Smith's story have appeared without the continuous support and enthusiasm of my wife, Jean. She gave me every encouragement from the beginning and then, at the very end, tidied up my final draft.

Claire Brown
Michael Carmichael
Tom Cotton
Marilynne Elliott
Samantha Hatzis
Alison Shepherd
Nigel Viney
Kelvin White
Kristine Ese (Lusaka)
Flexon M. Mizinga (Livingstone Museum)
Mazson Mundandwe (National Heritage Commission, Livingstone)
Alastair Robertson (Livingstone)

I also want to thank Dr Lester Crook and his colleagues at the Radcliffe Press. He held my hand and gently steered me along, whilst the team gave me every support and much practical help.

Prologue

'You can understand why the natives call them "Mosi-oa -Tunya", "the smoke that thunders",' shouted my father, cupping his hands round my ear. He, my mother and I were standing beside the Victoria Falls, dressed in oilskins and sou'westers, with spray streaming down our faces, mesmerised by the blur of the foam and battered by the noise.

That was 1932, when I was a small boy of seven.

A few days later, my mother and I were to leave Northern Rhodesia for the last time, and were making our farewells from the spot where David Livingstone had stood when, in 1855, he had discovered and named the greatest falls on earth; a spot we had stood upon scores of times before.

As the Zambezi roars over the sheer land-fault that slashed its course from side to side a hundred and fifty million years ago, the waters plunge 350 feet to the cauldron below, hurling thousands of gallons of spray three times that height to fall back, drenching the whole area, aptly named the Rain Forest.

Sixty years later, the scene is still secure in my memory. This is, I'm sure, because over all those years four large, sepia photographs of the Falls, taken and signed by the pioneer and photographer Percy Clark, in the first years of this century, have hung in our home.

One morning recently, I found myself staring at those photographs as long-forgotten memories crowded into my head; I seemed to be living back in Central Africa rather than in Southern England in the 1990s. So vivid were my recollections, and so poignant the moment, that I resolved, there and then, to set down the story of my father's life in Africa. I would edit it from the letters he had written home to his family before and during the First World War.

It would be a record of colonial life, 80 years ago... I would call it *Vet in Africa*.

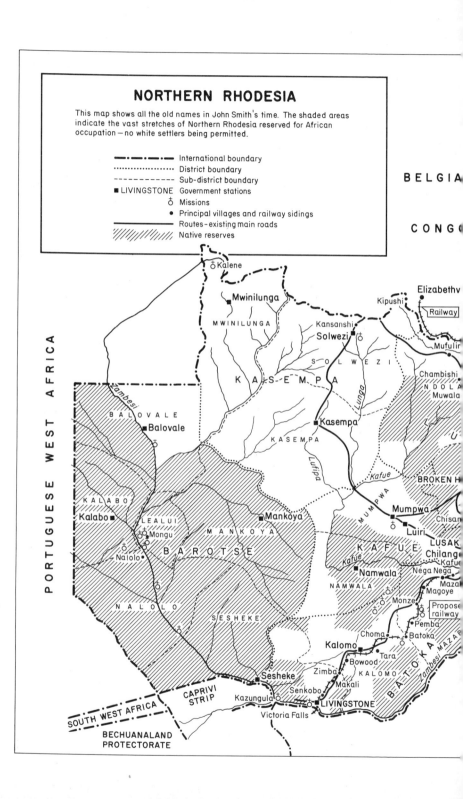

NORTHERN RHODESIA

This map shows all the old names in John Smith's time. The shaded areas indicate the vast stretches of Northern Rhodesia reserved for African occupation — no white settlers being permitted.

▬·▬·▬·	International boundary
··········	District boundary
----------	Sub-district boundary
■ LIVINGSTONE	Government stations
⚥	Missions
●	Principal villages and railway sidings
▬▬▬	Routes - existing main roads
/////////	Native reserves

BELGIA

CONGO

Kalene

Mwinilunga

MWINILUNGA

Kipushi

Elizabethv

Railway

Kansanshi
Solwezi

Mufulir

S O L W E Z I

Chambishi
NDOLA
Muwala

K A S E M P A

Zambesi

B A L O V A L E
Balovale

KASEMPA

Kasempa

Lufipa

Kafue

BROKEN H

KALABO
Kalabo

LEALUI
Mongu
Nalolo

M A N K O Y A

Mankoya

MUMPWA

Mumpwa
Luiri

Chisan

LUSAK

B A R O T S E

Kafue

K A F U E

Chilang
Kafue

Namwala

Nega Nega

Maza
Magoye

N A L O L O

NAMWALA

Monze

Propose
railway

SESHEKE

Pemba

Choma
Batoka

Kalomo

B A T O K A

Zambesi MAZAB

Sesheke

Zimba
Senkobo
Makali

KALOMO

Bowood
Tara

CAPRIVI
STRIP

Kazungula

Senkobo

LIVINGSTONE

SOUTH WEST AFRICA

Victoria Falls

BECHUANALAND
PROTECTORATE

P O R T U G U E S E   W E S T   A F R I C A

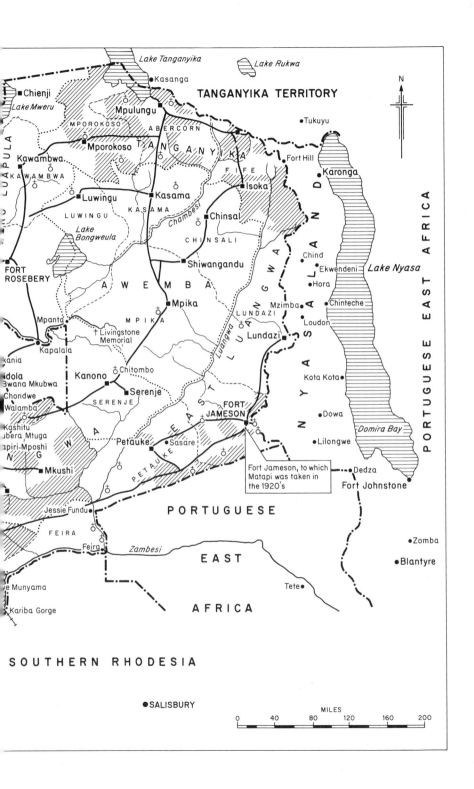

Lake Tanganyika · Lake Rukwa

■ Chienji · Kasanga   **TANGANYIKA TERRITORY**

Lake Mweru

·Tukuyu

Mpulungu

MPOROKOSO   A B E R C O R N

■ Mporokoso   T A N G A N Y·I K A   ·Fort Hill

Kawambwa   F I F E   Karonga·

K A W A M B W A   ·Isoka

■ Luwingu   ■ Kasama   K A S A M A   *Chambesi*   ■ Chinsal   CHINSALI   Chind·
·Ekwendeni   *Lake Nyasa*

L U W I N G U   ·Hora

Lake Bongweula

FORT ROSEBERY   A W E M B A   ■ Shiwangandu   Mzimba·   ·Chinteche

M P I K A   ·Mpika   LUNDAZI   ·Loudon

Mpanta·   † Livingstone Memorial   Lundazi■   Kota Kota·

Kapalala   ·Chitombo

Kanono   Kota Kota·

■ Serenje   SERENJE   ·Dowa

·Lilongwe

■ Mkushi   Petauke·   ·Sasare   **FORT JAMESON**

Jessie Fundu·   Fort Jameson, to which Matapi was taken in the 1920's   ·Dedza   **Fort Johnstone**

FEIRA   **P O R T U G U E S E**

Feira   *Zambesi*   **E A S T**   ·Zomba

·Blantyre

·Munyama   **A F R I C A**   Tete·

Kariba Gorge

S O U T H E R N   R H O D E S I A

·**SALISBURY**

P O R T U G U E S E   E A S T   A F R I C A

N Y A S A L A N D

L U A N G W A

L U A P U L A

MILES

0   40   80   120   160   200

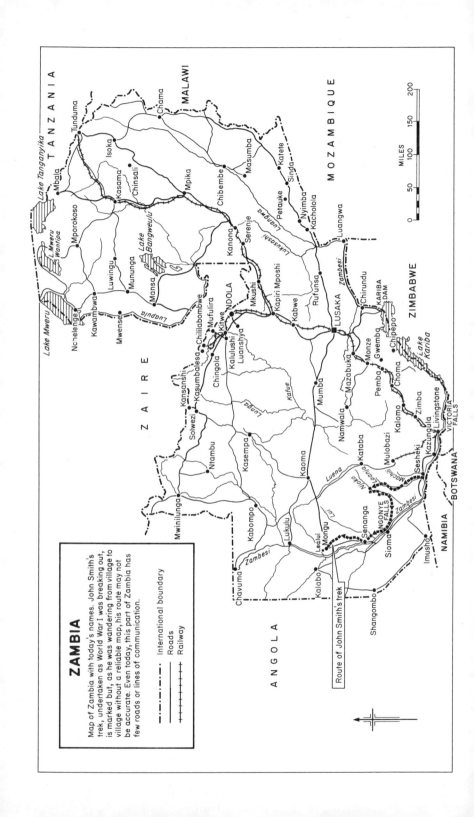

ZAMBIA

Map of Zambia with today's names. John Smith's trek, undertaken as World War I was breaking out, is marked but, as he was wandering from village to village without a reliable map, his route may not be accurate. Even today, this part of Zambia has few roads or lines of communication.

—··—··— International boundary
+++++++ Roads
++++++ Railway

Route of John Smith's trek

MILES
0   50   100   150   200

TANZANIA

Lake Tanganyika

MALAWI

Mbala
Tunduma
Moorpoko
Isoka
Chama
L. Mweru Wantipa
Kasama
Chinsali
Masumba
Lake Mweru
Mporokoso
Mpika
Chibembe
Katete
Sinda
Petauke
Nyimba
Kacholola

Luwingu
Mununga
Lake Bangweulu
Kanona
Serenje
Luangwa

ZAIRE

Nchelenge
Kawambwa
Mwense
Mansa
Luapula
Mkushi
Kapiri Mposhi
Rufunsa
Chirundu
KARIBA DAM

Mwinilunga
Kansanshi
Kasumbalesa
Chililabombwe
Mufulira
NDOLA
Kitwe
Chingola
Kalulushi
Luanshya
Kabwe
LUSAKA
Monze
Gwembe
Chipepo
Lake Kariba

Solwezi
Ntambu
Kasempa
Lunga
Kafue
Mumbwa
Mazabuka
Pemba
Choma
Zimba
Livingstone
VICTORIA FALLS

ZIMBABWE

Kabompo
Kaoma
Luena
Namwala
Kataba
Mulobazi
Kalomo
Kazungula

ANGOLA

Chavuma
Lukulu
Lui
Lealui
Mongu
Senanga
NGONYE FALLS
Sioma
Sesheke
Machili
Loanja
Njoko

Kalabo
Zambesi
Zambesi

Shangombo
Imusho

NAMIBIA

BOTSWANA

MOZAMBIQUE

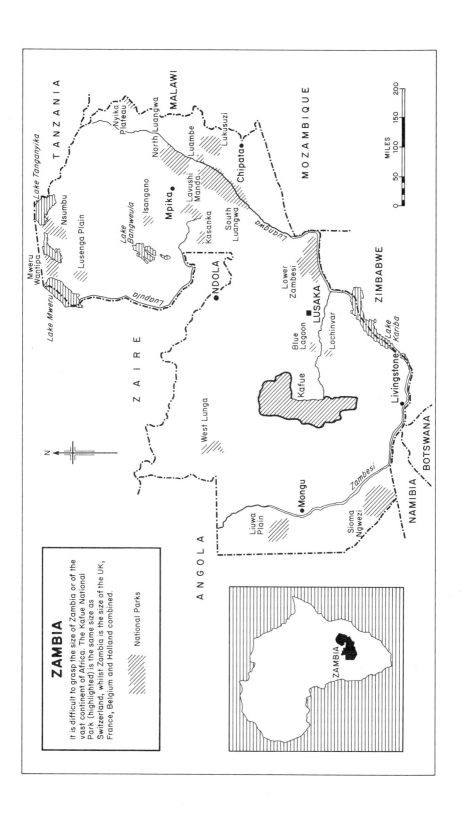

ZAMBIA

It is difficult to grasp the size of Zambia or of the vast continent of Africa. The Kafue National Park (highlighted) is the same size as Switzerland, whilst Zambia is the size of the UK, France, Belgium and Holland combined.

National Parks

MILES
0 50 100 150 200

N

TANZANIA

Lake Tanganyika

Nsumbu

Mweru Wantipa

Lake Mweru

Lusenga Plain

ZAIRE

Luapula

Lake Bangweulu

Isangano

Mpika

Nyika Plateau

North Luangwa

MALAWI

Luambe

Lukusuzi

Lavushi Manda

Kasanka

South Luangwa

Chipata

Luangwa

MOZAMBIQUE

NDOLA

West Lunga

Kafue

Lower Zambesi

Blue Lagoon

LUSAKA

Lochinvar

ZIMBABWE

Lake Kariba

Livingstone

Mongu

Zambesi

Liuwa Plain

Sioma Ngwezi

NAMIBIA

BOTSWANA

ANGOLA

ZAMBIA

Vet in Africa

Introduction

I was born in Livingstone, Northern Rhodesia, in 1925. My father always claimed that I was the youngest white child ever to see the Victoria Falls; it seems he had shown them to me, aged four days, when he had driven my mother and her baby son home from hospital.

Back in England, in 1933, I began to badger my father to write an account of his early days, before the First World War, when he was a junior official in Africa, but it was not until 1938 that he got down to the task. For my Christmas present that year he wrote, in his neat sloping hand, 180 pages about those days.

On a number of occasions my father had pondered the fate of the letters he had written home, but it was not until 1951 that they were discovered, in the loft of his family home, after the death of his sister, who had lived there all her life. There were 660 closely written foolscap sheets and, as I had the manuscript, I was given the letters.

The events of which my father wrote seemed to be so dramatically distant; they concerned native chieftains, the bush telegraph, crocodiles and prowling lions; all encountered, not on a well-rehearsed safari, but in the course of a day's work.

But John Smith must tell his own tale.

Kenley, Surrey
Christmas 1938
My dear Tony,
You asked me to write something of my experiences in Africa. Well, this is a start. I have tried to think of things that would interest you and which are of the Africa that is quickly disappearing. Conditions are changing, and much of the glamour is gone. The old African, such as I knew in Barotseland, was a fine fellow. The only way

really to get to know him was to move slowly through the country, as I did, living practically with him.

I tried to treat Africa well: it did well for me.

Perhaps you will read what follows with the greater interest because of your early days out there. Born, as you were, within sound of the Victoria Falls, I hope you will always remember those natives whom you knew, and who looked after you so well.

Your loving,
Father.

A few of the words and expressions we shall read may seem out of order today – offensive even – but they were commonplace before World War I. My father wrote of 'natives', 'boys', 'piccaninnies' and 'servants', all acceptable then, and widely used. Now, they may be distasteful. However, his true feelings for the African show through the language he uses; the admiration, trust and mutual affection are evident in letter after letter, as he recounts their experiences together. As he wrote in that letter, 'I tried to treat Africa well: it did well for me.'

My father's family were inclined to be straight-laced: they were pillars of the church and not what might be described as widely-travelled or worldly-wise. Also, they will not have found it easy to grasp how dramatically their ewe lamb's life had changed.

He, understandably, did not want to shock or upset his folk in Lancashire, so we can detect a certain restraint in some of what he wrote, particularly concerning illness or personal danger. It is interesting that he never told of the occasions when he shot lions or leopards, yet he did both; he obviously felt such news would cause undue alarm.

It might also be helpful to have a quick formula for translating sterling cost figures for 1913 into present-day equivalents. By happy chance, the Central Statistical Office began its cost comparison tables in 1914, so the reader has only to multiply by forty to get a rough reckoning.

1

John Smith, Veterinary Surgeon

H e was plain John Smith; his father, too, was plain John Smith, and they both came from Wigan. Yet these unromantic facts seemed to do neither of them much harm!

John Smith senior had been a machinist in a wool spinning factory and had married a local girl, Jane Heaton. Jane's mother had been a Bagnall and it was her name that my father, her grandson, chose to give to my sister and myself at our christenings.

By all accounts, my grandfather was a remarkable man. He graduated from minding a piece of machinery to being his own boss, with a considerable woollens business producing socks, pullovers and scarves. His affairs prospered and, in 1913, he built a large factory in the middle of Wigan and had the words 'Smiths Progress Works' picked out in bricks on the side facing the main thoroughfare.

This slightly pretentious name was, however, fully justified, as John Smith senior had many progressive ideas. Long before it was generally accepted, his employees all had paid holidays and were covered by a simple health insurance scheme.

A substantial part of the profits he made, from supplying woollen garments to the forces in World War I, was committed to helping build a new Baptist church, maintaining beds in a local hospital and providing funds to support missionaries in the Belgian Congo.

I cannot claim to remember my grandfather, but I recall my mother describing him as one of the kindest and dearest men she had ever known; this despite the fact that he had caused her to be reprimanded for knitting, one Sunday, for my unborn sister, whilst staying under his roof in Wigan!

Of my grandmother, Jane, I know practically nothing, except that she bore three sons and two daughters, and supported her

husband with many acts of kindness and generosity amongst the
all-too-numerous poor in that mining town so beloved of comedians.

On 4 May 1883, at 16 King Street, a son was born to Jane, the
last of her five children. He was christened John.

John's letters and essays give little away about what made him
tick. So I must try and paint a word picture, to show him as flesh
and blood, rather than an impersonal pen scribing his journeys and
adventures across the pages. Especially must I try to explain what
persuaded him, suddenly, to go off into the wild, what made him
such a dedicated veterinary surgeon, animal husbandrist and
agriculturalist and, above all, what caused him to throw himself
into a career devoted to improving the general lot of central
Africans.

My father was of slight build, weighing under ten stone; he was
wiry and sufficiently athletic to become an outstanding horseman,
an adequate golfer, a social tennis player and a keen walker. He
also claimed to have played the drums!

He was what would, in those days, have been called nice-
looking, with crisp, wavy brown hair and a neat moustache. He was
always well turned out, and cut a rather dashing figure in uniform.

Being almost totally unshy in the presence of both men and
women, he would have a go at most things, and was always in
demand for what are, rather unnervingly, called 'social activities',
amateur dramatics, party gatherings, picnics etc. Men found him
clubbable, whilst women could rely on him to be attentive and good
company.

He had a balanced sense of humour, and a splendid sense of
the absurd and of irony, although he somehow contrived to avoid
bursting into laughter, preferring a broad grin to signal his
enjoyment of a situation or story. He had a deep understanding and
appreciation of the Lancashire way of life and its humour, and was
a first-class mimic of its accent.

From time to time, however, grey clouds of melancholy could
gather and cast shadows over what was, fundamentally, a sunny
disposition. But he was unfailingly kind and always gentle.

He could be exacting in matters of discipline, but never stern.
He was forthright in his views and could be a touch intolerant; one

of his favourite comments was that 'so-and-so hasn't sufficient nous to run the last ten minutes of a thoroughly bad Sunday-school treat!'

My father was modest of his own achievements, never arrogant or self-opinionated; he was a polished speaker, and took pride in producing clear and succinct written work.

One of his characteristics was that he never panicked: the greater the drama, the calmer my father became. Major problems brought out all his strengths and, as friends and colleagues experienced this trait, they tended to gravitate towards him in times of crisis. He would have been a good man with whom to share a slit trench!

If John Smith was invariably at ease with his fellow humans, he was even more so with animals. As we shall read, he was, from his earliest days, determined to be involved with their welfare, having that gift of instinctively establishing a bond with all sick and hurt creatures.

My father's life falls neatly into three phases. Up to the age of 30, he was in England at school, university, and practising his veterinary and agricultural skills. Then, for the next 20 years, he was in Africa, except for war service. This volume will chronicle his life out there until he retired voluntarily, but prematurely, and found himself jobless back in England.

The story which follows needs to be enjoyed against the backdrop of his whole life so, before he sets sail from Southampton, it would be helpful if he tells us, in his own words, of those first 30 years. I will then tail this with a brief account of his later career, after he retired to England.

All my life I have been fond of animals and, although I was born in a large industrial town, I took every opportunity to get out into the countryside.

A few minutes from home, there were some Scottish farmers whom I got to know, and I used to spend a great deal of my holidays on their farm so that, by the time I was 16, I could milk, ride and drive horses, plough with a wheeled plough and do all sorts of jobs amongst the animals.

I was also fond of reading. My favourite author was Rider Haggard, and I knew every bit of such books as *King Solomon's Mines* and *She*: Alan Quattermain and Umslopogas were old friends of mine. So, of course, I wanted to go to Africa.

After leaving school, I became a student at the agricultural school at the Harris Institute at Preston. In the vacation, I was a pupil at the farm of the Lancashire County Council at Hutton. At the end of two-and-a-half years I received the diploma in agriculture and dairying.

By now, I had realised that it took far more money than I had to start farming; so I decided to take the veterinary course as the next best thing. I went up to Edinburgh University in 1902, aged 19, and moved with that veterinary school to Liverpool University in 1904. I qualified in 1906, and managed to win the gold medal for all England.

I stayed on at Liverpool for another year to take the first post-graduate course open to veterinarians, the Diploma in Veterinary Hygiene, known as the DVH.

I now had to get a job.

My first was with the London Roadcar Omnibus Company, whose buses were drawn by horses. I was to work on the feeding formula to reduce the cost by half a penny per horse per day. I failed! In fact, my efforts resulted in the cost rising by that very amount but, happily, the health and fitness of their hundreds of horses improved noticeably.

I wanted, however, to get amongst farm animals, for I was always more interested in them. My last year at Liverpool had been a training in housing, feeding and management of stock – what is now called animal husbandry – as this branch of veterinary work always intrigued me more than just the treatment of sick animals.

Eventually, I managed to become assistant in a large farming veterinary practice at Luton and St Albans. It was hard work with long hours. I seldom finished before 8.00 in the evening, six days a week, and 1 or 2 o'clock on Sundays. But I was thoroughly happy.

I was lucky enough to get some hunting and an occasional day's coursing. On the days when I was hunting – in my official capacity as attendant vet – I got up early and did some work, and then finished it off when I returned in the evening.

The farmers were all good sorts, managing large acreages; my agricultural training helped, as I knew more about crops and foodstuffs than the majority of veterinary surgeons.

I had made up my mind to start a small farm as soon as I could manage it, and keep myself going financially with veterinary practice, until I could afford to buy a bigger place and give all my time to it. Very soon, however, I began to get cold feet. Cars were arriving on the scene, and people were saying that they would replace horses altogether, even on the farms. The paying part of the practice was horses, a farmer not being able to afford to pay vet's fees – which could be large – on farm animals. Sadly, it was often cheaper to slaughter them.

I had stayed at Luton for three years because I was getting such valuable experience. But I had no wish to go on in practice all my life and so, after thinking it over carefully, I decided to try something else. I went back to Wigan to stay with my father, my mother having died in 1910, aged 67, whilst I was at Luton.

———•———

We will leave John Smith in the terraced house at 6 Clifton Crescent, in the late winter of 1913 and, leap-frogging the next 20 years covered in the pages which follow, pick up this brief biography as he joins my mother Beryl, my sister Diana and myself in a rather nasty and cheerless rented house in Surrey, exactly 20 years later.

———•———

Caterham, Surrey
January 1933

We were all depressed… the sun refused to shine, it was wretchedly dark and cold, and I was far from happy at joining my sister, for the winter term, at a girls' school just down the road. On top of it all, my father's spirits had, understandably, hit one of their occasional lows.

Four weeks earlier, in the blazing sun and blistering heat, he had been the toast of Northern Rhodesia, a very senior official, highly respected throughout the territory, and much loved by whites and blacks alike. He had been the Rt Hon. John Smith, OBE, JP, MRCVS, DVH, MLC. Suddenly, huddled before an inadequate and aged gas fire, he realised he was back to being plain John Smith, and out of work!

But, as is usually the case, within weeks things began to look up. We were offered a suitable and newly decorated house to rent, in Kenley, on a long and favourable lease; my father was asked to seek out, and buy, several hunters and hacks for our wealthy and generous landlord – a fellow Lancastrian – and my mother found herself in demand for tennis, mah-jong and tea parties. I started at a happy, if rather ineffectual, boys' prep school, incongruously named St Winifred's!

My father needed a job urgently, and began answering advertisements.

The whole western world was in the grip of the severest slump ever known, and unemployment was widespread. Because he had not been directly involved with domestic agricultural or veterinary matters for 20 years, he was not an obviously attractive proposition to UK employers. So it was a considerable achievement on his part, soon after he retired, to reach the last two in the selection process for the post of the first director general of the Milk Marketing Board, which was just being set up. After that, few suitable job opportunities were forthcoming. Still not 50, John Smith wanted, and indeed needed, full-time activity and income-producing employment. So, once again, his thoughts turned to farming.

He had, over a long period, made a study of pig breeding and management, and had formulated theories which, he believed, could enable farmers to enjoy a less volatile and risky occupation. He was keen to put these theories to the test and began to look for a suitable farm. But, when he couldn't find what he wanted after a few months, his courage began to fail him and, although he pursued this project somewhat half-heartedly for some years, he could not bring himself to cast the die and 'have a go'.

In the autumn of 1933, he was invited, out of the blue, to join the Colonial Advisory Council of Agriculture and Animal Hygiene. This was a highly influential body and my father was delighted. Quite suddenly, he found himself 'back in the swim' with committee work involving subjects of which he was a master. Gradually, he was being dragged back into the mainstream of his professional field, even if he still hankered after a more physically active and outdoor life.

By 1937, his contributions to the council caused him to be appointed chairman of its standing committee on animal health.

In January 1936, he was appointed a member of the Agricultural Research Council of Great Britain. This was a considerable feather in John Smith's cap. At last, three years after arriving back in the UK, he was officially recognised as one of the country's leading authorities on animal health and husbandry, and on agricultural research. His letter of appointment, signed by Ramsay MacDonald, the Labour Prime Minister, was on Privy Council paper with a broad, black border, a sign of respect for the recent death of King George V.

My father served on the ARC for almost ten years – an unusually long stint – and, over that period, was to be a member of the Loveday Committee on Veterinary Education which laid the foundation of modern veterinary training and practice, and also of the Poultry Technical Committee.

During these years, he was also chairman of the Army Veterinary Committee as well as, with the redoubtable Sir Merrick Burrell, an outside examiner for veterinary scholarships at Cambridge University.

Whilst John Smith was not, by instinct or inclination, a committee man, he was able to contribute significantly to the deliberations of those on which he served, because of his unusually wide and practical experience. In today's expression he had 'been there – seen it – done it'.

Although my father was now, a little surprisingly, a pillar of the agricultural and veterinary establishment in the UK, he was, in his terms anyway, far from fully occupied, and the 1930s slipped past without him enjoying the deep sense of satisfaction and achievement he sought; he desperately missed being in the thick of the action.

Then came the war, and John Smith was, instantly, back in his element.

He worked on projects connected with the production of food for both humans and livestock, and suggested a number of initiatives of material significance. He joined the Home Guard, firewatched in London and in the country, and energetically 'dug for victory'. As one would have expected, he was always calm, optimistic and resourceful, and a source of great strength to all around him, as well as to his two children in the forces.

But of greater importance, to the war effort and himself, was being called to London in 1940 as a special adviser on animal health to the Secretary of State for the Colonies, with the rank of under secretary. He was given an office immediately beside that of his cabinet minister and sought, and was given, a free hand to involve himself in any subject, or matter, on which he felt able to make a contribution.

John Smith was back on form, and began making up for what he regarded as the past years of relative inactivity by throwing himself headlong into his new post. I suspect he did not always endear himself to the permanent civil servants, as he was prone to cut procedural corners to achieve his objectives. In Northern Rhodesia, he had succeeded in getting things done with the minimum of delay and bureaucratic interference, and he set about operating in London in a similar manner.

During the war, he twice went to Africa, some of the way by flying boat, to try, once again, to reduce the scourge of trypanosomiasis and other devastating cattle diseases. Although he reached into Central Africa, he never managed to visit Northern Rhodesia again. When the war ended, he was asked to stay on for three more years to help get things back to normal.

My father served a number of secretaries of state, of both parties. The minister who impressed him most was Harold Macmillan, and we were often regaled with stories of his calm decisiveness. He never forgot, apparently, that he was a publisher by trade; one day, he wandered into my father's office with a new book in his hand. 'Smith,' he said, 'do you know how to recognise a really well-bound book?' He then bent the front and back covers until they touched. 'There, Macmillans of course,' he said, and ambled out of the door!

By 1948, my father had shed most of the responsibilities he had picked up since leaving Africa, but one last major appointment was to draw him, once again, into the heart of the life he loved so dearly. This time it concerned horses: his life had gone full circle, from horses as a vet in Hertfordshire in 1910, to horses in London and Newmarket in 1946.

In that year, his old friend and colleague, Dr W.R. Wooldridge, recommended that John Smith be invited to become a founder trustee and council member of the Veterinary Education Trust which was, a year later, to become the Animal Health Trust, by which name this widely respected organisation is known today.

A Miss Yule, the daughter of a wealthy family with trading interests in the Far East, was a great enthusiast of the turf and especially of the bloodstock breeding business. She proposed to put up a considerable sum of money to be devoted to the development of British racing bloodstock, and the many aspects of animal health associated with it.

John Smith's name was put forward, together with others which were then, and are now, amongst the more illustrious in the land. It was a source of much amusement to him that the trust's writing paper should carry the names: His Grace the Duke of Norfolk; His Grace the Duke of Beaufort; the Rt Hon. the Earl of Roseberry; the Rt Hon. the Earl of Iveagh... John Smith Esq.!

His involvement with the trust was a matter of considerable satisfaction to my father and he threw himself, once again, into this major project with great enthusiasm. He was to be involved for the rest of his life.

As John Smith moved through his seventies he settled into a pattern of, as he expressed it, 'poddling along'. He did some gardening, but in a rather desultory fashion: farmers and agriculturalists tend to make poor gardeners. He was a loving and attentive father and grandfather, but the sparks of yesteryear were now less in evidence as, somewhat before his time, he grew more frail in spirit as well as in body. The hammering the tropics had given his constitution, and the many diseases he contracted out there, had undoubtedly taken their toll.

He now spoke little of Africa, except to condemn what he regarded as the too-headlong and incautious plunge to independence. But that he thought, more frequently than he allowed his family to realise, of that earlier life, is in little doubt.

Whenever we watched him, as we so often did, hunched in his chair gazing intently into the fire's embers, we knew that his thoughts were many thousands of miles away in Northern Rhodesia.

He had left his heart in Africa and could never, fully, retrieve it.

2

Off to Africa

I was visiting old friends and colleagues, seeking advice and ideas on what I should next do with my life, when I ran into Mr Woods, who had been one of my college examiners. He told me that the British South Africa Company (BSAC) wanted a man with veterinary qualifications and, if possible, agricultural experience. They were sending a hundred pure-bred bulls, bought in this country, out to Rhodesia, and wanted someone to take charge of their acclimatisation, inoculation etc. I wrote, telling them of my background, and was invited to an interview in London.

I first saw Mr Calder, the secretary, who then took me to see Mr (later Sir) Dougal Malcolm. Finally, I was taken in to see Sir Starr Jameson; you can imagine how excited I was. Dr Jim, as he was always known, had been Rhodes's right-hand man; had led the first troops in Matabeleland and conquered Lobengula. He had, also, led the raid on Pretoria, and been condemned to death after being taken prisoner by the Boers.

It is wholly understandable that our 30-year-old vet was so excited to be meeting the famous Dr Jim. He was fascinated by everything African and, at that time, the reputation of this impetuous disciple of Cecil Rhodes was still untarnished. He had given the despised Boers a bloody nose and, despite being tried and actually imprisoned in Britain for his actions, was a hero to the vast majority of the British people. The hindsight of history, however, reports less flatteringly on him. His invasion of the Transvaal, on 29 December 1895, was a fiasco, a total disaster, which resulted in the virtual end of Rhodes's political career. He may have been a romantic hero to the patriotic young of Britain, but he was a reckless adventurer to more mature observers. Nevertheless, he still managed to assume, to a substantial degree, Rhodes' mantle by becoming Prime Minister of Cape Province and chairman of the BSAC operations in Central Africa at the time of John Smith's interview.

As the BSAC figures so large in this story, a few words about it might not come amiss. It was the brain-child of Cecil Rhodes and, incorporated in 1889, was granted a 25-year royal charter, to acquire and exercise commercial and administrative rights in southern central Africa. The Company became the means by which Rhodes's ambition to 'paint the map of Africa red' and drive the railway, and a road, from the Cape to Cairo, was to be achieved. It was, effectively, to be my father's employer for most of his time in Northern Rhodesia until, that is, the territory became a crown colony in 1924.

Sir Starr was a smallish cheerful man, and he kept me for a full half an hour. He then asked me to have lunch, and took me to the directors' dining room on the top floor. There I met Sir Henry Birchenough, chairman of Rhodesian Railways, and Mr (later Sir) Drummond Chaplin. I little thought, then, that I should work so intimately with the latter years afterwards.

Sir Starr said, 'Do you want to go to Southern or Northern Rhodesia?' Now, I didn't even know that Rhodesia was divided into North and South, in fact I knew nothing much about Africa beyond what I had learned from reading Rider Haggard. What made me say 'Northern', I will never know. It was one of the luckiest decisions I ever made.

I presumed they wanted me to go, but no-one had mentioned salary, conditions etc. However, Mr Calder took me back to his office and told me they were offering a three-year contract at £350 per annum, exactly three times the salary I had been earning, rising annually by £25. After three years, if all went satisfactorily, I would be put on the permanent staff. I was to learn that, for some reason, I was offered £50 a year more than the usual starting salary... I was to have free passage, a house and certain local allowances.

They asked if I could sail in a fortnight! I suggested a month. I had never had more than two weeks and two weekends off work each year, and felt I wanted a bit of time before I sailed.

I didn't know exactly what to take and I couldn't get any definite advice: 'Oh! Just anything you have, some washing suits for the daytime, and be sure to take warm things for the nights. They are often bitterly cold!' We got things ready at home in Wigan, and the house started to look like a shop: blankets, sheets, pillows, crockery, cooking pots and pans, clothes, bridles and martingales, saddles, guns, and all sorts of odds and ends. My father had a large packing case made at his works, but it was too big to go up the stairs, and had to be packed in the sitting room. Then it was too heavy to handle, and had to be unpacked, sawn in two and repacked! A lot of room was taken up by the woollen sweaters, waistcoats and thick underwear my father had insisted on giving me!

John Smith took a great number of inappropriate pieces of clothing, and lacked many necessities for life on trek, which he had to buy at exorbitant prices once he was out there. The many scarves, pullovers and woollens he took with him cannot have found a very ready home some 16° south of the Equator!

My father, brother and I travelled to Southampton, where the RMS *Edinburgh Castle* was berthed. A man named Wardell, who was of the Basuto Evangelist Mission at the Sefula station, and who had been in the territory for some years already, was going to Livingstone and I was to share a four-berth cabin with him.

I had hardly travelled before, and the *Edinburgh Castle*, 12,000 tons, and one of the latest of the Union Castle boats, seemed enormous. I also felt rather lost, as the rest of the passengers all seemed to know each other.

RMS Edinburgh Castle
Sunday 29th June 1913
Wardell and I strolled about last night, after supper, and listened to the band, then we turned in. The steward woke me with a cup of tea at 6 o'clock and, after a salt-water bath, I went for a walk round the deck before breakfast. By lunchtime, we were well out into the Bay of Biscay, but I'm all right! I haven't felt a bit bad, nor have I missed a meal. We are due at Madeira on Wednesday, then we don't touch land again until we berth at Cape Town in two weeks.

Monday 2 o'clock
We're right through the bay, and I am still all right! There are about half a dozen in their bunks, but it's smoother now. We ran into dense fog at about 4.00am this morning, and I was woken by the engines stopping: another vessel was sounding its foghorn.

Tuesday 7.00am
There is a Belgian officer on board, and he and his girlfriend are
a real nuisance; you never know where you'll find them next! We
told him, last night, to stick to one spot and then we should know!

Thursday 3rd July
We arrived at Madeira at 5.00am yesterday. The scenery is exactly
like a stage backcloth, dirty, squalid and buzzing with flies, but
marvellously pretty and picturesque. As one gets away from the
narrow streets at the quayside one comes, immediately, upon
luxurious growth. They have no winter here, and so everything can
grow: grapes, bananas, cherries, plums, oranges etc.

From the quay, we took a bullock cart to the train terminus, and
then the mountain railway to the top, 2400 feet above sea level.
After breakfast, and a good look round, we 'tobogganed' down in
a kind of chair. Two of us sat in it, and the two drivers steered us
down by braking with their feet. I held up a shilling, and promised
it to our men if they could pass the other two chairs. They nearly
went mad, got sworn at by everyone, but did it! I've never seen so
many beggars and flies: they buzz around in about equal numbers.

We had a dance on Wednesday, and another last night; we have
a concert tonight and a bridge drive tomorrow, when the sports
also begin. We passed the Canaries yesterday and so are, officially,
in the tropics.

Saturday
It is now a week since I left England. We are right in the tropics
and everyone is dressed in white. We had our concert last night:
some music-hall people on board turned out, and the two girl
dancers gave a splendid show. There was a full moon, and the boat
was as steady as a stage. There was boat-drill this afternoon.

Sunday
Church service was at 10.30, the Captain read the prayers and the
Chief Officer the lessons. We had three hymns but no sermon: too
hot! At 2.00pm, we ran into a terrific storm; the wind blew like mad
for about 10 minutes, and then down came the rain, in sheets,

16

flooding everything. It lasted about half an hour, and then the sun came out again.

Many of the people in our saloon are colonials, known for obvious reasons as 'returned empties', and are going back after leave. Some are from Cape Town, some from up-country, but no-one is going as far up as Wardell and I.

There is now no twilight, it is quite dark in two minutes, at about 5.30pm. I was leaning over the rail yesterday in full daylight and, quite suddenly, it was dark. Both yesterday and today we have passed shoals of dolphins, swimming along and jumping right out of the water. Then suddenly, in front of them, will rise up a shoal of flying fish, trying to get out of their way. As they fly, the water drips off them and the sun's rays cause a wonderful effect.

Tuesday afternoon
Last night we saw the Southern Cross for the first time, then had a dance, and as we crossed the Equator about midnight, you can imagine how warm it was!

Sunday morning
13th July
Last Wednesday afternoon the sports began. First the 'turtle pull'; then potato races; egg and spoon races; 'are you there?' and the 'bolster bar'. This last was the best. To my surprise, I found out that I was rather good! There were 86 entries and I stuck it out, without being knocked off, until there were only two of us left in. I then had to meet a Yankee, a cowboy who is going to give exhibitions of shooting, lassoing and rope-twisting. He weighs over 15 stone, I am 9 stone 2lbs! So I knew my time had come. 'I guess I'll make a hole in the atmosphere with you,' he said. And he did! I stuck it out for eleven smacks, and then I went with a rattle. But I won a special prize of a shilling. That same evening, we had another dance; then, on Thursday, a 'book dance': each wears something illustrating the title of a book.

On Friday came the fancy-dress ball. I have never seen such a collection of splendid costumes made on board. I had a great time making a costume out of all sorts of bits and pieces, to go as a 'Little

Girl'. There was nearly a drama when I started off up the companionway without any underpants! I had quite forgotten that my dress was made from butter-muslin which I had got from the butcher. Fortunately, the lady in the next cabin spotted me, and with her maid's help, and amid much merriment, all was put to rights! To my amazement, I won.

It is very rough today, but I seem to have got my sea legs. We had a marconigram yesterday, from the *Walmer Castle*, saying that there had been a serious riot in Johannesburg: 21 killed and about 150 injured. The people on board who live there are anxiously awaiting further news.

The mailbags are closing today, as we are due in Cape Town at 6.00am on Tuesday. I have made a lot of good friends and have invitations galore but, as nobody is going to my part, except an Italian count off to shoot big game, I shall not be able to fulfil any.

I have thoroughly enjoyed the trip, and now feel ready for work.

3

Setting Foot in Africa

—➤•◦◄⟸—

South African Railways
Friday 18th July 1913
I shall never forget my first sight of Cape Town. The city is situated
in a bay with Table Mountain at one side, towards the back: it is
a wonderful panorama.

I got the baggage agent into my cabin, gave him a list of all my
things and, after saying goodbye to a lot of people, went ashore and
set off to deliver my letter of appointment. As my gear was late
coming out of the hold, I had to stay in Cape Town a couple of
days before I could catch the train north.

I was given a first-class coupe to myself. Talk about first-class!
Well, mine is like the end compartment in the third-class trains at
home. It has only one seat on one side: dingy old leather cushions,
a bit of threadbare carpet on the floor and there you are. The dust
is terrible, but I'm told it's winter and there's not much dust... yet!
The nights are bitterly cold, and I was frozen in Cape Town. In
the daytime, it is like a lovely summer's day at home, but I had to
hunt around and buy a great big coloured blanket for the nights.

I find it strange that this letter, the first written on the continent of Africa,
refers to Cape Town in only 31 words. The approach to Cape Town is
sensational. The passengers will have risen early and crowded the rails as Table
Mountain slowly hove into view and the great harbour materialised. I would
not be surprised if the excitement, the apprehension and the magnificence of the
scene had not proved almost too much for this 30-year-old Englishman,
suddenly conscious of the dramatic change in his life.

There is another factor: the passengers had been at sea for all but three weeks,
in an unnatural and heady atmosphere; they had nothing to do except enjoy
themselves, make friendships and have fun. But the moment the ship docked,
the behavioural centre of gravity will have changed; everyone went his or her own
way again, old friends crowded the dockside, greetings were shouted and reunions

19

were everywhere. But John Smith had no-one to meet him. His new-found and, until this moment, intimate friends were already busy with their own, old lives, and he would suddenly have been, and felt, 'out of things': we all know the feeling. That, and the realisation that a totally unknown life now faced him, alone, will have brought on one of his momentary 'lows'.

It is extremely difficult to describe the scenery through which we are passing. It is composed of valleys and big hills extending for miles. With the sun on them, they look very grand. We stop about every hour at a station – at least I suppose it is a station because it has a sign up – otherwise nothing. We stay for a few minutes and the natives surround the train with their shoals of piccaninnies, as the native children are known. Then on we go again.

Going through the Karroo, I kept looking for the grass, as I knew it was the best sheep country in South Africa. I asked a farmer on which part of the Karroo the sheep were kept. He said, 'this is one of the best parts', and explained that the sheep feed on the small bushes that grow every few yards, and that it takes eight acres to keep one sheep!

Saturday 19th
My first night on an African train, and I've not done too badly. It is still bitterly cold, and through the night we kept on stopping at stations; each time I woke up. I'm writing this in my overcoat with my blanket over my shoulders.

We are now right on the veldt with occasional koppes (small hills) nearly all flat-topped. It is all very desolate-looking, with the only signs of habitation the huts at the side of the line for the maintenance teams. Last night, we came over a range of mountains during dinner. It took about an hour, and I don't think we progressed northward more than three miles. The train kept twisting and turning in and out of the hills; it gave some idea of what the original engineers had to contend with.

Livingstone
23rd
In Livingstone at last! I arrived yesterday morning, after four and a half days in the train! At Kimberley, I had a three-hour wait. It

was a great relief to get off and stretch my legs. I went for a walk round the town: it's a dirty, dusty hole and I was not at all impressed. No time to get permission to go round a diamond mine, so I went back to the station and had a meal.

From Kimberley to Mafeking we passed through a desert; you have no idea of the dust and the discomfort. All the apertures in the carriages have to be closed tight, and we simply sat and sweltered.

We arrived at 6 o'clock on Sunday morning. Again, it was bitterly cold, and I had my big overcoat on, buttoned up to the neck. Three of us went for a walk, saw the war memorial, a lot of the guns used in the siege and some of the old trenches. The town is small and quiet; we had breakfast at Dixon's Hotel and signed the visitors' book, which contained the signatures of those who had taken part, including that of Baden-Powell.

Next stop Bulawayo; three hours there also. It is a growing place with a population of about 4,000 Europeans. Some extremely fine buildings are up or going up.

We started off again at noon on the last lap. At about 5.00pm we struck the worst patch on the railway. It takes about seven hours to do that bit between Iwaii and Wankie. I am not exaggerating when I say that a quarter of an inch of dust creeps in per hour. The boys are constantly sweeping, and you can imagine the condition of the passengers. We sat and gasped; sleep was out of the question. Envisage yourself in a stifling room with people beating carpets all around you!

At last we got to the Victoria Falls. We just got a glimpse of them from the train, so I shall describe them to you when I see them properly. On the platform at the Falls Station, on the Southern Rhodesian side, I found the acting Chief Veterinary Officer looking out for me. At the main station at Livingstone, about seven miles from the Falls, another vet, Mr Woods, the brother of the man who had put me in touch with the job in England, was waiting to greet me. He had one of the buckboards belonging to the department: a buckboard is a four-wheeled vehicle with no springs, drawn by four mules.

I have a room at the hotel, and went straight there for a bath. I was beyond description after that night of dust. I am provided with all servants, except a cook who I will get when I have my own accommodation. My own native boy is about 14 years old, and is called 'Shilling'. I call him 'Eighteen Pence'. I haven't got used to a valet yet, and keep falling over him. When I last saw him he was washing a dress shirt: I tremble to think what it will be like when he has finished. It won't take him long to wash his own clothes, as I could put the lot in my pocket! At the office, I have a departmental 'messenger' and one other boy: I don't know what he is for yet. Between them all, they have about six words of English, so you can imagine the pantomime. I pay Shilling 5/- per month, and allow him 2lbs of maize and 4oz of salt per day, at a cost of 2/6.

Now let me tell you something about Livingstone. Its history really starts at the Old Drift, as it was known, which was the point at which the Zambezi was crossed before the Victoria Falls bridge was opened in 1906. It was about three miles above the Falls, where the river is narrowest and, unusually, shallowest, with no islands or outcrops of dangerous rocks. Barges and dugouts and, later, a launch moved people, cattle, goods and materials of every sort and description from the south into Northern Rhodesia.

'Mopane' Clarke was, probably, the first European to settle at Old Drift. He built a wattle and daub 'hotel' with two or three tiny bedrooms and a bar. He also started a store selling just about everything. It was named The Zambezi Trading Co., a name that was to live on in the area for many years. No story about the early days in NR could be complete without brief mention of F.J. Clarke. This considerable character was born in England, went to South Africa in 1890, then on to NR, where he was involved in recruiting labour in the very early days of prospecting. During this period, he negotiated with the great Matabele Chief, Lobengula, who named him for the mopane tree because he was, he said, 'tall, straight and hard of heart'! Having done well up in the mining district – it was, in reality, a vast area with a mere handful of hopefuls scratching around for an elusive fortune – he came south to Old Drift. He was then to move to Livingstone, five or so years later, and then to Kalomo, trading in cattle. He was now well-off, and his ranch on the fertile Kafue Flats boasted a 10,000-head herd, at that time the largest in NR.

At the turn of the century, there were six or so permanent settlers at Old Drift. This number slowly increased as the population of whites in the whole territory – remember that NR was the size of the British Isles, France, Belgium and Holland combined – reached the hundred mark.

The British South Africa Company set up its first boma – administration HQ – at Old Drift in 1901. Very gradually the settlement grew, with a couple more stores, a chemist run by Leopold Moore, a wheelwright, and a second eating house or small hotel. By late 1903, the population was 45 men, 17 women and six children. Their accommodation consisted of mud huts or wood and corrugated-iron sheds. Numbers increased again with the coming of the railway, which reached the southern side of the Falls in May 1904; the bridge was opened 12 September 1905. This was the signal for a good deal more activity and for the authorities – which, in practice, meant all the settlers – to think seriously about the suitability of Old Drift as a permanent township.

Besides the Zambezi, low-lying and all but flooded in the rainy season, Old Drift was one of the unhealthiest places on earth. Death from malaria and, especially, blackwater fever was tragically common as the sad, neglected cemetery bears witness. Most of the inscriptions record ages of between five and 40. In the region of one in ten adults and one in three children died each year. The decision was made to move the whole settlement five miles north, to a sandy ridge and beside the recently completed railway line. So Livingstone was founded in 1905, and named for the famous explorer.

In June 1907, with fifty Europeans resettled, the administrator, Robert Codrington, a widely-respected senior member of the British South Africa Company and personal friend of Cecil Rhodes, moved his whole staff, 35 of them, in one trainload down from Kalomo to Livingstone, having bought the North Western Hotel, which 'Mopane' Clarke had recently built out of the profits of his Old Drift enterprises, to house his administration.

Robert Codrington had been Administrator of North Eastern Rhodesia but, in 1907, was transferred to North Western Rhodesia with his HQ at Kalomo, with the brief to start preparations for the amalgamation of the two territories. He had been in Central Africa since 1890, being wounded three years later in an ambush in Bechuanaland. Whilst sailing back from leave in England in 1898, he met Cecil Rhodes who, much taken with this 27-year-old, immediately asked him to take over as Deputy Administrator of North Eastern Rhodesia. One year later, he became Administrator, with his HQ at Fort Jameson. Codrington was a first-class manager and a considerable character. His African name – 'Mara', or 'that is settled' – confirms his decisive manner. The story is told that, out on trek, he had a chest of drawers carried before him and an aspidistra behind him! In 1908, having known Dorothy Bird, daughter of the custard baron, only over dinner at Government House in Livingstone, Codrington proposed marriage and was accepted! But their happiness was to be tragically short-lived. Later that same year, on leave in London, he collapsed in the street and died, aged 39.

But to return to the history of Livingstone.

In 1911, North Eastern and North Western Rhodesia were amalgamated and Sir Lawrence Wallace, who had succeeded Robert Codrington in 1909, became administrator, a post he was to hold until 1921.

Between 1907 and 1913, the capital was not to grow substantially and now, in July 1913, is not much changed.

Livingstone consists of one main street, Queensway, a dirt track with sand inches deep and a length of only about 200 yards. Another track, Mainway, running parallel, goes the seven miles, via Old Drift, to the Falls. Again, by no stretch of the imagination could this be called a road.

Deep ditches run down either side of Queensway to carry the stormwater from the rainy-season downpours. But now, when no rain has fallen for months, the air is thick with dust 24 hours a day, as the long spans of 30 or more oxen drag the solid-axled wagons past offices, stores, hotel and dwellings. At the same time, mule carts are driven at a less leisurely pace along the same single track, adding to the confusion, dust and clatter.

On one side of the track is Government House with its 'English' garden, tennis court and stable block. Next to that is the United

Services Club, universally known as the Club, then some wood and corrugated bungalows – all the buildings are single-storeyed – and the Zambezi Trading Co. On the opposite side are the administrative offices, an hotel – just a row of little, hot bedrooms, each with two beds – a dining room with a long, low verandah open to Queensway, a grocery store, a butchery owned by the Susman brothers and a general store run by Beesley.

That is virtually the sum total of the main buildings, some of the Europeans being housed in brick and corrugated iron bungalows just off the 'town centre', along tracks which have not yet been developed. You might be better able to envisage what I have arrived to, when I explain that, just a few hundred yards in any direction from Queensway is dense, tropical bush.

The Veterinary Department, diagonally across from Government House, is the envy of all the officials, as it is a brand-new, stone building with six tiny rooms and a 25-foot verandah facing the road. On this blistering verandah stand six or so smart natives, all aged about 30 and wearing long blue shirts over khaki shorts with black, silver-badged fezzes on their heads. These are the government messengers – part servants, part sergeants and part bodyguards. They are all specifically chosen for their physique, integrity and loyalty, and follow their masters everywhere, always standing stock still unless on a mission.

The Club is very fine. It is the only centre for social activity, and is the cornerstone of life in Livingstone. The walls are covered with prize animal heads, antlers and horns, and there are lion and leopard skins all over the highly polished floor of African mahogany. There is a small library and reading room and a large saloon; everything is extremely well and comfortably appointed.

I have been made an honorary member until I can be formally elected. All the bachelors feed at the Club at a charge of £7/10/0 per month for all meals. No money changes hands: everything is signed for on chits which are settled at the end of the month. At meals, or in the saloon, a native servant in spotless white kansa – a long, nightshirt-like garment – stands motionless behind each chair, waiting to be called upon to fetch or carry; one's every wish and need is attended to immediately.

That is the Livingstone of which I knew nothing only weeks ago, and which is now to be my base for at least the next two-and-a-half years.

4

The History of Zambia

━━━━━►◦◄━━━━━

istory is modestly defined as being 'the story of the past'. The student of history discovers, examines and interprets the records of past human societies. Inevitably, in a country with no written material other than the scant amount bequeathed through European languages — mainly Portuguese, French and English — covering a period of less than the last 200 years, well-established historical fact is virtually non-existent. However, the following brief account tries to provide an historical perspective against which to understand some of the matters of which John Smith writes.

Zambia is the size of the United Kingdom, France, Belgium and Holland combined, and its peoples are mostly descended from the Bantus. Much of the country, which is land-locked with eight neighbours, lies on a plateau over 3300 feet above sea level. This plateau is deeply entrenched by the Zambezi river and its tributaries, the Kafue, the Luangwa and the Luapula in the north. Only the most southerly part, including Livingstone and the Falls, is low-lying with an appreciably hotter and more humid climate.

In the fourth or fifth century, the descendants of these early Africans, speaking Bantu and knowledgeable by now about iron-working, farming and cattle herding, moved swiftly down from the north in large numbers, displacing the short-statured bushmen who, a hundred or so years later, had all but disappeared.

The country then was much as it is today, a great sea of woodland, typical savannah with trees and tall grasses and a few island clearings for huts and crops.

The Bantus believed in a god-creator, but also in spirits of earth and sky and of the tribe's ancestors: they believed in magic, in witchcraft and in the power of charms to bring success to work, hunting and love.

The period 1100 to 1900 saw the emergence of both centralised and decentralised societies. Some developed into powerful states, either to protect their resources or to try to produce a monopoly in trade. The centralised states tended to be ruled by chiefs, whilst the decentralised societies were led by religious zealots or rainmakers.

A chief was usually the warrior-leader, the dispenser of justice and a link between the living and the departed ancestors. This was his source of authority and the legitimacy of his rule. During this period, there was much raiding, warlike excursion and subjugation of weaker by stronger tribes or groups of tribes. This fluid and restlessly hostile atmosphere between states and societies through this part of central Africa persisted until the end of the nineteenth century.

In the fifteenth and sixteenth centuries, Arab and Swahili traders, soon to be joined by the Portuguese, began arriving in what is today Zambia. This led to the gradual decline in the strength of many of the old-established chiefdoms. Ivory, by then in great demand, animal skins and slaves were traded for alcohol, cotton cloth, beads, trinkets and salt; some firearms were also imported. The process of commercialisation of central Africa, albeit on a tiny and local scale, is generally believed to date from about 1500.

At the end of the eighteenth century, explorers sought to draw a reasonably accurate map of the whole of Africa and, in 1798, one of the first Europeans to enter Zambia was the Portuguese Frasco de Larceda, who attempted to cross the continent from east to west. Fifty years later, Dr David Livingstone, a Scottish missionary and doctor, began a lifetime of exploration in Africa. He was shrewd in the ways of publicity and his lectures in London, and his writings promoted a tremendous enthusiasm for all things African in Victoria's Britain. On 16 November 1855, he gazed, spellbound, at the great waterfall which, for centuries, the Africans had called Mosi-oa-Tunya; in honour of his Queen Empress, he named his discovery the Victoria Falls.

The rush was now on to visit central Africa, if rush can mean a few hundred traders, hunters, explorers, missionaries and imperial agents – to follow the trail blazed by David Livingstone.

Many fairly soon returned; many died of tropical diseases, but a very few, mostly missionaries or traders, established reasonably permanent footholds.

The more formal colonisation of Zambia dates from the recommendations of the Berlin Conference of 1884/85. This marked the map of Africa with the somewhat arbitrary boundaries of each European country's areas of influence, although the actual boundaries were drawn a year later.

In 1890, a vitally important treaty was negotiated by Frank E. Lochner, acting for Cecil Rhodes's British South Africa Company, with Paramount Chief Lewanika of the Lozi tribe, which occupied Barotseland, the north-western 'half' of what is now Zambia, an area larger than the United Kingdom.

Cecil Rhodes, still only 37, already dominated the South African gold and diamond mining industries. His ambition was to fly the union flag from Cape to Cairo and, in 1889, he persuaded the British Government to grant a royal charter to his new company, through which he intended to stake claims of control throughout southern central Africa, to the exclusion of, mainly, the Portuguese, Belgians and Germans. The whole territory was to become, essentially, a 'company state'.

In these ambitions he was substantially successful and, by 1889, his administration had been imposed throughout what was, in 1964, to become the independent Republic of Zambia.

At the turn of the century, present-day Zambia was split, for administrative purposes, into NW and NE Rhodesia, the boundary between the two being the Kafue river. But 12 years later, in 1911, the two were joined to become Northern Rhodesia, the whole administered by the BSAC. This vast territory thus became, in practical terms, if not in name or fact, a British colony from 1911 to 1964, although it was not formally declared a crown colony until 1924, at which time the BSAC relinquished their controlling interest.

By 1930, Southern Rhodesia, now Zimbabwe, which had always been more advanced in social, economic and administrative terms, began to lead a move by both territories' white populations towards federation. This was a not-untypical proposal by those who sensed that they had an opportunity to enlarge and enrich their fiefdom, and extend their area of influence. It is interesting to note that, as early as 1914, Sir Starr Jameson, in a speech in Southern Rhodesia, had suggested that amalgamation might be beneficial to the two Rhodesias.

In 1936, at a conference held at the Victoria Falls, white politicians from both sides of the Zambezi argued that amalgamation would be in the best interests of all their people, black and white alike. But two years later, the Bledisloe Commission, appointed to study a larger federation of both Rhodesias with Nyasaland, found that the Africans were opposed.

The clamour for amalgamation increased, however and, in 1941, Sir Roy Welensky's Labour Party was formed to try to achieve this aim. Welensky had, as a much younger man, been a driver on the Northern Rhodesian railways.

By 1948, enthusiasm for amalgamation began to wane in favour of the federation proposal which was, again, finding favour. In 1953, the federation of the three territories took place but, after the political shilly-shallying of the last twenty years, there was now a deeply entrenched restlessness amongst Africans and, in 1963, the barely ten-year-old federation was dismantled.

There was now fervent nationalistic activity in a widely-felt desire for independence, which was given added impetus by the fact that Ghana and Nigeria were already there, with Uganda, Kenya and Tanganyika well on the way. On 24 October 1964, the independent Republic of Zambia was born.

Zambia's history from 1964 has not been without its dramas and disappointments. The heady atmosphere of success tended towards policies which underestimated the fundamental need to strengthen the country's basic economic structure.

Today, Zambia is a friendly and proud nation of some eight million cheerful souls who, unhurriedly but not always efficiently, smile their way through life. After several years of crippling drought, its people may, perhaps, be able to summon up the energy to start the long haul to put their house into effective order. If this were to happen, the tourist potential of this fascinating and beautiful country could begin to be realised.

5

Ready for the Bulls

Maramba Camp
July 1913
A few days after I arrived, one of the officials from the department came in after a 12-month trek. He had with him a remarkably tough pony, and I managed to get hold of him. Another of our team, the Mr Woods who had met me at the train, is off next week to patrol the Belgian Congo border, watching out for rinderpest – a vicious cattle disease – and he expects to be away for 18 months!

News has just come that the first batch of pedigree bulls sent out from Britain, and for which I have been employed, is due to arrive in ten days. The whole thing about this project is that no British cattle have previously been imported, because of the very high death rate from the disease. My job is to accept the bulls, try and give them immunity against disease, and get them sufficiently healthy to be distributed up-country to help improve the quality, ultimately, of all the herds in the country. It is a most ambitious programme.

The camp for this operation has been set up at Maramba, about seven miles from Livingstone, but in the centre of what was, just a week or so ago, virgin bush.

But first, let me describe a little outing I had just before I moved down here.

I was told to go off to the Victoria Falls and inspect some cattle on the border between Northern and Southern Rhodesia. I was given six natives to carry my gear and get me around. The first leg of the trip, which was seven miles in all, was by trolley, pushed by my boys along the main railway line. This trolley is about 10 feet long, and five of us, with my gear, perched on it whilst two natives took turns to shove it along the track, a most novel way to travel. When we got to the Zambezi, after about three miles, we transferred to a dugout canoe which was waiting with a scratch crew of paddlers. At this point the river is about one-and-a-half miles wide. The banks are rich with palms and tropical vegetation and, at the river's edge, scores of crocodiles were sunning themselves with just their great snouts showing. The currents are very swift and unpredictable and my paddlers kept having to change direction.

Everything is so still, just the rhythmic dip of the paddles and the synchronised grunt of the paddlers. The whole countryside is strangely silent, and I am finding it hard to get used to. Occasionally, one of the boys would quietly point with his paddle, and it would turn out to be an especially large crocodile, or some other matter of interest. Once, the head boy pointed out a pair of hippopotamuses coming downstream, just their snouts showing. They stopped paddling and we all sat quiet until they had passed: I wasn't sorry when they had gone!

We finally reached the famous Victoria Falls Hotel. I stayed the night there, whilst my six native paddlers rolled up in the blankets each had brought, and slept outside my room on the verandah.

My inspection of the cattle resulted in three having to be shot and, as I had a day to spare, I decided to see as much of the Falls as possible. It is utterly impossible to describe them. The roar can be heard 40 miles away, as the one-and-a-half-mile-wide Zambezi plunges 350 feet over a sheer land fault. Spanning the gorge of 'boiling' water just below the Falls is the great railway bridge, 630 feet above the cauldron, and the highest bridge in the world. The spray rises a thousand feet and the sun, shining through it, produces a vast and almost permanent rainbow. It is twice the height and twice the width of Niagara.

I had heard that, with an expert dugout crew, it was possible to paddle across the river to Livingstone Island, which provides a dramatic close-up view of the Falls' edge. I called my six boys together and indicated what I wanted to do. They are all tip-top, hand-picked boatmen, and they struck out and paddled magnificently to the island. I climbed a rock, looked down into the cataract, and was rewarded with a view which literally took my breath away. I was, of course, drenched with spray, but that didn't matter. Ever since I was a small boy at home in Wigan, reading everything I could lay my hands on about Africa, I had dreamed of seeing the Falls and here I was, four weeks after leaving England, standing in the middle of the Zambezi, gazing down at the seething mass of water below.

Now, back to Maramba.

Preparations had begun before I had arrived but, as always, there was an almighty rush to complete the work by the day the bulls were due. An area of about five acres, five miles from Livingstone, had been cleared from the bush. The camp was beside the railway line and the so-called road; both led from Livingstone to the Falls. The far end of the clearing reached down almost to the Zambezi whilst the Maramba river, which feeds into it, flowed along one side. It was not the best site, but work was too far advanced for me to make any changes.

There were two British stock inspectors working with me – both vets – and three European carpenters supervising a workforce of 200 natives. In addition, 100 long-term prisoners were drafted in to help. We had armed guards surrounding the camp, and we three had to carry our revolvers.

The camp consisted of stabling for 120 bulls, with a surrounding stockade of three rows of barbed wire five feet high. It is absolutely vital that none of the bulls breaks out. Beyond the stockade, and a little apart, is the native village, with individual huts for the married men, who all have their wives, often plural wives, with them as well as hoards of children, or 'piccaninnies' as they are called.

This is quite an undertaking and yet, amazingly, all the huts were put up in a morning! Small trees are cut and trimmed to make uprights; smaller branches are then fastened across these uprights and long grasses, not unlike our thatch, are spread as a roof. Palm leaves, cut into strips, are used as binding, and the floor consists of swept, bare earth.

My own quarters, with three rooms, are made of wood and corrugated iron. I have a bed-sitter, a laboratory and a lock-up store. My own servants are quite close in their rather more palatial huts, whilst my two veterinary colleagues are in tents.

My cook arrived yesterday with his wife and their baby, slung across her back by a shawl, this being her only wearing apparel! At this stage, I have about twelve words of the local dialect, the cook has the same of English, so you can imagine what a pantomime it is arranging meals! But he knows his business: our first dinner, served in my room, consisted of meal soup, tinned kippers, curried rice with tinned bully-beef. A feast!

The logistics at Maramba are formidable, especially for someone like myself with no training or previous experience of this sort of operation. This is a camp of about 200 natives, with about as many again camp followers. Then there will be 100 bulls needing food and water; the latter is pumped up from the river by motor pump, the petrol being sent down from Livingstone in eight-gallon drums loaded on ox wagons. Each native receives a weekly ration of 14lbs of maize meal and 4oz of salt. The meal, mixed with all sorts of weird concoctions, is eaten by old and young alike.

I have just made an inspection to reassure myself that all is ready for the bulls. Yesterday, the whole landscape behind my 'house' was virgin scrub. Today, it is covered with huts, before each of which burns a fire, day and night. The families squat, play and laugh, which they seem to do unceasingly. As I walk round, which I do last thing every night, all the natives, except the children, stand up and remain motionless until I have passed. I find this particularly hard to get used to.

Friday 1st August

I got a wire on Wednesday, to say the first 46 bulls would arrive at 2.00pm the next day. The train they were in, and had been in for nine boiling days, with temperatures of nearly 100°, was to be shunted straight into the camp, along a short slip-line we had laid especially.

I turned the whole camp out at sunrise to fix the mangers, which had only just been delivered, and to handle the cattle feed, which arrived only hours before the bulls.

Suddenly, they were here – 46 young, highly-bred bulls which had been cooped up in this heat for well over a week. The natives had never seen such magnificent animals, and the atmosphere throughout the camp was electric.

I had been advised, by a wise old settler, to use this occasion to impress the natives by behaving as if this was an everyday occurrence. So I, with my colleagues, opened up the first truck and, armed with shamboks – rhinoceros hide whips – turned out the bulls. Some of them were extremely nasty, kicking and bellowing. The natives just stood and gasped. We seemed to acquit ourselves quite well, as my head boy came to me the next day, and said the whole camp had been discussing our action and they 'have much please with us'!

The unloading did not go wholly without incident: a particularly restless Friesian charged out of the truck, laid out two natives and got a third against the barbed wire. We managed to beat him off the boy, but he turned on me and I had to jump to the top of the stockade to avoid his horns. The native was badly cut about so I had to assume the role of camp doctor, stitch him up and cleanse his wounds. Fortunately, the PMO (principal medical officer) in Livingstone had sent me a full medical kit. Incidentally, I've also had a case of pneumonia and what I diagnosed as smallpox. Fearing the worst, I had a six-mule cart sent from Livingstone with Dr Aylmer May, but he was able to set my mind at rest, as 'smallpox' proved to be chickenpox!

Back to the bulls. My colleague, Thomas, took some photographs of this little Friesian adventure, but the boy to whom he handed the camera dropped it, and the back flew open. Thomas's language was colourful, but unintelligible to the native who, nevertheless, guessed he was not popular!

You can't imagine the mess we were in when we had finished, soaked with perspiration and covered with dust thrown up by 40-odd crazed bulls thrashing about in the sand. We were all black from head to toe, the Europeans I mean! I had two cooks making tea continuously, tea is a great reviver in really hot weather.

Finally the bulls were secured in their stalls, fed and watered, and we could all stand down and clear up for the day. My boys carried up three eight-gallon drums of boiling water, straight from the fire, and I wallowed in the best bath of my life. Then, in clean gear and dressing gowns, we tucked in to supper. We had our one statutory, large whisky and sat on our little netted veranda, looking out over the compound of native huts. We then noticed rather more and bigger fires, which were being more constantly attended than on previous evenings. I went off to enquire the reason, and learned that a number of leopards had been spotted prowling around the camp. As no one seemed concerned, I followed suit: such is the speed with which one falls into the drill out here.

6th August

I received your letters by runner last Saturday. I have now established that letters, posted in Wigan on a Thursday, arrive here on the Friday or Saturday four weeks later. They are sorted in Livingstone and sent on. Thomas is especially eager to get his mail, and sits on the top of the shed with my glasses and watches for the boy to arrive at the appointed time. As he approaches, going at the usual jog-trot, Thomas shouts and waves to urge him on to greater speed. The awaited letter has a decidedly feminine slant to the handwriting!

The long hours and the dry heat make us extremely hungry. Fortunately, I have a treasure as a cook. Let me give you last night's dinner menu: bean soup, tinned bloaters, mutton with sweet potatoes and pumpkin, fish paste on toast, boiled and fried currant pudding. I can't imagine where the mutton came from, and have already learned that it doesn't do to ask too many questions.

We turn in at about 9.00pm and I sleep like a log until about 6.30am, when my boy brings me a cup of tea. I get dressed and am at work at 7.00. It is surprisingly cold at night, at this time of year, and so the whole camp is out and about early, to benefit from the delightful warmth of the rising sun, and to get essential work done before it gets too hot.

We have had an eventful day. First thing this morning we noticed that all the native cattle and the transport oxen were covered with ticks, the type that carries the disease redwater. I immediately had a dip trench dug, 15 yards long and seven feet deep. We counted 3000 gallons of water being tipped in from cans. Then I got some arsenic from the stores, and mixed the dip. We pushed the beasts in at one end, they swam along and scrambled out at the other. It is an interesting fact that these cattle are the first to have been dipped in the whole of central Africa, as no-one had thought of this treatment before I arrived. We plan to dip the cattle for the whole area at a charge of 3d per head; this should recoup the £120 the arsenic cost.

Four of my bulls are very ill: they are those to be passed to the Farmers' Association. A deputation from them visited the camp yesterday. It seems that enormous interest is being shown by all the farmers, throughout the territory, in my operation at Maramba. If I can only pull the bulls through, and make them immune, it will be a mighty big feather in my cap. I must confess, I would rather have been experimenting with cheap local cattle than with expensive, prize bulls brought all the way from the UK. Last night was particularly lively: we were all up, three times, to recapture and restall a number of bulls that had broken loose.

I am writing this letter at my desk, it is most primitive. My chair is a barrel of Epsom Salts, and I share the desktop with a complete laboratory kit, set out exactly as I used to have it at Liverpool University Veterinary School, all those years ago.

On Tuesday afternoon, I made my first excursion to try and shoot some game. I took two native trackers, my shotgun and my .303 rifle. After I had shot some doves and pigeons, we got onto the spoor of six kudu, very large buck. We followed them for a good three miles, but then had to turn back, as it would soon have been dark. I have sent one of the boys out today, to see if he can find where they are going for water, and I will then see if I can get one.

Major Gordon, who has a farm not far from Maramba, came over on Sunday. He told me he had shot three lions in the past five weeks. One of them got into his kraal and pulled down a 17-month-old heifer. The lion then managed to manoeuvre the body across its back and jumped a 12-foot stockade with it. As it landed, the major shot it dead. Apparently, it was a magnificent specimen. He has asked me to stay with him, and will take me along to try and get another lion.

My boy Shilling has left me. He had heard, in Livingstone, that I would be trekking in due course, and that was not to his liking. Judge Beaufort has recommended an older boy to me; he is more expensive, 15/- a month, but is already looking after me well. He was educated at a Baptist mission in the Congo. Happily, he speaks a little English but, already, I am picking up the language fast – I jolly well have to! But I make some funny mistakes. Yesterday, I wanted my pony, so shouted to 'Sixpence', my pony boy, 'Tenga n'mba suppano leno'. Now, 'n'mba' is a house, 'cavalo' is a horse. I should have said 'Tenga cavalo suppano leno', which means 'Bring my horse at once'. No wonder 'Sixpence' looked flabbergasted when I asked him to 'bring a house at once!'

Let me tell you about this pony. He is called Champagne, and is probably the most uncomfortable ride I have ever had, but he is tough as nails. There are practically no horses in central Africa because of horse sickness, the cause of which is unknown and against which no remedy exists. A very few do recover, and are then immune or 'salted'. This is the case with Champagne, about three others in Livingstone, four in Barotseland and a few scattered amongst the farmers and settlers along the railway line. He is totally sure-footed; I ride him up to Livingstone five miles away, sometimes in the evening, and he brings me back, through the bush in pitch blackness with never a falter.

I have also managed to acquire(!) four magnificent, matching bright chestnut mules, all 15 hands high, from a batch which has just arrived in Livingstone. They are hardly trained and very fast when driven, four-in-hand, in a buckboard. The other evening, I took Thomas with me to the Club in Livingstone, for dinner, and to bring two friends back for the night. I took two natives with me to mind the mules. We were a bit late returning, and the mules were mad-fresh; I had great difficulty in holding them. But I knew that if we could only get them to the point where the road, so-called, becomes a sandy track, all should be well; this turn-off was marked with a stout post. As we approached the turn, I realised the mules were taking it far too sharply. We hit the post with the rear wheel, the buckboard turned over, throwing four Europeans and two natives into a heap, whilst the mules kicked themselves free and set off for home. We trudged two miles through thick sand, and found the mules happily waiting to be fed and watered. A new rear wheel and sundry bits of harness made all as good as new in just a matter of days.

Our track from Livingstone is much improved, but it still takes 20 oxen, spanned in pairs, to pull the supply wagons through the deep sand. Each team has a piccaninny at the head of the lead pair, pulling away at a thong attached to the leaders' horns, whilst the native driver walks alongside the span, trailing a very long whip. He is so skilled that it is said he can flick a fly off the lead ox, or from a wheeler, from the same position beside the team.

The other night there was a new moon and, about 9 o'clock when it was pitch dark, the natives began singing and beating a tom-tom. Suddenly, one of them jumped up and began dancing in a frenzied way around the fire. Then a second boy joined in, and then another, and another, until all the men, except for the tom-tom player and the two playing native pianos, were dancing and singing round the camp. It was fascinating and, I learned later, is a sort of rite, always performed at the new moon.

Here am I, sitting on a verandah with two Europeans, watching 200 natives dancing to the moon, only five miles from the territory capital, which was not in existence six years ago, and yet I am only a few weeks out of England.

Last night proved to be another one of action with the bulls. At about 7.30pm, we heard a terrific din, and found that three young bulls were fighting, having broken free. I shouted for the boys, but only about six turned out. We managed, at last, to secure the culprits, but it was hard going and not a little dangerous. Afterwards, I made all the boys parade whilst I gave them a piece of my mind. I was good and mad and, despite the language difficulties, they were left in no doubt as to my feelings. I then gave the six boys 3 pence (a silver coin called a 'tickie') each. Then I dismissed the whole lot to their huts.

Little was I prepared for the consequences! The six began to rebuild their fire into a huge blaze, and to dance and sing a chant which, it seemed, consisted of variations on the theme 'our master is good' (B'wana m'webe). This they kept up until 11pm, having directed their attention, at half time, to mocking the remainder, who had decided to skip recapturing the fighting bulls.

12th August

One of my bulls is dead: he had pneumonia and pleurisy badly but, as I had kept him going for four days, I had hoped he would recover. However, on Sunday, when it was extremely hot, he suddenly keeled over. I carried out a postmortem, but it was nothing sinister. Still, it's a worry, as I haven't even started the immunisation programme yet. As I finished the pm, the natives set up a great racket, and I suddenly realised they were after the carcass. As there was nothing to harm them, I let them loose on it and, in no time, it was picked clean.

I was invited to Livingstone last night. It might seem strange to you, at home, to be riding by pony, dressed up in a dinner jacket, through the tropical bush and forest, to a dinner party: it's common practice here. I bathed and changed at Maramba, and set out on Champagne, with my pony boy at his head, at 6 o'clock. Suddenly, it was dark. This still throws me, but happily there was a full moon and, after a while, it was almost as light as day. I arrived in good time, had an excellent dinner, played some bridge, and set off back at about 11.00pm. All was quiet and eerily still; I was, as usual, carrying my revolver, just as a precaution.

The second batch of bulls is due on Friday. The camp will then be full, and I shall have to start on the really important part of inoculation and immunisation. So far, I have been in the preparation stage; my biggest problem is estimating the amount of virus I need to inject, to achieve immunisation without it proving fatal. There really are too many unknowns for me to feel confident about what to do.

I must tell you of a possibly serious incident last week. The three of us were about to relax with our nightly whisky when Thomas, who had taken a gulp, spat it out and gave a warning shout. The boy, quite unknowingly, had filled the decanter with a strong and corrosive brown disinfectant! It was a little unnerving, as I had already heard of three bachelors, sharing digs together in Livingstone, almost being killed when their cook put insect poison into the soup instead of pea flour. Fortunately, the doctor lived nearby, and all was well.

Thursday

There is an almighty wind blowing today, and the temperature has dropped 40°. It is bad for the bulls, as they catch cold easily in such conditions.

I've had my first experience of trouble with my natives. There have been three or four trouble-makers on whom I've had my eye, but it came to a head when they complained about working on Sundays. On Tuesday, I found out that one day's rations for the whole camp had been stolen from the stores and, on doing my rounds, saw evidence of it having been distributed in the huts, so I stopped their food for the next day. The majority took it well, but I found the three or four suspects trying to rouse the others to rebel. Yesterday, at call-out, a number came to my house and said they would not work. So I gathered up my messengers, and told those willing to work to stand to one side. The remainder we formed up into a column with myself, revolver in belt, on Champagne at the head, Thomas bringing up the rear and the messengers on either side. I told the natives they would be marched to gaol in Livingstone. We had only gone a few yards when the column broke up, and they all started working with the others.

It is an odd experience when three Europeans and a couple of native sergeants have to discipline upwards of a hundred natives. Anyway, I went to the native commissioner, who asked for the ring-leaders to be sent to him; he said he doubted if I would have any more trouble as they were, typically, just testing to see how far they could go. I am certainly having to learn fast, without anyone to teach me!

Friday, a week later

I can't write much, as the boy will have to set off to Livingstone soon to catch the mail. Your letters won't be here until Sunday, as the train is 24 hours late, owing to a washed-away section down in South Africa. The news came first from the natives, passed by drums – the bush telegraph – all the way from the south and was faster, believe it or not, than our telegraph. It is a weird, and somewhat uncanny, state of affairs.

Today, I have given my first injections, just small doses, and I expect reactions – slight I hope – in about nine days. After that I shall increase the dose.

I've managed to get a dugout canoe down to Maramba, as there are a number of good paddlers amongst the boys here. I hope to have an outing on the Zambezi, to try to shoot a crocodile. I shall, however, steer clear of the hippopotamuses until I'm safely back on the bank!

21st August

What a week! 46 more bulls arrived on Tuesday; we've had to settle them on top of nursing some very sick ones as a result of the injections. One of the new bulls is a particularly nasty customer, and laid out three natives before we managed to get him in his stall. I am really up to my eyes, as I am having to do all of my laboratory microscope work on top of watching over new arrivals and a lot of sick animals. But it is enormously exhilarating.

The weather is getting hotter, and will continue to do so until, about Christmas, it will be in the region of 120° in the shade.

Last Saturday, I received a runner giving me two hours' notice of the governor's visit, which I had been half expecting for the past two weeks. The governor is Sir Lawrence Wallace who, having arrived out here in 1896, has been in this territory since 1901. He is a South African with a French wife who is, I gather, very charming.

I called out all the boys, and we had a great scamper round tidying and cleaning. I had told the natives that 'the Great Chief' (b'wana m'cuba) was coming and, as they are apprehensive of him, they put the place to rights jolly fast. His Excellency, universally known as HE, arrived in a buckboard drawn by eight fine mules and, having toured the camp and asked innumerable questions, stayed to tea with me. I had my personal boys in clean kansas, and they behaved beautifully. The two messengers acted as body-guards and then they, and my servants, stood behind our chairs in my room, quite motionless. It is uncanny how still a native can stand, and for how long.

I feel the visit was a success. I was congratulated in a most fulsome way when HE left and then, a few days later, an official letter of congratulations arrived. So I am pleased.

It is quite hard going now. Every day I have to take blood from every bull, examine it microscopically, and then bring my records up to date, as well as progressing the programme of immunisation. I also have natives on the sick list, two of them with bad fevers. This is partly caused by the strange weather pattern just now. Every afternoon, at about 2 o'clock, a terrible wind gets up and blows sand and dust into everything. The temperature at night is still low and the natives stuff every crack in their huts and then go out, naked, into the cold morning air.

Tuesday

My bulls, which have been inoculated, are all doing reasonably well, although many of them have temperatures of up to 106°.

Last evening, the three of us officials decided to have a sing-song after dinner, which is always a long, drawn-out affair. We try and finish outside work at about 6.30pm, then we write up reports and diaries, have a good bath and change into fresh clothes, so we start dinner at about 7.30pm. Anyway, last night we started singing everything we could think of until about 10.30. We even tried to sing the various parts in 'For unto us…' in the Messiah! Finally, at Thomas's insistence, we ended up with 'God Save the King'. Thomas is a stickler for etiquette. On Wednesday, one of our courses for dinner was sardines on toast; our boy served it as a first course and Thomas nearly went mad. He then spent about fifteen minutes, with the aid of a dictionary of sorts, trying to explain that this was a savoury dish, and should be served after the joint. I pointed out to him that we didn't have a joint, unless a tin of bully-beef was called a joint, and, anyway, the food was getting cold by the minute. He then told us that this was the price – cold food – that we must pay for teaching our 'poor, black, heathen brethren the ways of society'! It was a rather charming, if incongruous, little episode.

This morning, one of my messengers was limping badly, and I discovered he had an abscess on his foot. When he saw me pull out a scalpel, he began hollering and wriggling like mad. It took me a good half-hour to calm him down, and persuade him that all would be well. Yesterday, a boy reported that he was 'very sick'. His pulse and temperature were normal, so I guessed that he wanted the day off. I mixed him up a big dose of salts and also gave him two pills known, locally, as 'Livingstone rousers'. About six hours later I sent for the boy and told him it was time for some more 'make well' but he informed me he was feeling much better and didn't need any more!

26th August

On Monday, I had to go into Livingstone to see the administrator. He is going back on leave soon and, as the acting chief vet is away at some meetings, it seems I am to act as chief. As I can't possibly leave all the sick bulls at Maramba, it has been arranged that messengers will bring and collect letters and papers four times a day.

On Tuesday, I tested my new cattle for tuberculosis and found that two were infected: they were supposed to have been tested and passed in England! I went into Livingstone and reported the situation to the Governor. He said that he left it all to me, and would support whatever I decided to do. I had no alternative but to shoot them, and a post-mortem confirmed my diagnosis. But, just to be on the safe side, I have inoculated some rabbits as further proof. These carcasses provided meat for a big feast for all the natives, and this was followed by much merry-making and dancing round the fires.

Each time I meet HE I like him better. He is extremely helpful and understanding. He told me, on this visit, that when my Maramba project is finally completed, I must write up the whole programme, in a full report, and he will see that it is published.

Last night I had a bit of a fright. I was awakened by a dark form bending over me and trying, very excitedly, to tell me something. I jumped up in a bit of a panic, and became hopelessly tangled in the mosquito netting which completely covers each of our beds. He pointed out of my room, and I saw a native hut ablaze, across the compound. The occupants had fled safely, but they lost all their belongings. Foolishly, they had built a fire inside the hut to try and keep warm.

Ten days ago, a grand old Scottish farmer came over to see the bulls. We had a good chat about Edinburgh – he had not been back for 40 years – and today, one of his boys arrived with some preserved fruit, a great treat.

Summer is coming on apace; it is getting very hot and out are coming the flies. I move nowhere without my switch, which is made from a buck's tail stitched onto a carved wooden handle. Eating with a knife and fork and switch in one's hands is not very easy!

Last Saturday, all of us in the camp had quite a surprise. A motorcar ploughed through the deep sand and out stepped the British South Africa director who had engaged me in London, Mr Dougal Malcolm. 'Well, Smith, I told you I would see you before long,' he said. He was on one of his periodic tours of inspection, and had brought a car up with him on the train, solely to impress the natives. That he most certainly did! As he arrived, half of them fled, screaming into the bush, whilst the others just stood and gaped. As this was the first car in NR, we were all pretty impressed.

All the first batch of inoculated cattle are as ill as they can be. Of course I expected it, but some of them are very bad indeed, and I have been up most of the night with them. I feared two of them would die, but they seem better now. So far, I have had no deaths from inoculations, and am hoping to pull them all through. I had allowed for a ten% loss but, if I manage a 100% success, I won't know what to do with myself! In South Africa, their best success rate on all inoculations is 87%, and they have never dealt with more than 40 bulls at a time. But I have some time to wait before I can be sure.

My tall messenger, Mohenda, asked me about a month ago to send for his wife from his village. I wrote to the Native Commissioner but received no reply, so told Mohenda to off and fetch her. He wanted five shillings advanced on his wages, so I gave it to him. Soon after he left here, he met her, coming in the charge of a boy from the native commission. The NC had written me a note, saying that Mohenda must pay the native who had accompanied his wife, but he had blown the whole five shillings on a piece of vivid yellow material as a present for her. Mohenda, his wife and escort stood before my rooms with the former grinning from ear to ear! He told me he hadn't any money left but, because he was such a fine fellow, and because I would be pleased that he had got his wife – a girl of about 15 – with him I would want to make him a present of two shillings for the escort! I couldn't help but laugh, and told him that, as he was a married man, I would increase his wages to 12/6 per month, and would take the two shillings out of it. He gave me at least six salutes at this and went away as happy as a sandboy. In so many ways, these natives are just like children, and they cause me much amusement.

My pony boy gets twelve and sixpence a month, and asked me to hold back his money and give him 25/- next month as he wants to buy a wife: she will cost him £1. All wives have to be bought from their fathers, the price depending on the social standing of those involved. Another of my headmen is a chief's son, and his wife cost £5. He wears a different head-ring to denote his rank.

On Saturday, I was invited to a dinner for the governor, before he goes on leave. I have to wear full evening dress. So I shall be riding my pony, in white tie and tails, five miles through the bush, and then back again in the pitch dark. I shall take my pony boy, two messengers and a hurricane lamp. What a strange group!

I have been having an awful struggle with two of my bulls, and have been pouring medicine into them all week. On Thursday afternoon, one of them was so bad that I got another strong bull, threw it down beside the sick one, and opened both their jugular veins. Then I passed a tube between them, and the blood flowed from the strong to the weak beast. It was a chancy business, as I had to improvise all the equipment, but it seems to have done the trick.

Later

The governor's dinner was a great success. After the meal, we were all required to do a turn. I managed a recitation and 'the German at the telephone'! When I finally got away, and rode the five miles back through the bush, still in white tie and tails, it was well into the small hours.

The temperature is now about 106°, and a squad of prisoners is cutting reeds to provide more shade for the bulls, as I have now lost three from heatstroke. The whole camp is surrounded with armed guards, as the convicts are mainly serving long sentences for major crimes.

Ready for the Bulls

18th September

I've had my first orders to do a job outside Maramba, because of the senior men being away. It is a bit of a risk leaving the bulls, but as they are between two lots of reactions, I can slip away for a week. I am to take the train to Lusaka, a 300 mile journey that will take 36 hours. I shall be met there by a guide with a mule cart, and am to travel to the Sable Antelope copper mine, to investigate an outbreak of a strange disease which is killing the oxen pulling the wagons. It is good game country, so I will take my rifle and shotgun, and will be looked after by my messenger and my personal boy. I'll ship my bed, bedding and bath with me, so that I can be pretty self-sufficient.

Maramba is like an armed camp: each morning a white sergeant marches the convicts down from Livingstone, and leaves them with armed native troops, who surround the camp. We three officials carry revolvers, and I am trying to get used to the almost endless saluting which takes place. Africans adore ceremonial, and go out of their way to salute as frequently as possible. Amongst the convicts are sixteen murderers, of which six are chiefs. If a native chief is disobeyed, their 'law' requires that the offender be put to death, but the chiefs cannot realise that those days are over. The older ones still carry out their 'law', and some are not caught, but those that are get life sentences. One old chief of about forty – natives are getting old at that age – told me he had never done any work and that it was 'plenty hard'. He had killed six natives with his own hands, because they did not obey him. But he still cannot understand why he is in gaol: his father did what he did, why not him?

28th September

I travelled to Lusaka on Friday. I had a compartment to myself. My boy unrolled my cork mattress over the seat and I snuggled down under my blanket. The man sent to meet me was there, and we spent that night in a grass hut.

Lusaka consists of two tin shanties and a few grass and mud huts, and is mainly a dumping ground for displaced Dutchmen coming up from South Africa. (*The author's rather abrupt dismissal of Lusaka, now the capital of Zambia, was not too unreasonable. Only weeks earlier, on 13th July 1913, Lusaka had been declared a township, but, despite this, there were still no real buildings and the score or so of whites were mainly concerned with the railway sidings and the handling of supplies for the Sable Antelope copper mine near by. The whole area was lion-infested, and it was not uncommon for oxen, out-spanned beside the railway siding and waiting for the next day's train, to be killed and dragged off during the night.)*

When I discovered that the oxen I was to inspect were 85 miles away, through the bush, I refused to go. I could not possibly be away long enough to make that journey both ways. However, after making some enquiries, I discovered that some cattle 20 miles away were showing the same symptoms and so, on Sunday, we drove out with a buckboard and four mules to see them. My guide was a Dutchman; he had brought no tent and very few provisions. 'We can shoot our food,' he said. I was minded not to go on, but decided that two days away was bearable. We arrived at nightfall, and ate some tinned meat and drank tea, then I rolled up in my blanket under a shanty. Next morning, I examined the cattle and, from my microscope, discovered that they were suffering from a form of sleeping sickness (trypanosomiasis).

I got my Dutchman to drive me to within 12 miles of the station, and then decided I would rather walk the rest of the way. I persuaded three natives, from a nearby village, to carry my gear, and promised them 2/- each. Halfway, they downed loads and refused to budge unless I paid them 2/6 there and then. I didn't know a word of their language, and my boy only had a few words, but their intention was clear. So I pulled out my rifle, loaded it, and suddenly all was sweetness and light! In future, I shall never, never travel without a messenger, my own tent and proper provisions. I had learned an important lesson.

Later

I've finished my first batch of bulls: they were sent off around the country on Friday; the others go next week.

Last weekend, travelling to Lusaka, I saw my first lion – from the carriage window – a magnificent specimen. The long trek I missed from Lusaka would have taken me through the finest lion country in the world. Incidentally, I was offered a tiny leopard the other day – for a pound. It was a beautiful, fluffy, cuddly ball of fur, just like a kitten. But common sense prevailed, and I politely declined.

I'm finding the languages very confusing: each tribe, and there are 72 of them, has its own dialect and all are quite different. There are four in this camp alone! So I've decided to try and become proficient in one, and then just pick up the others or, at least, some of the more important ones. But I'm fearful of making the wrong choice. I am, however, very lucky in my cook, as he speaks eight dialects and fairly good English, so I get some help from him. The thermometer has just touched 110° in the shade, on my verandah. It is very hot for us all, and for my poor bulls.

On that 600-mile round trip to Lusaka, I was again surprised at the countryside. There are no railway stations; the train stops beside a small corrugated shanty, which serves as the station offices, and a couple of mud huts complete the picture. Two or three farmers stand beside the track to receive their mail and catch up on the gossip: that is that. This vast country consists of a railway line and tiny outcrops of habitation beside it.

3rd October
The rains have started. At about 5 o'clock last Tuesday, it suddenly began to get dark, then a terrific wind sprang up. The dust was awful, coming in great clouds, through which it was impossible to see anything. Then the thunder and lightning began, and appeared to be directly overhead. The noise was deafening, the whole place seemed to rock and the lightning, a combination of sheet and fork, lit up the countryside for miles around, flashing every few seconds. Between the flashes it was pitch dark. I put on a coat and sat on the verandah, totally transfixed by the utter majesty of it all. Then, suddenly, the wind dropped away completely, and down came the rain, in absolute torrents. But it did cool everything from the 120° it had been earlier.

I am having to lay some of my natives off, now that the main part of the Maramba job is finishing. They are entirely philosophical about it, as they only work to accumulate the hut tax. Beyond that, they leave it to the women to do everything. Those that were going lined up outside my hut on Thursday to be paid. I came out onto the verandah, and they all raised their right hands and shouted 'Shala gaiehla Inkoos' ('Go in peace, oh Chief'). Then each came up in turn and gave me a chief's salute.

It is quite a complicated business paying natives. There are no coppers: the threepenny piece – a tickie – is the smallest coin, and by far the most used. I paid one boy four half-crowns, but then another ten separate shillings, and had the devil of a job explaining to the first that he had received the same as the second, despite having six coins less.

One of your letters mentions my wearing khaki trousers in the towns. Livingstone is the only town! This is a vast unexplored country, with only about 30 or so white farmers, quite often separated by hundreds of miles. One farm or ranch can easily be 100,000 acres but maybe only a few hundred of them are cleared of scrub and forest. Some parts of NR have never been crossed by any white man although, of course, our officials are scattered through the areas where there is some native population.

Tuesday morning

I had a bit of an outing last Saturday. It was so hot that I couldn't face riding into Livingstone, and managed to get a government mule cart sent down to pick me up. I got to the Club at about 5.30pm, and then went on to dinner at the Drews' bungalow. It was quite a gathering and, after dinner, we had some music until about 1.00am. I stayed the night, and at 6.00am the boy brought coffee. As I was drinking it, the acting administrator walked into my room. He had come for breakfast, and began questioning me about Maramba and my work there. Things certainly happen here in a most unexpected way!

On Wednesday week, there is a *café chanson* in Livingstone with a play *A Pair of Lunatics*. I have been persuaded to play the male lead opposite the major's wife (he is at the barracks commanding the King's African Rifles). I've learnt my part and, yesterday, rode back into Livingstone for our rehearsal. Mrs Stennett is driving out in a mule cart on Friday, and we will rehearse again, this time in the open air. The performance itself will be in the Barotse Gardens as there is no suitable building available. That night, I have been asked to stay at Government House. You can see we all work hard to provide our own entertainment.

10th October

I've had my first dose of malaria. We all take quinine tablets regularly every day, but as this camp is down by the river, it is practically impossible to avoid mosquitoes. *Maramba was only a few hundreds of yards from Old Drift, which had so many deaths from malaria and blackwater fever.* It is about two weeks since I went down and I'm practically fit again, but I did feel extremely unwell for a few days. Unfortunately, I couldn't let up on my microscopic work, and so just had to make the best of it.

I have been keen to get out in the cool of the evenings, so encouraged some of my natives to make a dugout canoe and paddles. This they do in next to no time, hacking out the centre of a tree trunk for the hull, and fashioning the paddles from branches. So, most evenings, I go off with two paddlers about a mile downstream and then back. It is perfectly beautiful: the banks are lined with palm trees, some over 300 feet tall, whilst canaries fly about in droves and are a wonderful sight. On my outing yesterday, I stopped to watch a couple of baboons swinging and jumping through the trees. They must have been well over six feet tall. There are a great number, with monkeys, in one of the groves not far from my camp.

I've had trouble with my personal boy. He is a frightful liar and, after finding a number of my things in his hut, I had to get rid of him. I had given him three warnings, but the fourth time was too much. I caught him wearing my wristwatch, also a pair of my white trousers. A week later, I found him wearing my gear as he was leaving to visit his village, so I had no alternative to chucking him out. Major Stennett is trying to find me another boy. It's all rather a pity as he was a good worker and knew his job, but I would never have had a moment's peace.

The real rains are still not here, so we're having to put up with excessive heat. It's quite impossible to do anything between noon and 2 o'clock. The temperature today was 116° in the shade, the hottest day so far for me. I just lay naked on my camp bed as the sweat rolled off me onto the blanket beneath. There is no wind and a cloudless sky. I believe the rains, when they do come, will be equally dramatic.

The natives looking after the bulls have abandoned all clothing and have shaved their heads. Even they are uncomfortable in this heat. One boy has scrounged a great big overcoat and, believe it or not, is wearing it every day, such is the power of pride!

There is a saying out here that the moon is so bright that one can read a newspaper by it. Well, last night I tried: I couldn't manage a newspaper, but I did read a book! The moon is very beautiful, hard-edged and casting sharp shadows everywhere.

19th October

I've started drafting my report and will be able to claim a 94.6% success rate. I'm quite pleased, as most people feared it would be considerably lower. In fact, I believe I've set a new record as, previously, the best figure was 87.4% in Southern Rhodesia, with considerably less virulent cattle diseases.

Yesterday, I went to Livingstone to greet a new vet arriving by train from the Cape. He is very young and just qualified, and is to be stationed right up north at Fort Jameson. That means the 36 hours in the train to Lusaka, and then a six-week trek to the fort. He won't be able to take a pony, as he will be passing right through the middle of the 'fly' (tsetse fly) country and no pony would survive. But the compensation is that he will be going through what is regarded as the finest game country in the world. Out here, one is certainly thrown in at the deep end! He will simply have to set out on foot and learn everything as he goes. It's quite a frightening prospect being the only white person for hundreds of miles, when the only forms of transport are your own two feet or being paddled in a dugout.

Our *café chanson* evening seemed to be a great success, and our little bit of theatre went splendidly from start to finish. As there were some important visitors staying at Government House, Major Stennett said he would put me up at his place at the barracks. There was a real panic just before dinner on the evening of the show. I had sent one of my boys ahead with my evening clothes, giving him a note to the clerk at our office asking for a messenger to take him to the Stennetts. The clerk was pretty silly, and sent my boy off with a lad who didn't know where he was going. I rode in at 6.30pm... no gear. Crisis! Eventually, just in the nick of time, one of Stennett's policemen brought my boy and the messenger in. It seems they had simply gone from building to building standing still until questioned. If it was not the right house, they just moved on to the next, and so on. All was well in the end. I've written of this at some length to illustrate how natives, unless they are exceptional, will never use any initiative or be conscious of any sense of urgency. One has to be aware of this and operate a 'fail-safe' system of explanation. Every request must be spelled out at great length and in great detail. After the show, a crowd of us moved to the Stennetts and continued the party until 3.00am.

The natives reacted interestingly to my taking part in the play. News of it had got round the camp, somehow, and some of them got permission to stand at the back, for the performance, and watch. The next day, when I returned, the onlookers stood outside my hut grinning from ear to ear! They hadn't, of course, understood a single word but, at one stage, I had to pretend to hypnotise the leading lady. My boys were hugely impressed, and believe I have the power to put people to sleep!

Monday 20th October
When we set up this camp, I promised my assistants, Thomas and Woods, that if all went well with the bulls, I would throw them a dinner here to celebrate. Well, the great day has arrived. I've sent a couple of boys to the Zambezi with instructions to catch a bream or else! This is our menu: olives, soup, tinned prawns and fresh bream, curried kidneys, chicken, mince pies and custard, caviar on toast, papaw, oranges, nuts and coffee, not necessarily in that order! The meal to be washed down with champagne and South African wine. Try and picture the three of us, dressed up to the nines in dinner jackets, solemnly sitting round a small table, surrounded by huge fires burning outside scores of native huts, eating *à la*

Claridges, although we are out in the deep bush and five miles from the nearest other white man!

This is my last day at Maramba. I am to return to Livingstone for two or three weeks, to prepare for my trip north. I will stay in the Government House guesthouse, so will have a bit of luxury and being pampered before ploughing off into the bush.

So I have now completed, successfully thank goodness, the special commission for which I was specifically engaged in England six months ago. My life will again change dramatically, and I'm much looking forward to this next challenge.

6

Preparing to Trek

3rd November 1913

I have now moved into the guesthouse. Apparently, in 1910, the Duke and Duchess of Connaught – he was better known as Prince Arthur, and was the brother of King Edward VII and son of Queen Victoria – visited Livingstone, and a bungalow was built to accommodate his staff. When the acting administrator visited me last week, I plucked up courage and asked if I might use it whilst preparing for my trip. A smile spread across his face and he said he would see! Anyway, a note arrived from the secretary saying that I might use it, so I am extremely comfortable after roughing it a bit down at Maramba.

My orders are to work in the Sesheke district, which lies northwest of Livingstone and forms part of the vast native reserve of Barotseland, itself covering about a third of NR. Sesheke is 180 miles through the bush without any road or rail link. There is a native commissioner (a white official responsible for all native affairs) at this post who has his wife with him, and a French missionary. That is the sum total of 'civilisation' I can expect for the next six months or so.

The Barotse, the tribe inhabiting this huge reserve, in which no white people are allowed to settle, are a fine people. They are cattle farmers, and count their wealth by the numbers they own. Their king, or paramount chief to give him his proper title, lives in the centre of the territory, but his son and heir, Litia, lives close by Sesheke.

It seems that, for some time, the Barotse tribe have been losing thousands of cattle from disease. I am to tour the territory for six months or so, trying to pinpoint the problem and suggest remedies. I shall establish a modest HQ at Sesheke with my laboratory equipment, but will carry sufficient gear to do the necessary diagnostic field work.

Perhaps it will help to put the whole operation into perspective, when I explain that Barotseland is very nearly the size of England. All travelling is on foot, along bush paths or tracks, or by dugout canoe on the rivers, the largest being the Zambezi itself, into which many, many other rivers and streams feed.

I am to be allocated seventy native carriers or porters, each of whom will carry a 60lb load, his own blanket, his cooking pot and his armoury of a knobkerry (a wooden club with a small axe blade set in one side) and one, two or three assegais or spears. I shall have a further seven natives comprising my 'staff', so I shall be totally responsible for feeding, watering, protecting and looking after the health and well-being of about 80 human beings, and one pony!

I am busy making lists and buying provisions and stores, a daunting task for someone who has never done this before. I simply cannot afford to forget anything, as I shall be away from all supplies for at least six months, and maybe even longer. Fortunately, the extremely helpful stores manager, universally known as Mac, has vast experience of officials going out on trek, and he has guided me, not least by adding all the little necessities I was in danger of overlooking.

It is only practical, in this weather, to carry about two days' food for my boys, and so I have to be sure to shoot enough meat and fowl to see us through. Their meal, ground from mealie maize, will be supplied from the villages we are passing through although, of course, I am to 'pay' for these provisions with sixpences and threepenny pieces (tickies), of which I shall carry quite a quantity in canvas bags.

Setting myself up for this journey has cost me all the balance I had in the bank, and some more, but I am determined to be as well equipped as possible. I have had to buy a second rifle, as my .303 is not capable of stopping lions and buffaloes. I managed to get a .375 off a man returning to England, after I had got the armourer at the barracks to check it over. I will need these guns if I am to provide all the food we will be consuming day in and day out.

You will still get my letters, and I yours, fairly regularly, as a native runner leaves Sesheke each week with the mail and official papers. He has to run – or jog-trot actually – through the bush the 180 miles to Livingstone, so there is bound to be some delay. I think some of my letters may be quite five weeks reaching you.

Two of my messengers come from Sesheke and so, yesterday, I told them we would be off there in a few days. You should have seen the look on their faces. The grins broadened until they stretched from ear to ear. I asked one of them what he was so pleased about, and he replied, 'M'kasi wanga adipo' ('my wife is there'). 'How many wives?' 'Two'. He has lately been giving me his money to keep, and now he has 22 shillings saved, so I bet he plans to buy another.

Unfortunately, the native dialect I needed at Maramba will be no use in Barotseland, so I have to brace myself to learning theirs. Happily, both messengers will be able to help me to begin with. I'm pleased with my senior messenger, Matapi. He was offered the post of head messenger at Livingstone but refused it, preferring to stay with me. He would have earned £1 per month, so I managed to increase his pay from 12/6 to 15/6 as some compensation.

My stores are being divided up into 60lb loads, almost every load containing a little of everything. This is a precaution against losing some vital provisions or equipment during, say, the crossing of a river. It is also time-saving at making and breaking camp every day. Salt, as I may have mentioned, is a very scarce and precious commodity. I already have several loads, but need yet more. It is necessary for my carriers in their mealie-meal food and is, of course, a very popular present for village heads and lesser chiefs. I've invested in a large galvanised tin bath for myself. All the pots and pans will be carried in it, constituting a load for two boys, who will carry it with a pole passed through the handles. I fancy it may prove to be a bit difficult to carry through the dense bush, and will certainly create quite a clatter! I've also bought a large tent with two fly-sheets, one of which will provide a sitting-out verandah at the front.

The key men on this trip, and on all such trips, are the messengers. They originally got their name because, in a land with no written word, the passing of messages is often of vital importance. So 'messengers' memorised and delivered important government instructions, and then stayed to ensure they were carried out. Matapi, my head messenger, is a chief's son, and was once a paddler in the *Naliquanda*, paramount chief Lewanika's state barge, which is almost certainly the largest dugout canoe in the world. It was fashioned from one massive tree-trunk, is about 70 feet long, and needs 30 expert paddlers, standing up, to take it upstream against the current. The senior boy, after the messengers, is 'Shilling', as he has been with me since I arrived in NR. He stands a good 6' 3", and is built in proportion. He is an expert assegai thrower: I've seen him dislodge a shilling piece at 30 yards. He carries my guns, and is always at my elbow when I'm on the move.

I am, of course, taking Champagne, but I won't be able to ride him all the time, as we have to travel through two 'fly' belts, one 27 miles wide and the other 19. Champagne will be sent on ahead, travelling through these areas during the night, for it is only then that the flies do not bite. Otherwise I would risk losing him from this pernicious disease.

Whilst in Livingstone, I've managed to go to St Andrew's Church a couple of times. As virtually all business here is conducted by 'chits', with little cash changing hands, I found the collection operated the same way. It does mean, though, that how much is given by each churchgoer does tend to get known to a good number of inquisitive people!

I was anxious to have a pretty comprehensive medicine chest, so asked the PMO if I might raid his stores. He let me do so and, when he saw what I had collected, said, 'Well, you've practically cleared me out. Do you realise this lot must be worth at least £30'! But he let me keep it on condition that I didn't mention it to a soul.

The climate is certainly not pleasant at the moment. We get terrific downpours which arrive quite suddenly, and yet the shade temperature is moving towards 120°. The damp has brought out every conceivable fly, beetle and creepy-crawly. We spend our days and, particularly, our nights, pulling off and sweeping away a host of horrid creatures from our clothes, our hair, our food and our drinks. It is extremely disagreeable.

24th November
My carriers have still not arrived, so I am spending this spare time making sure my arrangements are as good as I can get them. I will have: 20 boys with food; 20 on tents, my furniture(!) and personal gear; 10 carrying my laboratory equipment; four with my clothes and then four or five loads of assorted items such as spades, pickaxes, buckets etc. One boy is carrying all my medicines: I hope nothing happens to him. I have also bought a large cover for my messengers, their wives and hangers-on, and a shelter for the cook.

If I have some luck shooting on this trip, I shall try and send some trophies, such as horns and skins, back to you in England. Everywhere you go here, you see splendid horns and lion and leopard skins. There are also many fine examples of native carvings from a central area. Some of the native women are hardly able to move for the bangles they adorn themselves with. I have seen several with bangles all the way from ankle to knee and then knee to thigh. Some even encircle their bodies with hundreds of them from waist to shoulder, although these are usually the wives of chiefs. The women here do practically all the work, as well as all the carrying. It is not unusual to see a woman carrying her baby strung across her back in a shawl, with a huge three-feet-cube load on her head and with both hands full, whilst her husband walks a few paces ahead, with only his knobkerry and a bunch of assegais.

1st December
I am still at Livingstone and champing to be off. Would you believe it, we are expected to take dinner jackets so that if we meet another European we can dine together in style in evening dress, in the middle of nowhere! It is almost beyond belief! In fact, as I shall be trekking right beside both German and Portuguese territory, I shall be expected to do some 'official' entertaining, if you can call it that!

This is the last mail to reach you for Christmas, so I wish you all a very happy time and all prosperity in 1914. Think of me on Christmas Day – we are about two hours in front of you – sitting down to Christmas dinner in a temperature of about 115°, looking and feeling as if I am in a Turkish bath!

Sir Starr Jameson, who engaged me in London (the great Dr Jim) arrived last Friday and I met him again, this time at the Governor's garden party. He had read my report, and discussed it at great length with me.

The native band from the barracks played throughout the afternoon. It consists of about 60 uniformed and very smart natives, not one of whom can read a single note of music! The bandmaster, a European, gets all the players of one instrument together, and plays their part to them over and over again, until they have grasped it. He then sends them off to practise that bit until they have learned it. He repeats this rather laborious process with each section of instruments, until he judges it is time to put it all together. Then he gets all 60 of them going, and beats out the time for all he is worth. It is really surprisingly successful and, amazingly, the standard is not far short of some bands I have heard at home!

Yesterday, I went to church: it was full, with 48 of us. I have joined the choir, and we all sang with terrific gusto, which was pretty creditable considering the heat in that tiny building. Our suits were soggy with perspiration! Our parson is a baronet, Sir John Key, a great enthusiast but not a very effective preacher. He must be conscious of this because, as with yesterday, he tries to get missionaries and visitors to preach. He and his wife are an eccentric, but charming pair. She wears thick tweeds, on the principle that if they keep the heat in, they should, equally, keep the heat out! There are many delightful tales told of her absent-mindedness. Major Stennett called on her one day and stayed a while. Suddenly Lady Key said, 'Dear me, it is 6 o'clock, I have forgotten my native class. I left them at 2.30 to learn a verse of poetry.' Apparently the boys were all still sitting in exactly the same places, calmly gazing into space! This is one of the unnerving traits of natives: if told 'Luida' ('Stay here') the native will stay and not move for hour after hour, until somebody tells him otherwise.

Here are my carriers! At last! I must break off.

7

My First Trek

———————•◦•———————

Kalamhora's Village
Barotseland
5th December 1913

I t is only four days since I sealed up my last letter, but such a lot
has been happening. After days of relative calm, all was hustle
and bustle in a near-chaotic situation. The carriers had been
several days on the road to Livingstone and were tired, filthy and
suffering, in some instances, from sore feet. So the messengers set
about getting them looked after. I decided I would take things very
easily for the first few days, and try and get them back into shape
to face the couple of hundred miles we will be walking to Sesheke.

I'm afraid this letter will be much delayed. I tried to establish
where I could catch up with the mail runner on his way down to
Livingstone, but something went wrong and I missed him. I have
to make detours to all the villages en route, to inspect their herds,
so am constantly leaving the main track used by the runners.
Anyway, here I am on the third day of my first 'ulendo' in Northern
Rhodesia, feeling fit and extremely happy to be off at last.

By daybreak on the day after I closed my last letter, all was ready
for the off when a runner came in to tell me that I must carry seven
days' food for my whole camp, as the villages we would be passing
through, this first week, are badly short of maize. It seems that there
is a general shortage throughout the territory. The villages nearest
Livingstone have sold everything they could lay their hands on,
ignoring the fact that, in due course, they themselves would have
to go short. I also got a last-minute message from Sesheke, again
by runner, that they are out of salt, and would I please bring up
an extra 250lbs!

It is all a bit difficult, as I have no spare carriers, but I managed
to fix for a mule cart to bring four days' food and the salt to this

village to meet up with me here. Kalamhora is on the Zambezi, as is Sesheke, so I have told the village headman that he must provide me with a dugout and paddlers to take some of our gear and the salt up to Sesheke, so that my carriers can take up the extra maize.

Well, after all that, it was after 11 o'clock on Tuesday before my 'caravan' of 80 set off. I waited behind, saying my goodbyes, for a couple of hours, and then rode off on Champagne to catch them up beside the Sindi river, where I planned to make my first camp.

I reached the site a little before my carriers, and was much impressed at the procession as it wound into view. Out in front walked a messenger with my own boys, two of whom had my guns and my travelling gear; then came the seventy carriers with a second messenger in the middle; the rear was brought up by the third messenger. Each boy has a pole across his left shoulder. At one end is tied his 50/60lb load which is counter-balanced at the other with his blanket, cooking pots and calabash of drinking water. In his right hand he holds his assegais and his knobkerry. He carries these over his shoulder, and under the pole, to lever some of the weight off his left side. The whole procession made me feel uncomfortably like a slave-trader!

Every now and then a messenger called out 'M'sanga, m'sanga, m'sanga' ('Faster, faster, faster') but it seemed to make little difference. I judge we are progressing at about two and a half miles per hour.

Let me give you my routine yesterday. My cook was up at about 4.45am, and had breakfast ready for me soon after 5.00. I ate it at my small folding table which had been set up under a tree, laid with a cloth and my silver and china. Whilst I was eating, the boys were packing up my tent and furniture, such as it is, and getting ready for the trek. Daybreak was at 5.30 and, about ten minutes later, we were off. We walked until 11.00, when we rested and I had lunch. At 2.30 we were off again until 4.30, when we found water and stopped to make camp.

One messenger took twenty boys to cut and collect firewood; another took twenty more to carry water, whilst the rest pitched my tents and got the whole camp set up. During all this activity, cook was busy with my dinner. By the time I finished my meal, darkness had fallen, and the fires had been built up to the size they would be kept all night. After a long day, I was happy to turn into my camp bed with fresh, clean linen sheets at 7 o'clock. I slept like a log.

I arrived here at 12.30 today, and will stay put, as water is 10 miles further on, and my carriers could do with taking it fairly easy for a day or two. The going is very rough, and a number of them are still having trouble with their feet: it is bare feet all the way, and they simply cannot avoid sharp stones, thorns and potholes, and all the hazards of rough bush tracks. It is a wonder there isn't more trouble in that direction.

It rained hard in the night, and the boys had no protection except for their blankets and what little shelter a few branches and reeds could afford. Then they had to march, carrying 50/60lb loads plus their own things. They manage all that on 2lbs of maize plus whatever meat, fowl or fish I have been able to provide.

I always supervise the distribution of food myself: the bags are brought to my tent, and the messengers weigh it and serve it out. I got used to doing that at Maramba. Last night, this new lot of carriers tried one of their favourite tricks out on me. It is quite usual for one boy to collect meal for two or three others; he holds up his fingers to show the number of helpings. I knew the way the game was played, so counted carefully, but kept quiet. Eventually the full quota had been served, but one boy stood by the scales still holding up three fingers. I promptly said 'Chapweno, palcha sappano' ('Good, all finished now'). The boy simply walked away. He muttered something under his breath which I did not catch but the messenger, grinning, translated 'The master is good, he is not a fool like some'. In native psychology, the boys will think more of me for having spotted the trick than for doling out extra food.

I am beginning to feel really fit again, and have walked practically all the way today but, in consequence, have a badly blistered heel. We've had to cross two rivers, and Champagne swam splendidly with me on his back, trying to keep out of the water. I told the carriers to put their loads up on their heads and they managed to keep them all dry; well, all but one, who had a good ducking. I was afraid he might have been carrying flour but, happily, it was washing soap!

The second morning out, I saw the sun rise on the great Zambezi river, a most beautiful and awe-inspiring sight which I shall never forget. It rose in about 10 minutes, and all the huge, tall palms – well over 200 feet high – were reflected in the shimmering surface of the water. It was breathtaking.

Today, we began striking some larger villages. As we approach each one, a messenger goes on ahead and, by the time I arrive, all the inhabitants, with children, goats and chickens have turned out, with the chief standing in front. Then they all drop on their haunches and begin to clap their hands in rhythm, quietly at first, then getting louder and louder and faster and faster, and then all dying back. This is called a 'candalella', and is the greeting afforded a chief or white official. In a large village it can be quite deafening.

I called at Chomo's village this morning – each village is named after the present chief – and was provided with a gourd of fresh milk, the first I have had since leaving England six months ago. I had forgotten just how delicious it is. In return, I gave Chomo about as much tobacco as would fill a pipe, and he almost split his face, such was his grin of pleasure. I also managed to buy a chicken for sixpence. I handed it to my cook, who promptly strung it up by its legs, still very much alive, to one of the carrier's poles. He said that way it would taste better at dinner!

I have recognised how different – and difficult – it would be to trek here without messengers. They wear a uniform, which is immediately recognised, and it strikes the fear of god into all and sundry. Messengers have the power of arrest and considerable authority, and no one dares to trifle with them.

The three messengers and cook have their chief wives with them. The ladies left Livingstone dressed like Solomon in all his glory, with perspiration pouring off them in their unaccustomed finery. But common sense has prevailed, and the four of them have reverted to the simple, long loincloth, but nothing else.

5th day
Ngweze River

I didn't write anything yesterday as I was extremely tired. We covered 20 miles to get back to the Zambezi, so as to be sure of water, as the rains have been light in this area, and the sun has baked the earth hard. As a consequence, the boys are still suffering with their feet.

We camped at Mowhowa's village, and I went off to try and shoot some food. I saw scores of pheasants and guinea fowl, and four bribi – small buck rather like deer – but just couldn't get a shot in because of the density of the undergrowth.

The route, yesterday, was quite the most pleasant so far. The track was straight through a very large forest; the paths were only three or four feet wide, which made it difficult riding. It was even worse for the carriers, as they had to twist and turn, and duck and weave to get their loads through without them being caught in the branches. The tracker boys out in front are quite remarkable: they seem to have a sixth sense on which to rely, and very rarely make a mistake. Once again, I found myself tucked in bed by 7.30pm.

This morning we started at daybreak and headed straight for the Ngweze River, but when we reached the banks we found it bone dry. The next dependable source of water is 19 miles further on, and I judged we simply could not manage that. So I began to search around. After a good hour, I found a small green patch on the river bed. I set the boys to dig, and we struck water at about seven feet It took simply ages, as all the soil was lifted up from hand to hand. When we finally got to it, you could hardly call it water, but it was wet! I shuddered at the thought of drinking it, but the boys tasted it and pronounced it 'very good'. I am taking no chances and am having it well and truly boiled, but I have to say that my tea didn't taste too bad.

This little episode has brought home to me what a responsibility I bear for the 80-odd natives travelling with me. They need food and water every day, day in and day out. If we hadn't found that brackish, muddy water, I suppose there would have been nothing for it but to battle on for another 19 miles, as we only had five quarts left, and that would not have gone far amongst the lot of us.

All today we have travelled over the open veldt: no trees, no shrubs, no vegetation of any sort. As there is no water, nothing grows and, in consequence, there is no game. We are heading for the Kasai River, which is large, and then the day after, with a bit of luck, we will reach Sesheke.

I can't remember if I told you of the natives' eating habits. They never have any breakfast and so do a long stint of marching, carrying their loads, on empty stomachs. In early evening, they put their mealie meal (ground maize) into their iron cooking pot, over a fire, and add water until it forms a paste-like consistency. They stir it with their assegais, and then fist it out with their fingers, adding pieces of meat or fish. All the time, they are sitting on their haunches, a position they can quite comfortably maintain hour upon hour. After this meal, they build up their fires and curl up, with or without a blanket according to the night, and go off to sleep.

Sesheke

Tuesday, 8th December

I must dash this off in a great hurry. I arrived at 10.00am this morning, having been walking since 4.00, some of it in the dark, only to find that the mail had been sent off by dugout on the Zambezi two hours earlier. Anyway, it has been agreed that I shall send these letters down to Livingstone by special runner. As it is 180 miles, and he has only four days to catch the mail-train to Cape Town, he will have to go like mad: 45 miles a day in these conditions is pretty good going!

I've met Mr and Mrs Jack Venning – he is the district commissioner or magistrate – and they seem awfully nice. I'm to have lunch with them, and then tea with the assistant native commissioner and his wife, Mr and Mrs Ingram. The 'house' I should have had is badly riddled with white ants and is being repaired, so I am to occupy two huts such as the natives use, kept for just such an eventuality.

We have all had a big disappointment: the mail from England arrived but, on opening the sack, we found newspapers but no letters. Apparently, this happened once before and, as a consequence, it was nine weeks between letters and news of any kind from home. As you can imagine, the four resident whites are pretty mad, and a stinging letter goes off with mine to the postmaster in Livingstone.

I will write next week. All best wishes for a New Year full of happiness, prosperity and good health.

8

An Unusual Christmas

Sesheke
Barotseland
10th December 1913

I am now well and truly settled in, if occupying two large native
huts, with practically no furniture or belongings, can be called
that! I don't suppose it will matter too much, as the two white
couples here are so hungry for outside company and recent(!) news
of England that I shall be spending much of my free time with them.
I say 'recent' news, which it is to them, but I have to keep reminding
myself that I have been away for about six months.

I'm making Sesheke my HQ for the next four months or so, and
have paid off my carriers, as I want to recruit local natives as and
when I need them.

But I'd better pick up where I left off, at the Kasai River a day
or two back. We tramped through a forest beside the Simalaha
Flats next day. This is a noted area for lions and, although I didn't
see any, I did see the spoor of what was obviously a huge one, each
paw mark the size of a large soup plate, with each pad the size of
a saucer. That night we took no chances, and built up extra large
fires. The natives crowded inside them around my tent, with
Champagne tethered right in the middle. But we weren't disturbed
and I slept like a log.

Last Tuesday was the high spot of my trip so far but before I
tell you about it, I need to explain how things are run up here in
Barotseland.

As you already know, Lewanika, an old man of about 80, is
paramount chief of all Barotseland, but as his 'kingdom' is roughly
the size of Britain, with no communication other than by dugout
or runners or, of course, by bush telegraph, he is assisted by others
of his family. Some of the power and authority is devolved to

Lewanika's eldest son, Litia, and some to his sister and her daughter, known as the Moquai and the Little Moquai. They, rather confusingly, rule over various tribes within the part of the country ruled either by Lewanika in the north or by Litia in the south. Put simply, it works like this: northern Barotseland is administered by Lewanika himself although his sister, the Moquai, looks after certain tribes within that territory. The southern part of the country is administered by Litia, with some tribes being looked after by his cousin, the Little Moquai. It is all rather difficult to sort out but, in practice, it seems to work.

Now let me try to explain, roughly, how the country is actually ruled. The Paramount Chief is advised by a khotla which is, to all intents and purposes, like the British Cabinet. The members each have responsibility for an activity or department, much as ministers do at home, the difference is that all the members of the khotla are chiefs – senior chiefs – in their own right. The khotla has a special meeting hall, where all their deliberations take place. Whilst the Paramount Chief listens to all the advice he is given, he is free to accept or reject it as he pleases. Then, over everyone, our British Administrator guides, advises and oversees all major decisions and pronouncements, although he tries to interfere as little as possible, whilst seeing that law and order are maintained and justice administered.

It is important to appreciate how powerful these rulers are, and what loyalty they command. They all have many servants and retainers around them, and live and travel in considerable style, comparatively speaking!

Anyway, after that diversion, back to Tuesday and the high spot of my trip.

I was to visit Prince Litia. His 'capital' is about half a mile away, across a small plain from our HQ. The government station was set up here, at Sesheke, specifically to house the resident commissioner who advises him. Natives are great enthusiasts for ceremonial, and so the whole day was laid out according to the recognised ritual. First, we sent a messenger to Litia to say we would visit him. The messenger was sent back to tell us that it would give the chief much pleasure, and it would be a great honour, if we would visit him. We promptly went off and had lunch! This ensured that we would keep Litia and all his people waiting, thus raising the status, not only of us in their eyes, but also of Litia in the eyes of his people! A strange business!

Coming back with our messenger had been an induna, or headman, to act as guide, so he had to wait too. When we had eaten, a procession formed up as follows: the Prince's induna, three of Jack Venning's messengers, Jack and myself on ponies, three more messengers, six native policemen from the NR police in very smart khaki uniforms, two pony boys and, finally, two personal boys.

Litia has a most imposing set up: the British Government had supplied some bricks and so some of the buildings had solid walls. The other native huts are of considerable size, with very finely patterned thatch and most cunningly finished walls and entrances.

All the way to the village, our route was lined by hundreds of natives squatting, on either side of the dirt track candalelling. It was quite moving, if noisy. When we reached the gateway, a huge candalelling crowd greeted us, as Litia walked out to welcome us. He is a fine figure of a man, aged about 50, tall and good-looking, with great courtesy and beautiful manners. He was dressed in a white suit – the first native I have seen thus attired – and was attended by all his chiefs and headmen. He led us in procession to the audience chamber, which is a large and imposing native building with three huge carved chairs, a standard lamp with pink shade, and many magnificent woven mats and animal-skin rugs on the floor. An enlarged photograph of King George V and Queen Mary seemed a little out of place!

The prince sat on the largest of the chairs, with his headmen squatting on the earth floor behind him. Jack and I sat opposite. Venning, of course, speaks the language fluently, but etiquette requires that there be a 'mouth between', and so an interpreter passed the conversation backwards and forwards. It is a slow business, especially as, again, etiquette requires that a well-rehearsed formula is followed. This always happens unless the meeting is established, beforehand, as being informal.

Prince: 'It makes me glad to see you so well.'

Venning: 'It gives me much pleasure to see you so well.'

Prince: 'I trust Mrs Venning is well.'
Venning: 'Thank you. She is very well.'
Prince: 'The administrator and all your people are well?'
Venning: 'All are very well.'
The conversation, through an interpreter, went on like this for a full 15 minutes, then ended with:
Venning: 'Does your aged father (Lewanika) carry his years well?'
Prince: 'His years do not trouble him'.
Suddenly the ceremonial ended, and the atmosphere changed when Venning said, still through the interpreter, that something had displeased him. It seems a murder had been committed in an outlying village, and no evidence was forthcoming. In a most courteous but authoritative way, Venning pointed out that, unless some evidence was produced to assist in the administration of justice, the villagers involved would be held collectively responsible. I gathered that, although the prince almost certainly knew nothing of the murder, he would see to it that those responsible were brought down to Sesheke to be tried.

After this exchange, I was able to join in as Litia is well-known for his interest in, and knowledge of, cattle and everything concerning them. I explained that I was going to set up an intelligence system, so that I could keep myself informed of all diseases and problems, and I asked that word be sent out to all the villages for the information to be passed speedily to me. As I explained my plans, Litia asked extremely well-informed questions and kept turning to his senior councillor behind him, saying 'See that this happens'.

Our meeting lasted from 2.15 to 4.30. As it drew to a close, the compliments resumed along the lines when we arrived. The procession then reformed, and back we came to the station. It was all quite fascinating, but being in a white linen suit and tie after weeks of bush shirts and shorts was very testing indeed.

After this, Venning took me to be introduced to the missionaries. Interestingly, all of them are French and Protestant; there are no British at all. The Rev. Roulet, his wife and young assistant are all charming and most friendly. Unhappily, their little boy is quite ill with blackwater fever, but is just about over the worst. This is a particularly bad spot for malaria and about every kind of tropical disease, and is especially so in this, the rainy season.

Incidentally, I am already earning quite a reputation for my medical prowess! Whilst with Litia, I was asked, at great length and with numerous compliments, to have a look at one of the Prince's sons who had given himself a nasty gash with an assegai. I also had to see a senior chief's favourite wife who was down with a fever. I did my best for them both, but was stymied when a native arrived with a large, bulging hernia!

Sesheke is magnificently sited on the banks of the Zambezi, where it is about half-a-mile wide. Across the river is a thin strip of German territory, known as the Caprivi Strip. In 1890, German South West Africa was granted this bit of land, along the Zambezi, so that they could have access to it for a railway which, in the event, they never built. The German foreign minister, at that time, was Count Caprivi, after whom the 'strip' was named. The German resident's house is plainly visible, set amongst huge palms, which are all in flower with every kind of exotic colour.

The British station consists of the resident's house, the native commissioner's house, my 'house', the office with the union flag flying, the prison and huts for the six native police — the askari — and the 20 government messengers. Behind these dwellings are huts for servants.

I'm beginning to settle in, and have fixed with Litia's induna to send me three quarts of milk, night and morning, at a cost of 10/- per month. I'll then show my boys how to make butter. I've also bought some laying hens and should soon be having my own eggs.

Incidentally, it was just about here on the Zambezi that David Livingstone crossed on his way south from Lake N'Gami in 1855.

Last evening at about 5.00pm, Jack and I decided to take a dugout, and a couple of paddlers, and try and shoot some duck. We were just ready for the flight when the heavens opened and it truly fell down. The rain was so torrential that we could only see a few yards. When we got back, I found that the office gauge showed that 2.02 inches had fallen in 30 minutes!

As I shall be stationed here for some time, Jack has 'sworn me in', which means that, in the event of an emergency, I could be called upon to take command of a group of natives and messengers. To this end, we three Englishmen have rifle practice each Saturday. I badly need this, as I have been shooting very poorly at ranges over 300 yards. Venning is acknowledged as a superb shot: he has lots of trophies, and holds the record for the largest buffalo horns in the territory.

It seems that, every Christmas, the Vennings give all the government boys and their families a great blowout, so I am resolved to get back to HQ before the 22nd. That evening, Jack, the French missionary and I are to set off with trackers and paddlers to a favourite spot for game. We will camp for a couple of nights, with a full day's hunting in between. We'll need a big bag to satisfy all the boys, their wives and children.

But before that, I am to make a week's trip to try to solve a difficult problem. We've had a message to say that a French trader was tracking through Portuguese territory, not far from here, and has strayed into German territory by mistake. On hearing that the German authorities were out to get him for illegal entry, he crossed the river into our domain, about 60 miles away. This is, in itself, illegal but he is travelling with some cattle, a number of oxen, mules and a horse, which means he is also contravening all sorts of government regulations on importing and exporting animals. I'm expected to do something about it all, but just what, I can't think. Jack has suggested that I quarantine the lot for a year at Sesheke, then we can purloin the oxen, mules and the horse for our own use: not very helpful!

Saturday, 13th December
The rains have arrived with a vengeance! It starts raining at about 4.30pm and in the past two days we've had over four inches, but it will do my vegetable patch good.

The general shortage of mealie-meal has affected us now. There is absolutely none on the station. So we plan a day-break start tomorrow, to a promising game area about 15 miles down-river.

We will take a big dugout and a good crew of paddlers, to try and replenish our larder.

We've also been visited by another French missionary, on his way through to open a station about 500 miles north of here. He is short of dugouts and paddlers, so Jack is fixing for Litia to supply both.

Yesterday, I travelled out a bit and examined some cattle belonging to a white trader who had received permission to keep them at a village not far away. I discovered that over 50 beasts had died in recent weeks, but nothing had been reported, as is required by regulations known to all. I caught up with him later in the day and, innocently, asked how his cattle were. 'Splendid!' he said, 'no deaths'! His scheme was to conceal the deaths, so that he would get permission to move his herd out of Barotseland, when he hoped to sell them. The upshot is that I have sent off a summons for him to appear before Jack Venning. I have confiscated and quarantined his cattle, and am glad of the opportunity to show the natives that white traders get no preferential treatment over them.

My 'house' is nearly ready, but I shall be terribly short of furniture, and would dearly love a chest of drawers, but I shall have to make do with shelves made out of old packing cases.

In a dugout on the Zambezi, opposite German territory
19th December
Since I left England, you have had letters written in some strange places and in unusual circumstances, but none more interesting than this! I am sitting on a rug in the bottom of a 40-feet native dugout canoe, under an awning of reeds to keep off the sun. Despite its length, the dugout is only about 24 inches wide, with a couple of inches freeboard. One paddler, standing, is in the fore part of the dugout in front of me, whilst six more, also standing, paddle behind me. They have astonishing balance as they all remain upright, despite the quite frightening rocking caused by the rhythmic plunging of the paddles. I am having to write in pencil, but I think you will still be able to read it. Behind this dugout, another of similar size carries my tent and gear, also Tolani and Matapi. I am on my way to see the cattle, oxen and mules illegally

brought across the frontier by that Frenchman. I had to ask Litia for both dugouts and paddlers, and he readily supplied them.

I set out yesterday, at daybreak, and travelled with very few stops until 1.00pm, going up against the stream, which was flowing strongly after so much rain. I plan to get to Katima Mulilo's village tonight, leaving me a five mile trek to get to the Frenchman's camp. I then plan to make the return trip, with the stream, in a straight 13 hours.

These paddlers are extremely fine specimens of men: all have enormously developed shoulders, but with noticeably spindly legs. They can, and do, paddle for hours on end, only pausing occasionally to scoop up a handful of water from the river to drink. Otherwise they never break the rhythm. I tried my hand at paddling yesterday, but had to steady myself with two assegais, driven into the craft, to prevent myself from tipping over into the river. I was dead-beat after a pitifully short time, and can hardly conceive how my boys keep it up, flat out, for six or more hours at a stretch.

The Zambezi is very wide, getting on for a mile at this point. The Germans occupy the opposite bank, with Portuguese territory a little further upstream. Both strips of land are narrow, being planned to give each nation just enough access to the river. The scenery is spectacular, with long views of waving palms and tropical trees, glinting in the sun.

I have a line out behind trawling for fish and, so far, have caught eight: some must weigh as much as 10lbs. A paddler can easily eat his way through a couple of these for his single meal of the day. Yesterday, I shot a goose and a couple of duck and had one of the duck for dinner: it would have tasted less tough a good three years ago! A short while ago I passed two hippos, but I didn't want to waste time now, as I'm determined to get back to Sesheke for our pre-Christmas hunting trip.

Sitting, rocking in this dugout, I have been reflecting on the parties I am missing in Livingstone. I was asked out on Christmas Eve, Christmas Day, Boxing Day and New Year's Eve, with a lot going on during the days between. But it doesn't do to dwell too much on 'what might have been': there is little profit in that.

Later
I called at a village after writing the above, and established that my quarry was camped up above some substantial rapids, the Kachekabwe. So I asked the chief to let me have two experienced paddlers to help my crew up through that stretch. The cost of sixpence, for both to go up and back, can't be complained of!

Am writing this slap in the middle of the rapids; the boys are working like mad; I'm scrawling away with these few lines, because I feel sure nothing has ever before been written in such a situation. More later.

6.00am Sunday, 21st December
It is two days since I wrote whilst ploughing up through the rapids. Shortly afterwards, we were forced to stop by a torrential thunderstorm and pitch camp on an island in the middle of the Zambezi. We were all drowned, and the whole camp was awash. The next morning, I packed all the paddlers into my dugout, left my gear in the other tied up at the island, and pushed on as fast as we could go, to a spot on the bank which left me just two hours from the Frenchman. When I got to his camp, only his cattle were there. So I examined them and, as everything was in order, I decided the only course of action that made sense was for me to go back to Sesheke and talk over with Venning what, if anything, either of us could or should do.

I'm now on my way back, going with the stream, and hope to reach Sesheke about tea-time.

It was extremely exciting going up through these rapids, with the narrow channels through which a dugout could just scrape, and through which the water rages. At times we seemed to be making no headway at all, and the boys called to each other to paddle harder. Every now and then, a boy would jump out of the boat on to a rock, give a great shove, jump back inboard and pick up paddling, all the time the dugout rocking wildly. One boy did miss his footing and, to the great delight of his colleagues, fell in! To peals of laughter, he swam to the bank, ran upstream, and then jumped back in at the next opportunity. Being river people, they can all swim like fish.

But by far the greatest thrill is to come down the rapids with the stream. This was my first experience, and a good part of the time I stood up, holding on for dear life to the roof of the latunka, partly for a better view but partly, I must admit, to be ready for any eventuality, as it did seem a rather dangerous moment in my life! Fortunately, I had collected two extremely experienced paddlers on the way up and, as they practically live on the rapids, they knew every rock and eddy: they took the two vital bow and stern positions.

As we approached the rapids proper, which I estimate fall a good 20 feet in quite a short distance, I could feel the pull of the current. The boys then simply hold their paddles in the water, to steer and act as a brake. The bowman decides the channel to take, with the least number of rocks and the least turbulent water. Into the first channel we plunged; out went the bow's paddle against a rock to swing the bows clear, then the stern-man would do the same to clear the rest of the boat past the danger. The natives react like lightning, changing sides with their paddles and leaning this way and that to prevent the dugout being swamped. A laden dugout has a freeboard of only a couple of inches at the best of times, so there was a good deal of water slopping around. As we came to the most testing reach, the bowman shot me a split-second glance. I guessed he wanted to see how this raw white man was taking it all! Then we were well and truly in it again, twisting and turning, and swinging from near-miss to near-miss!

Suddenly we were through, wringing wet, but tremendously exhilarated by the sheer skill and boatmanship of my boys, who stood up in a 40 feet by 24 inches dugout right through. As we slid into the still-swift, but comparatively calm stream, the bowman called out 'On o my yo', to be answered by the others with a resounding 'Yo' as they dug their paddles even deeper, and lifted the dugout with the sheer power of their strokes. I looked back at the second dugout: it was a very dramatic sight as it followed after us. Our bowman's call is difficult to translate and is only to be heard on the river. The nearest I can get is 'Now, let's really go!' Sometimes, when I do my stint at paddling (kneeling down I have to admit), I have called out 'On o my yo', back would come the answer 'Yo', and the dugout would surge forward with the extra effort. As the paddlers strike the water, in perfect rhythm, they breathe with a peculiar hiss and grunt, which adds drama to the whole affair.

After the Kachekabwe rapids, we called again at the village to drop the two extra boys and to pay them off. As my bowman stepped ashore, he said to me 'Ki kehoma, Morena?' ('Was that good, chief?'). I replied that it was very good, and was rewarded with a huge grin.

Just past the rapids, yesterday, we came upon a shoal of 13 hippos, but as I was suffering from a wretched migraine headache, I didn't want to risk just wounding, so had to let the opportunity pass. These hippos are simply huge. They shove their snouts above the water to breathe, then sink and re-emerge some way away. The hides are most sought after, and fetch £4, as they are cut into strips and used for harness on wagon oxen. As an ox cart can be drawn by no less than 30 or 40 beasts, a goodly supply of hippo hides is needed.

Four of my paddlers are from Litia's own barge and are a much higher caste than the carriers. Yesterday, they kept going for six hours without a single break, despite the fact that they had done sixteen hours without a bite to eat. They live virtually all their lives on the river, and are quite unused to travelling any distance by land. Being on the river by day at this time of year is quite beautiful, but the evenings and nights are more troublesome. The downpours are so sudden and spectacular that it is extremely difficult to get or to keep dry. My camp-bed, which has been pitched in some pretty odd places since I left England, is wet right through, and is rather uncomfortable.

Saturday, 27th December
The day after I got back from my river trip, I received my Christmas mail. It was wonderful timing, having only taken three-and-a-half days by runner all the way from Livingstone. These boys really are marvellous! It was a great joy getting all your family letters, and quite a few from friends as well.

The day after the mail arrived, Tuesday 23rd, we set off early on our Christmas hunting trip, but it was all rather a disappointment. Firstly, Jack couldn't come, as he had to hold a sudden enquiry over slavery: some tribes still practise it, despite strenuous efforts to stamp it out totally. Secondly, we found that the heavy rains had driven the game back into the bush, the 'we' being the French missionary and myself. I only managed five beasts despite tramping through the undergrowth for two solid days. Towards the end, I crawled flat on my stomach for 45 minutes, trying to get a large buck about 300 yards off, but he saw me and bolted. I fired, but only hit him in the shoulder, so had to crash through the bush again for a good two miles before we caught up, and I could finish him off. Altogether, it was a rather frustrating trip, and the Rev. and I were dead-beat on our return. Thankfully, I slipped into my camp-bed at 8.00pm and slept the clock round.

Next day was Christmas Day, my first out of England. It was to be a stifling hot one with a shade temperature of over 100°, a far cry from reindeer, sleighs and snowball fights! The Vennings have an old wind-up gramophone, a portable HMV, and I was awakened by one of their boys standing over me, holding it while it poured out 'The First Noel'. They gave me a beautiful buck hide for my floor.

But the really big event of the day was the official opening of the Paris Evangelical Mission Church, which the Roulets, the Rev. and Mrs, with their assistant, had been building for months. They were, naturally, terribly excited, and it was an occasion I shall never forget. The mission is on the banks of the Zambezi, about one mile from our station, and it was decided that Jack and I should officially represent the British government at this French occasion. So we went the mile up river in state, in one of Litia's ceremonial dugouts with twelve paddlers and a capito, or head-boy, overseeing everything. Ahead of us, acting as escort, was another dugout with six messengers and six askari, all got up in their best uniforms and standing up in the boat *à la* Royal Marines on a battleship! We were met at the tiny landing stage by the Rev. Roulet and Litia who, also, was making this a ceremonial occasion: around him he had all his retinue of chiefs and headmen.

Off we all went to the brand new church, dressed up to the nines in a great variety of outfits! The church, which can accommodate about 500 souls, virtually all standing, is a brick-and-wooden structure and is most imposing. The missionary had baked the bricks himself in a home-made kiln, and done all the joinery as well: it really is a tremendous effort.

When we were all gathered, a procession formed up, with the children leading and all we dignitaries(!) bringing up the rear. We paraded round the church whilst blessings were intoned, and then in we trooped. The native congregation was segregated into male and female, with the children squatting on the sandy floor in front. Benches were arranged for the Europeans, all five of us, and for Litia, who sat next to me. Then the service began. As it was in Sekololo, the local dialect, I couldn't follow it all but joined in, in English, at the bits I knew by heart, including the opening hymn which began 'Yes, I'll sing the wondrous story'. 500 enthusiastic, and perspiring, natives belted it out most impressively. The *bouquet d'Afrique* was almost unbearable, especially for poor Mrs Roulet, who was battling away at the pedal harmonium with perspiration pouring off her.

The second hymn, 'All hail the power of Jesus' name' was an even greater success. The almost-naked children in the front, and the gaudily dressed adult natives behind them, practically lifted the new roof! Litia had his outsized Bible and hymn book carried before him on a cushion by a native servant. He and his headmen regularly attend services, but are not 'members' because they practice polygamy.

The Rev. Roulet gave a short sermon, and then something happened which was almost unbelievably strange. It was a part-song which the participants had obviously been working at for weeks. I could hardly believe my eyes and ears. The parts were sung by: Litia, the Little Moquai (his cousin), Litia's favourite wife, his prime minister and his three most senior headmen. They sang amazingly well, and with considerable confidence. It was a most stirring performance, deep in remotest Africa on Christmas Day, and in front of a handful of white Europeans.

As the part-song was being sung, I could not prevent my mind from dwelling on the incongruity of the whole situation. Litia's father, Lewanika, had, with his own hands, killed the six men who had opposed his claim to the throne. Then, in the war against Lobengula which followed, he and his tribesmen warriors had slaughtered every single man sent against them. They had also caused the death, by starvation, of hundreds more by the simple ruse of luring them onto an island in the middle of the Zambezi, and then stealing their dugouts in the darkness. Lobengula's men couldn't swim but, even if they could, they would have been eaten by crocodiles.

The Little Moquai's mother, who is still alive, had murdered, or arranged the murder, of three of her husbands, and had personally cut the throat of the fourth. Yet the offspring of these multiple murderers were calmly and cheerfully standing up in church, singing their hearts out to the glory of God! It was a unique occasion.

Next, Litia spoke. He recalled how the missionary came to teach his people, how far he was from his family and friends in France and how he had never asked for anything, but had built the church, with his own hands, for the benefit of all the natives. Next, the prime minister and the three headmen added their appreciation. The service ended with another hymn.

There was a huge Christmas feast for all the mission natives, and we were asked back to their house by the Roulets, but we politely declined, as it might have been an embarrassment to them, which we would not wish.

We later had a simple meal with the Ingrams, and all repaired to their rooms to sleep through the worst of the heat. Then we all got dressed up again for Christmas Dinner with the Vennings. What we were to eat was no surprise, as Jack and I had gone out in a dugout with two paddlers to shoot our meal! We hid in some tall reeds at the water's edge, and managed three duck and a paw, which is not dissimilar to a turkey, weighing about 40lbs.

It was a merry evening but, inevitably I suppose, we were all feeling a long way from England, family and friends and, in a way, were relieved to turn in at about 11.30pm

So ended my first Christmas away from England. It had been a strangely moving one, from the scratched strains of 'The First Noel' and the dramatic and totally unexpected dedication service, to the meal with a handful of English men and women, drinking each other's health, and that of family and friends back home, beside one of Africa's greatest rivers, hundreds of miles from any hint of civilisation.

9

Sour Milk and Crocodiles

<hr/>

I have just had a most interesting chat with one of the local chiefs, and have learned some fascinating things. Chief Nalissa is a very old man indeed, and too frail to move, so I went to his village, which is not far away.

He recalled that it is 60 years since he saw David Livingstone leave the Zambezi at exactly the spot I left it three weeks ago, at Katima Mulilo. He was the first white man to be seen in Barotseland, and Nalissa was able to describe the whole episode in great detail. I was riveted by it all. He also put me right on the Lobengula/Lewanika story I wrote about the other day, and which I had slightly wrong. It seems that Lobengula, the legendary Zulu chief and one of Africa's most dramatic characters, had sent his impis, the fighting regiments consisting solely of six-foot-plus warriors, over a thousand miles north, to try and wrest Barotseland from Lewanika, who was already earning himself a considerable reputation as a powerful leader.

The Zulus had made a mistake, and had travelled north on the wrong side of the Zambezi, along the bank opposite where Lewanika had gathered his fighting men. At his council of war, attended by the youthful Litia, it was agreed that Lewanika would pretend to sue for peace, offering to send boats and paddlers to carry the impis across to his bank for discussions about terms. The Zulus fell in with the suggestion, and were picked up by Lewanika's dugouts. But instead of paddling their 'guests' to their own bank, they took them to a large island which, from the opposite bank, looked as if it were the mainland. The impis landed and then, suddenly, the paddlers shot off, leaving the Zulus stranded. As they are not river folk, none of them could swim, indeed even if they had been able to, they would have had short shrift from the crocodiles. The Zulus were left to starve, hundreds of them, while Lewanika and his people sat half a mile away and looked on.

This elaboration on the story made the events in church, on Christmas Day, even more bizarre. Litia, with his large Bible and hymn book, and his participation in the part-song, was the same Litia who had sat with his father, 30 odd years ago, watching hundreds of human beings, fine brave Zulu warriors, starve to death under their noses.

I remember explaining how Barotseland was ruled through Lewanika and his sister the Moquai up north, and Litia and the Moquai's daughter, the Little Moquai, in the south. As she was also in church that day, I should tell you something of that daughter as, to an extent, she is cast in the same mould.

Moquai Ininyani, the Little Moquai, lives at the native village Sesheke, for which our station was named. This is only a short distance from her cousin Litia, whose village is called Maondo. She is an extremely hard case, with an aversion to being interfered with by white officials. She frequently gives us no little trouble, quite unlike her cousin, Litia. The drill is always to visit her in the afternoon when tea is served, but none of us wants to do that more often than is absolutely necessary! I always seem to have something to complain of, or have to insist upon and so have experienced some unpleasant audiences.

The Little Moquai is a handsome woman, but with a violent temper which ensures that her retinue of relatives and servants is extremely careful about the way they conduct themselves in her presence. One of her little peculiarities is getting rid of her husbands. Some of them having disappeared in puzzling circumstances. The husband is in a difficult position: he is her subject, and has no share in his wife's authority as a ruler but undoubtedly, under native custom, has a husband's rights over her. However, none of the past spouses exercised their rights, except one who gave her a good hiding, thereby establishing his proper position in the household. Sadly he died, from natural causes surprisingly, and the present husband was chosen to take his place. The 'victim' could not refuse; had it been possible to do so he most certainly would.

As you can see, much of what we have to assume as a reasonably civilised way of life is but skin-deep, and old attitudes and patterns of behaviour often still lie just beneath the surface.

Although we are a long way from the centre of activity at Livingstone, and have to go without many of the things most of us tend to take for granted, I must admit I am glad to be based here. Jack has been kind enough to tell me that the natives I've come in contact with have let it be known that I'm 'all right': so far so good!

I have virtually nothing to spend my money on here except food and ammunition, yet I find it almost impossible to save. The cost of food is simply prohibitive, and this leads to much swapping and bartering. I make butter, but too much for myself, so I swap it with the Vennings for other foodstuffs. Just the other day, they got a ham sent up from Livingstone. It was a great treat, and I managed to swap a duck and a goose for a couple of slices! Jack, apparently, simply adores ham and is guarding it with his life. He told his boys that if any of them so much as lets one fly get at it, he will have them brought before him and given 10 years hard, without the option! The tiny bit he has got left, he has refused to swap for anything less than six months' extra leave! Such is our little life on this station.

None of us, the whites that is, moves more than 20 or 30 paces without being accompanied by a messenger. This is not for any reason of status or importance, but is a practical precaution against anything and everything, and I'm not meaning against natives. We have to be on our guard, all the time, against wild animals, snakes and, especially, crocodiles. As we have no medical facilities and are days away from any help of that nature, it is simply not worth taking chances.

I now have about 15 fowls, which I have bought at 9d each and, although they are wretched layers and I'm pretty certain the boys pinch the eggs, I hope soon to be able to vary my diet a little. I also have the fresh milk from Litia's herd. The other morning, the milk was sour. I told Matapi and, the next day, a native was sitting on his haunches outside my quarters. He was the culprit, apparently, and Matapi was conducting a long monologue which went on for a full 15 minutes, the boy not being allowed to get in a single word in his own defence. Matapi told him 'Shangive' (the medicine chief, my native name) was very angry. 'How could such an important man be expected to drink sour milk? It is offensive to him. He is a great chief and comes from over the greatest river in the world. So how can he be expected to drink sour milk. He makes the cattle sick, then he makes them well again. Whatever he pleases, the cattle do. He has great powers and much magic, and so cannot be expected to drink sour milk.' Natives simply love to go on and on and on like that; to take everything slowly is to enhance one's reputation, whilst any sign of haste is interpreted to the contrary. For instance, if a chief comes to see me about some cattle, I take no notice of him for a good 30 minutes. He just sits, motionless, outside my office. Then I send for a messenger, one of whom stands on duty close by the entire day, and then keep him waiting. Eventually the chief is escorted to me and, by now, is hugely impressed by the importance of the man he is being seen by: me! This will, in turn, reflect to his own greater glory when he repeats the whole story, which he surely will, when he returns to his village. It is a wearisome, but absolutely vital, routine.

I went to Litia on Tuesday to complain that things had not been happening as he and I had agreed. We sorted it out at this 'indata', interview, and then he gave me tea in some lovely little china cups he had ordered from England. He also showed me some of his photographs. The Duke of Connaught, on his visit to Livingstone in 1910, had given him a camera at the reception which Litia had attended: it is one of his most prized possessions. His quarters are quite palatial, and very interesting, and he impresses me considerably with his intelligence, his courtesy and beautiful manners.

The other day I was trying to explain to my messengers about England, its size and the number of its people. I had found a photograph of Queen Victoria's diamond jubilee and showed it to them: they just could not comprehend such a vast crowd. Explaining numbers is tricky, as a native can only add up to 10, five fingers on each hand. He will calculate the passage of time by cutting notches on a piece of wood, noting the passing of the months by marking the new moons. All I could say to them was that the crowd – it happened to be a picture of the Queen outside St Paul's – was just a tiny part of her 'tribe', but it was obviously way beyond their grasp.

This is a most unusual rainy season. It has been dry for the past two weeks, and the crops desperately need water. If we don't get the amount of rain that is usual, the mealie-meal crop will fail right across Central Africa, and we will face actual starvation for thousands of natives. They are notoriously improvident, and never take account of such circumstances as drought. Year in and year out they each – the women that is – till and plant a patch about the size of a tennis court for their whole family. It is just, but only just, enough for a normal wet season. If the rains do not materialise pretty much to time, their crops fail, but the natives never learn. They seem to see it as the will of nature.

I told you that I had a pet monkey here. Well, he is a pet no more, having decided to slip his harness and disappear back to the bush. I can't say I blame him.

I am making some interesting and, potentially, most important discoveries on the health of cattle. It has long been thought that only the tsetse fly carried sleeping sickness. But I am discovering trypanosomes in some cattle here, as well as two other species of fly, so I am expanding my experiments using monkeys, dogs and cattle. I have to be thankful that the anti-vivisectionists are not out here to obstruct me. If my fears prove to be founded, it will be of paramount importance right throughout Africa and beyond, and I will need to write up my findings for publication. But it is early days yet, and I am still waiting for a separate small hut to use as a laboratory, so that I can do more detailed studies. If I could really get the answer to these diseases, I would feel all my discomfort decidedly worthwhile.

At last my house is finished! It was the original residency some time ago, but was ravaged by white ants, as is every single wooden structure throughout Africa. Anyway, it's finished, and I've got Litia to send a team of women to put the finishing touches to it. This involved plastering the walls, which they did with their babies slung across their backs in shawls. They mixed ant heap, dung and water and, using their hands as trowels, achieved a passable finish which, of course, dries in hours. I managed to find some chalky soil and mixed it to make a crude whitewash. You should have seen my women when they had finished: as much on themselves and their babies as on the walls! Afterwards, they all trooped down to the Zambezi, stripped naked and washed themselves, their babies and clothes. This is a dangerous business because of crocodiles which can, and do, lie a few feet from the water's edge, with only the tip of their snouts showing, waiting for unwary bathers.

The payment for plastering and whitewashing was one tickie plus some salt each. I can't think HM Government can jib at that!

I was struck again, today, by how seldom I hear a baby cry out here. I wonder if it is because they spend the greater part of each 24 hours cradled across their mother's back. I can think of no other explanation.

Yesterday, one of our native commissioners came through Sesheke on his way back to England on leave. He was tremendously excited, as he only sees white men for a couple of days, once every six months, as he is in the depths of Barotseland. He said he was genuinely confused at having to speak English for several hours on end!

9th January

I am hoping to move into my house tomorrow evening, but it won't take long, one deckchair, one folding chair, one camp-bed, some food boxes for drawers, one shelf for photographs and some hooks for clothes. That's it!

We are having great trouble controlling the movement of cattle. The whole matter is to do with containing disease and conserving grazing, so that there is enough for all and, especially, for the natives whose country this is, and for whose welfare we are responsible. To this end, I had to send an urgent message to my boss in Livingstone. I called a messenger – I now have eight – and said 'Tisa, tiwa Livingstone, tiwa Morena Lane. Kapiri, kapiri'. He saluted and said, 'Morena'. I had told him, 'Take this message to Chief Lane in Livingstone. Quickly, quickly'. He replied, simply 'Yes, Chief'. He showed no emotion, no concern, nothing. Off he went to his hut, collected his blanket, some food, two assegais and trotted off. I never cease to be amazed at this sort of behaviour.

We have some really terrific news. For months now, a huge and exceptionally audacious crocodile has been helping himself to men, women and children along the banks of the Zambezi by the mission. All the residents have had a go at him; in fact, Jack and I, in the short time I have been here, have seen him twice, but each time he has slithered off before we could get a shot in. Well, on Tuesday, Litia and some hunters finally got the brute. They speared it and managed to haul it back on land, which was a good thing as crocodiles are cannibals. Jack and I shot four over the past few days and, as they rolled back into the river, they were set upon by their colleagues(!) and torn to bits in minutes. A very unnerving and spine-chilling sight. Litia's monster, 13' 2" long and with a girth about the size of a bullock, was found to have quite a collection of human bones inside him. The rejoicing at his demise was considerable. It is particularly pleasing that it was Litia who masterminded the operation.

Sunday

It has been a bit hectic over the past few days. The Administrator, His Honour Mr McKinnon, who is number two to the Governor and is acting Governor at the moment, suddenly decided to bring his wife with him on a river trip from Livingstone to Sesheke. He has served in Barotseland for years. They are both very fond of the country and its people, and so get away from Livingstone whenever they can. They arrived yesterday in a veritable flotilla of boats, all, of course, dugouts paddled by natives. We were warned of the visit only one day in advance, so we posted runners to report on their progress and to warn us when to be ready to greet them. We also alerted Litia.

Our squad of six askari, native police, was paraded by their corporal, and I inspected them, before despatching them to the landing-stage to form the guard of honour. Our messengers lined up opposite, and the sight was really quite impressive. Then Litia brought all his headmen and chiefs with him, and a vast crowd of natives lined the bank for hundreds of yards. Litia had sent runners out, and had used his bush telegraph to round up all the natives in outlying villages to witness what, for them, was quite a considerable occasion.

As His Honour, wearing full-dress uniform with sword, and Mrs McKinnon stepped ashore, the askari and messengers snapped to attention and, at a sign from Litia, a quiet, deep murmur began from the many hundreds of natives present. It slowly grew in volume until it was a great roar and then, again at a signal from Litia, every single native, with the exception of their chief, leapt in the air and then threw himself, or herself, on the ground and remained there, silent and motionless. This is the royal salute, and it was the first time I have witnessed it carried out by such a number: it was both exciting and moving. Such was Litia's apprehension at the arrival of such a senior official – to him anyway – that he was grey with anxiety, and perspiration was streaming down his handsome face. As he stepped forward to greet the McKinnons, he was almost speechless with nervousness, although he had seen and spoken to them a good number of times before.

I looked round the vast crowd, but could detect not even the blink of an eye. The askari and messengers might as well have been cast in bronze. Natives have this extraordinary ability to remain motionless in just about any position for a very, very long time, hours if need be.

This sudden and unexpected visit is making life much easier for me. A number of problems have been dealt with, on the spot, and it has also been agreed that a carpenter will be sent up from Livingstone to build me some quarters for my experiments with animals, as well as a hut for my clinical and microscopic work. He will also make me a few extra sticks of furniture, I hope!

His Honour has given me full powers to do exactly as I feel necessary to try and improve cattle health and conditions throughout Barotseland. This is splendid news and results, Jack has told me, directly from the success of my work at Maramba with the bulls which, I gather, is being discussed as a major contribution to the Northern Rhodesian farming economy. So I feel pleased with my first six months out here.

I am now installed in my house, bare as it is. My shelf of photographs greatly intrigued my boys who had, unknown to me, invited all their village pals in for a squint. I caught them at it and there was a great and sudden exodus.

Saturday

All yesterday I was at a village, eight miles from here, examining cattle and inoculating a good few of them. Suddenly, I saw a flight of crested cranes, which are huge, and not unlike secretary birds, but with beautiful golden crests sticking up over their heads. This is the emblem of NR, so I hope I won't be flung into gaol for shooting one, but I wanted to inspect it at closer quarters.

Mrs Venning is off next week to Cape Town to have her baby: she and Jack are going to Livingstone by dugout. One can only admire a heavily pregnant woman travelling in such a manner, camping at nights and sleeping rough, when the nearest medical help is 180 miles and many days travelling away. She is extremely stoical and cheerful but will, I'm sure, be glad to get out of this heat in her condition.

I intend to meet Jack a short distance downstream on his return, and we are then to trek together. I need to see a lot of cattle and he, with me, plans to try and sort out a possible slavery situation at a village a good distance off which, it is believed, has never hitherto been visited by white men. It should be interesting.

Perhaps I can demonstrate the violence of our tropical storms at this time of year by telling you that, the other afternoon, lightning struck the missionary's herd of cows and killed nine out of twelve at a single stroke. That same night, I was woken by an almighty crash. I jumped up and could just see, through the torrential rain, that my kitchen hut had collapsed completely, burying all my gear, and bending and smashing a good many of the pots and pans and most of the chinaware. It may have been lightning, or simply the weight of rainwater. I could do nothing about it then but, at dawn, we set about retrieving what we could, and rebuilding the kitchen.

But, let me end this letter on a rather more optimistic note. My garden is looking really quite respectable, and I'm beginning to feel rather more excited at the prospect of actually having some green vegetables after months without. I've got beans, peas, tomatoes, lettuces, carrots and onions. I've also set a handful of potatoes, and am waiting for them to come up. I shall treat myself to one binge with them, but keep the remainder for further seed stock.

10

Shangive: Medicine Chief

I should now be on my way to meet up with Jack Venning as we planned, but a couple of days ago Tolani, my treasure of a cook, went down with an extremely bad attack of blackwater fever. This is a serious complication of malaria, produces a very high temperature and calls for hospital treatment with blood transfusions and continuous nursing. As you can imagine, all this is impossible. I carry a modest supply of the most commonly used medicines, as does Jack, but beyond that we have to rely on care, the fitness of the patient and a pretty thick slice of luck. My cook has been more or less unconscious for the past 36 hours with terrible sickness. I am doing my damnedest for him by injecting strychnine, which is all I have that is remotely suitable. I am, after all, a vet and not a doctor. At about 3.00pm yesterday, I was sure he was dying, and upped the strychnine, adding whisky in the hypodermic as a last resort. I am hoping that was the moment of crisis, as he seems fractionally less ill this morning, although still wracked by violent sickness. Again, I have no remedy for this, so I blistered his stomach to see if that would help.

I dare not, and would not, go off and leave him, as I believe he would surely die, if for no other reason than that natives, once they are at all ill, chuck in the sponge and exhibit no will to fight and live: it is a problem.

Tolani and Matapi are by far the most important natives around me. Tolani does a lot more than just prepare and cook my meals: he manages the stores, supervises my personal boys and, because he speaks eight languages, acts as my interpreter.

Perhaps it is timely to give you some idea of the problems of sickness out here, especially in the wet season. Violent changes in the temperature and humidity, the fact that we are often sodden to the skin for hours on end, and the existence of, literally, clouds of mosquitoes give rise to any number of unpleasant fevers and sicknesses. Malaria is, of course, our deadliest enemy. It can vary from a mild attack, with sudden high temperature, shivering and profuse sweating which lasts a few days, to virulent attacks that need to be treated in hospital. Our only recourse against these wretched, buzzing, vicious little creatures is to take, every single day without fail, a substantial dose of quinine, to cover the entire body from top to toe the moment the sun sinks and, also, to sleep under special cotton netting which is suspended over the bed of every white person in the land. It is quite impossible to avoid every mosquito. Stagnant pools and swamps, of which there are hundreds of square miles, are prolific breeding grounds for these malaria-carrying creatures. I suppose it is just one of the things summed up in the phrase, 'the white man's burden'.

Being at HQ, if three houses and a cluster of huts can be called that, is resulting in a certain sameness of diet, especially as Jack's cook is not a patch on mine. For the past week I've had chicken for every meal, and some pretty tough chicken at that, and could well do with a bit of a change. But that will have to wait until I am, once more, out with a gun.

You would be amused at the way we buy these chickens. Native traders appear, with a long pole over one shoulder from which are strung a dozen or so scraggy fowl, tied by the feet to the pole. This doesn't seem to fuss them, as they make no attempt to flap their wings or squawk. The native lowers his pole, straightens up the wretched birds and, after candelelling, squats outside my office or house waiting to be spoken to. I notice him but, in compliance with etiquette, do nothing, as do my messengers. Eventually, I am told he is here with chickens to sell, but it would be quite wrong for me to be involved, in any way, in the ensuing negotiations. It is deemed to be beneath my dignity to have anything to do with such a domestic arrangement. Having consulted with my cook, the messenger will begin a long bartering session, during which each will hold forth at great length – often for 15 minutes or more – on the virtue of the birds, and on the importance and fussiness of the official for whom the birds are being bought.

All this is a total charade, as there is a market price for all cocks and hens and absolutely everybody knows what it is: 6d for a cock and 9d for a hen. But the whole rigamarole has to be played out to the bitter end.

Eventually, a deal is struck(!), but the next problem is that no native, especially raw bush ones such as these, can count or calculate. So each bird that has been bought is laid out, still tied, and the appropriate cash is placed beside it. Only thus can the trader see that he is being paid the correct amount. As we only buy hens, a sixpenny piece and a tickie are placed on the ground beside each hen. At long, long last the deal is concluded, to the satisfaction of both parties.

There is something strange about the tying up of chickens. No matter where they have been reared, or last lived, a bird that has just been released from bondage will never stray from its new environment. When I was living in my hut, my birds roosted every night in a tree beside that hut. When I moved to this house just 30 yards away, the boys caught the birds, tied them up and brought them to the yard beside the house. They left them trussed for a couple of hours before releasing them. The birds then slept right beside the house, and made no attempt to wander over to, or roost in, their old tree, although it was only a few yards away. Very strange.

I am writing in the middle of a torrential downpour. Already, in only half an hour, over an inch of rain has fallen. The Zambezi is rising steadily and will, soon, just about double its width, with the water lapping only about 30 yards from our doors. I suppose that will make it in the region of a mile wide. Up until recently, the rains have been regarded as being particularly light, but everything can change in such a short time out here. As this is early February, we only have about three or four more weeks when it is likely to be wet, then the dry season will last right through to November, a full eight months of drought!

The other day, I presented our askari corporal with a photograph of himself I had taken a few days previously. Later that day, I saw him at the centre of a crowd of at least 30 of his village pals, all pressing round trying to catch a glimpse. A camera is regarded as a very special piece of white man's witchcraft, and is an object of great curiosity and fear. I tried to explain to my boys how it works, but I could see that they had no intention of abandoning their own theories on its purpose. I opened mine up to show them the works, but they firmly believe a spirit lives in the case, and this often makes them reluctant to pose for a snap, yet they are mighty proud to be given a photograph of themselves, which they can then boast about to their friends. When I am on the march, one of my messengers always carries my camera, and I can see that he regards himself as the high priest of the genie inside. When I was last developing some film in Jack's tank, I took my senior messengers in with me. Seeing the blank film first show a negative image, then see that change, gradually, into a photograph seemed to them the very height of magic, and they now have a new regard for the darkroom and its contents. My microscope, too, is an object of great interest. The boys are fascinated when I stain slides with blood samples, and stand with their mouths open, ready to bolt from the room. The other day, I needed to decolour some stains on a test-glass, so shook a few drops of acid onto the stain which immediately turned a neutral colour. The boys watching let out a sudden yell, and jumped back. They are convinced I practise magic, and was showing them some of my tricks!

I am also regarded as some sort of 'medicine man', indeed, my native name is Shangive, which means 'the medicine chief'. Apart from my poor cook-boy, I am constantly having to administer first aid and various remedies. I need to have them take the physic under my nose as, otherwise, they prefer to ditch it unless it smells sweet. I have, also, discovered the best way to get my treatments carried out instantly. I hold a large veterinary hypodermic syringe in the other hand, and my patients take their medicine as the lesser of two evils. As with most of us, they would do anything to avoid a prick!

Recently, I have found myself acting not only as a vet, doctor and surgeon, but also as a dentist. A native, suffering from tooth trouble of any description, agrees to lie flat on his back whilst a couple of pals perch on his chest, arms and legs. A third friend(!), sitting by his head, grasps an assegai in both hands and jabs at the offending tooth until the sufferer is parted from it. After the 'extraction', the patient springs up, grinning through the blood, and warmly thanks the 'dentist' and helpers, while holding out the wretched tooth for all to see.

I decided that, in the interests of hygiene, not to mention human suffering, I should introduce a less drastic treatment. Now, sufferers from toothache etc. come to me with only one friend in attendance. They both sit on a log outside my hut; the patient's head is held back, mouth wide open, by the helper, and I give the time-honoured 'twist and tug', as practised by the village blacksmith at fairs back home!

It is a huge success, but I suppose that when I have moved on it will be back to the assegai etc!

Natives' feet, and the soles especially, have to be unbelievably tough and hard. The other day, I had to cut a thorn out of the sole of one of our local natives; the skin was at least quarter of an inch thick. Although I had to use a scalpel, he seemed to feel nothing, and calmly walked away when I had finished. Only a day later, I watched one of the boys, who had just returned from a long dugout trip, calmly scraping the skin which had become softened by standing long hours in water, from both soles, with a piece of rusty tin which he had found on a rubbish dump. He kept going until he reached the hard layer underneath. It was exactly like scraping the top off rotten leather.

Later

This has not been my week! My kitchen was wrecked; my pony boy has now gone down with malaria; one of my messengers is still recovering from it and Tolani is still very far from well. He is conscious now, and the fever seems to be subsiding, so I have high hopes of pulling him through, despite his determination to the contrary! But he is frightfully weak, and it will be some time before he is up to anything.

Little did I realise, in England last spring, just what I was letting myself in for out here: I am marriage counsellor, magician, doctor, dentist and building engineer, all rolled into one. Whatever the problem, from a quarrel with a wife, to a broken cooking pot, it is brought to me.

My food is ready and so I will stop. As it has been raining continuously for 15 hours, I feel in need of a good, hot dinner, although I suspect it will be chicken again!

11

Slave Trade, 1914

Sesheke
12th February 1914

Our mail, which, for a good time, has been getting here from Livingstone on Monday afternoons, was several days late this week. Apparently, a large piece of railway track was washed away somewhere in Southern Rhodesia, with our letters on the wrong side of the track.

Jack arrived back last Sunday evening, heartily sick of the torrential rain through which he had trekked virtually all the way up from Livingstone. The river I had found bone dry on my last few days before reaching Sesheke was so full and swollen that Jack had to swim across. Because of all this, we've decided to postpone our trip in the hope that the weather will improve.

The box of Christmas goodies you all sent me so kindly came to light in Livingstone recently, and is now on its way here on an ox-wagon, which is being used to bring up a good deal of gear, but as Jack passed it well and truly stuck in the mud only a shortish way out of Livingstone, goodness knows when the parcel will arrive. I do hope it's watertight!

Last Saturday, yet another part of my estate chose to fall down in a storm, this time my store hut. It all collapsed in a most frightful mess of straw, woodwork and mud. The tinned stuff was all right, but I lost 50lbs flour and 50lbs sugar, as well as all sorts of other provisions, which were absolutely sodden before we could get to them. I called out the boys to try and salvage what we could, but it was pitch dark, pouring with rain and running with mud. But, the good news is that Tolani really is recovering and, although terribly weak, is slowly beginning to gain strength.

I can almost see the grass growing. It's hard to believe that the ordinary grazing grows about six or seven feet high. Around our

HQ, it is set on fire as soon as it will burn, and then lush, new shoots spring from the ground, which is perfect for all game and stock to graze off. Of course, out in the bush, it makes shooting hugely more difficult, as game are virtually invisible, and spoor is much more difficult to follow.

A party of native prisoners has been put to clearing up around my house and compound, as the crashing of two huts, and the effects of the flood have produced a sorry sight. My stores are now housed in my dining/drawing room, and I've had to retreat to my bedroom for my meals, and to sit down.

I've managed to qualify as suitable to command in time of trouble by passing my shooting test. We fire at 200, 500 and 600 yards, with eight shots at each. It's a pretty daunting test, as the bull's eye is 6 inches at 200 yards; 12 inches at 500 yards; and only 20 inches at 600 yards. I managed to pass with flying colours, and the practice has done a lot to restore my confidence in long-range shooting. Six hundred yards is more than a third of a mile away, and I grouped my bullets nicely into the 20-inch bull.

Jack and I have decided to send for about 35 carriers from a tribe of big, strong natives up in the bush. He warns that they can, sometimes, be awkward to handle but agrees they are just the answer for a trip such as we envisage. They should be here in about a week, and we will start immediately. We will also take eight messengers, our own five personal boys, the two pony boys and six native askari policemen. We will be shooting for over 50 mouths, as we don't expect to pick up any meal from the villages en route. Our ponies may have to leave ahead of us, as they must swim the three-quarters-of-a-mile-wide Zambezi, and then walk up along the opposite bank to meet us after our river trip, which will take us up past the German territory. The shooting should be good. Last time Venning went in that direction, he got 50 head, including five lions and a leopard.

I seem to remember that you asked how the bread was made. Tolani mixes his flour and water, and then adds some native hops, which he guards with his life. As it rises, he puts the dough in an iron pan or bake-pot and then scrapes hot ashes over, under and round it. Sugar is also added to the dough to sweeten the taste of the hops.

Exciting news! My box of Christmas goodies has arrived here and will be delivered to me shortly. I can't wait to unwrap it, and feel just like a small child on Christmas Eve! I suspect Jack will jolly soon be round to see what he may be asked to share.

Later

I've just finished unpacking the box and am sitting on the floor, in the centre of my room, enjoying some of it. I am drinking fresh tea, eating a mince pie, stuffing in a chocolate and smoking a cigarette, all at the same time!

What a feast: peaches in syrup, pears ditto, Camembert, Gruyère, duck, chicken, beef, Christmas puddings, mince pies, chocolates, potted meats, steak and cigarettes. Jack and I are both really fond of cheese, so tonight, we plan three courses: duck, Christmas pudding and cheese with a good cup of fresh tea afterwards, rounded off with a fresh cigarette! I do thank you all, very much indeed, for all the food. I shall use it sparingly and make it last as long as possible.

That box had quite a trip, rail from you to Tilbury, boat to Cape Town, rail to Livingstone, ox-wagon to Mambora's village, stuck in mud, carried by natives to the Kasai river, which they swam with the box on a raft, carried to the Zambezi, dugout to Sesheke and, finally, carried to my door.

Saturday

Two days ago, three of the Paris Evangelical Mission team from up country came through: M and Mme Ellenberger and M Arnot. The latter is extremely ill. We have done what we could for him, put him in a machili, a hammock, and given them one of our messengers to keep discipline, and to see that they get supplies of milk and eggs on the way down to Livingstone: the messenger's uniform is widely respected, and he will be obeyed. I'm afraid I have my fears about poor M Arnot surviving such a journey in these rains, with no proper medication or protection from the elements. But it is all we can do for him in his plight.

This is the well-known F.S. Arnot who, with Sherpa Pinto, Cameron and Selous went north 25 years after David Livingstone came through. They trekked large parts of the country preaching Christianity, and brought back stories of the barbarism of some of the tribes, of the slavery then widely practised, and of the wealth of game of just about every description which abounded throughout the territory.

M Ellenberger recounted a most alarming experience he had a few days ago. They were on the Zambezi, when he heard some guinea-fowl cackling up a tree and, as they needed food, they pulled into the bank and he jumped ashore with his shotgun and got one. As it dropped, he heard a rustling, and a lion jumped out, feet from him, seized the wretched guinea-fowl and bolted with it in its mouth. What a blessing he shot that bird as, otherwise, the lion might have had another kind of meal. He disobeyed one of the rules of survival: he did not take a rifle as well as his shotgun, and did not take some natives armed with assegais. He was jolly lucky.

The German resident may be joining us for our two-day river trip, as we plan to have a concerted hippo hunt. Spoor, which is massive and very easy to follow, showed that two hippos had been feeding quite close to my house, but we failed to find them. As they slide down the bank into the river, it is easy to trace their tracks, but then they disappear into the water and are gone. Hippo skins fetch £5 and, as this is exactly the price of a game licence – mine is overdue – I could do with getting one. (*The licence prohibited the killing of: vultures, owls, ostriches and also, elephants, rhinoceros, zebra and duiker. Restrictions were also in force on the numbers of other game allowed to be killed.*)

Our boys are very excited at the prospect of our trip, as it means some hunting, which all natives love, and, particularly, plenty of fresh meat. You would be astonished what a hungry native can stow away. Jack was out a little time ago and failed to kill anything, leaving them all to go without food for two days. He was getting desperate on the third day, when he came upon the spoor of roan antelope. He trekked after them, came up with the herd, killed two and wounded five. He followed up the five, as we always do, found and finished them off. So, there were seven buck the size of cows and 42 natives. He told me they sat up all night eating and, in the morning, one boy could have carried away all that was left. Goodness knows where they put it all, except that one can see their stomachs visibly swell as they gorge themselves.

I've suddenly remembered to tell you what a lot of leprosy there is in this part of Africa. Every village has its lepers, who live and move about as if they were normal members of the community. Some day, we will have the medical resources to start tackling the problem but, at present, all we can do is to exempt them from paying taxes. I try and avoid close contact with them, and my boys keep them from coming too near, but it's not possible to quarantine them.

The creepy-crawlies that try to spoil our lives are legion. Great flying beetles suddenly drop into our soup, whilst a cup of tea or coffee left unattended for a few minutes attracts a host of flies on the surface. I would have been ill at home, but have learnt to take it all in my stride. By the same token, I dare not go near my kitchen for fear it would put me off my food for life! I did once: never again!

Wednesday, 25th

I'm lying in bed sending you a few lines, but will try and write at greater length later. At 1.00am on Sunday, I woke up shivering and shaking, and started to vomit violently. This kept up for a good time and, at 6.00am, I started to sweat profusely. I was so wet I had to keep on changing my pyjamas and bed linen. I recognised that I had another bout of typical local fever – malaria – and dosed myself accordingly. By Monday, I was feeling a bit better, but had sweated all the energy out of my system, so was very limp and wobbly. Fortunately, our carriers had not yet arrived, so I am not wasting anyone's time. It's just a wretched nuisance, as I shall have to get fit as quickly as I can, so as not to be a drag on the rest of the party, especially Jack and the German.

Saturday

I'm beginning to feel a bit more like living. I'm eating well, so can't be about to die yet, but I have to admit I do feel terribly lethargic. Fortunately, I've been able to take things easy, and l have caught up with some reading and paperwork.

Sunday 1st March
I'm feeling sad, as news has just reached us that M Arnot has died. I feared he would not survive the journey. He was buried beside the Zambezi he loved so dearly.

The carriers are here, and we will be off first thing tomorrow morning. I am feeling much, much better, and am keen to get away, and down to the practical business of making myself fit and strong again.

This should be a most worthwhile excursion. Much of the territory we plan to cover has, as far as we can learn, never been crossed by white men, and we will make a rough map of it for future expeditions. So, it's all hustle and bustle, despite the fact that we shall travel light, relying on our combined shooting skills to keep the larder stocked.

I really ought to explain what this trip is all about. My part is very straightforward. I need to visit tribes and villages as far up into Barotseland as possible to examine their cattle, and get a better picture of the conditions for pasture improvement and disease control. But Jack has an altogether more dramatic objective. There is a chief, named Kaliangula, up country who rules a most ill-disciplined, marauding and primitive tribe. They have never been visited by a white man, and have never paid any tax. They are, in short, a law unto themselves. They are also reputed, still, to raid neighbouring villages and to carry natives off, male and female, young and old, to be sold into slavery for the benefit of tribes much further north, and for the Portuguese. So Jack has asked me to accompany him on what ought to be a most interesting and important expedition but, as no authentic information about Kaliangula has ever been forthcoming, because he has never been seen, it may be that we are on a wild goose chase.

Later
I am writing this in our tent by the light of an oil lamp, so I hope you can decipher my writing. Three days into our trip I am 100% fit and well again. We are on the opposite bank of the Zambezi, and I will try and describe the rather exciting events of the past few hours.

We set off this morning at daybreak and, at 1.00pm, we struck the Zambezi at the point we judged would make the best crossing. But the river is a good three-quarters-of-a-mile wide now, and the current is quite fast-flowing, so we had no choice but to get our gear, and ourselves, over in relays. Jack set off first in a not-very-large dugout we had commandeered. He took a full load, and made camp on the other side to receive all our natives and baggage as it came over in batches. But, as you can imagine, it was an extremely slow and tortuous business, three-quarters-of-a-mile over, and then the same back.

The first trip across, after Jack's, was to take his pony. He hated it and, halfway over, stopped swimming and had to be towed by the paddlers. Eventually, they got him across, and back came the dugout and Champagne was driven, extremely reluctantly, into the water. He fought like mad, and managed to slip his halter. Thank goodness, the pony boy and some others lassoed his head and, finally, landed him safely. By now, quite a wind had sprung up and, as I watched our gear and the boys – we finally landed up with 63 all told – bobbing about in midstream, I was sure some of it, or them, would go to the bottom. Miraculously, the dugout did not capsize. The carriers came from an inland tribe, and were absolutely terrified of the whole operation. All the time, too, we had to keep a number of natives doing nothing but beating the surface of the water and shouting to scare away the crocodiles. At long, long last I left with the final load, and wobbled and splashed my way across to join Jack who had, thank goodness, managed to bring some semblance of order to the camp.

I have to admit to feeling about all in. We've been at it for the best part of 14 hours, so I'm just going to have a bath and a meal which Tolani, now much recovered, is preparing, and then turn in, as we have to be ready for another daybreak start tomorrow.

2.00pm, four days later
Somewhere near the convergence of Portuguese, German and British territories
I'm going to write a few lines while we rest, and before Jack and I go off to try and shoot some game. We are now extremely short

of food, as it has been impossible to find anything in grass that is nine or 10 feet high. We've shot one wild pig only, and badly need to get something this evening as, otherwise, the boys, and ourselves for that matter, will have to go without tomorrow.

But I must pick up my story. After crossing the Zambezi, we marched for four days through dense forest. There were no paths, and the almost-constant rainstorms made progress extremely disagreeable. It wasn't possible to ride because of the trees and bushes, so Jack and I have needed to be able to keep up with our very fit carriers, who keep going without any sign of fatigue.

We are in most interesting parts. The natives hereabouts are veritable bushmen, living on berries, herbs and game, with no crops for meal. They have hunted, and been hunted, for scores of years, for slaves to be traded in Portuguese territory, and so have adapted their lives accordingly. They are nervous and edgy, and always on the alert, and have no villages as such. They build temporary grass shelters, so as to be able to move on at the slightest sign of trouble, then they scurry away and hide in the deep bush, of which they are profoundly knowledgeable.

As we approached the area – and remember, our objective was to find the tribal chief Kaliangula – we spread out and, suddenly, came upon a woman foraging for food. She tried to make a dash for it, but a messenger caught her and, eventually, she led us to the tribe's village, just a collection of shelters.

We surrounded the area and all hell broke loose. One of the natives threw his assegai at me but, fortunately, it flew past my shoulder and Matapi, ever vigilant beside me, laid out my would-be assassin with his knobkerry. Jack and I had deliberately not taken our rifles so as to cause as little alarm as possible.

All the natives, to a man, were almost sick with terror. They clearly thought it was another raid, but one by men the colour of whose skin was quite new to them. We did our best to calm them down and explained, slowly and painstakingly, that we came in peace, that they were living under the care of the great white king from across the widest river in the world, and that we wanted to take them to a place where they would be safe from raiders, and able to live in peace and security.

Eventually, we persuaded one of the tribe to guide us to Kaliangula, whose camp was, apparently, some distance off. We left the carriers to continue the good work of acclimatising the still-terrified bushmen, and made our way to try and find this almost mythical figure of a chief. We took six messengers and two of the askari policemen and, after another longish march, came upon the camp and surrounded it. As we moved in, most of the women and men managed to break out through our ring. They are all past masters of this art, but we managed to grab hold of about a dozen. Right in the middle of the clearing was a ramshackle hut and, inside, hunched on the floor, was the old man himself, surrounded by half a dozen of the women.

From what we gathered I was, indeed, the first white man he had ever seen. He was almost inaudible, and was nothing but skin and bone, very deaf and unable to walk without help from his women. We calculated that he must have been almost 100 years old. He tried to convince us that he was in German territory, and wriggled and wove his way through a pack of lies but, finally, he saw that the game was up. He wore no clothes, but was covered with string upon string of beads with, literally, hundreds of bracelets and bangles on his legs and arms.

There is no doubt that Kaliangular has been one of the great troublemakers in this part of Africa. He has, until recently, ruled with a rod of iron over a lawless, cruel and wretched tribe, and has been responsible for much hardship and tragedy for neighbouring natives. Now, one suspects, his power is gone. The whole episode seemed to me as if we were participating in a piece of history, back in David Livingstone's days.

We camped beside Kaliangula's kraal, having taken three of his able-bodied men prisoner. I have never seen natives like this before. The women behave more like animals than humans, and crawl about on all fours around the camp, only standing upright to go longer distances. They are the embodiment of what the word 'primitive' really means. It has been a weird experience!

We were off again at 5.00am this morning and, three hours later, surprised another group of Kaliangula's people. We were more successful this time, and caught 10 of the men.

My part of the trip has not been so rewarding, as I have found no cattle at all in these parts. They simply do not exist, for the reasons I have explained.

12th March
In the Marshi country
We are still trekking, but have decided to turn back tomorrow. The problem is, quite simply, food. We now have 80-odd mouths to feed and, because of the rains and the tall grass, have not been able to find any game. Last Tuesday, I spent eight hours, crawling on my stomach and fighting my way through thick bush – we haven't seen a path for days – to try and find something we can live off. At last we came upon the spoor of a large eland bull: the tracker boys can determine the size and sex of just about anything, from the hoof marks. We followed him for three hours, but were beaten by darkness and had to turn back. My boys instinctively brought me straight back to camp, although there were no stars or moon and we were, to all intents and purposes, in the middle of a forest without paths. They have this uncanny 'bump of locality'.

When, at last, I staggered into camp, I found Jack had had a bit more luck. He had stumbled upon two wildebeest, and had killed one and wounded the other. He found the latter an hour later and finished him off. So we could, at last, provide our camp with some much-needed food. Tantalizingly enough, we had been amongst plenty of giraffe, but they are strictly protected. We resolved, however, to ignore that if need be, as our natives and ourselves were still desperately short of food for the return journey. Happily, we fell upon two sissebe yesterday morning, and so have enough for today.

It is 9.00am, and we are still tent-bound because of the rain. Last evening, we carried out a raid on a village that has been causing all sorts of trouble, and have added the chief and six men to our haul of prisoners. So we now have a camp of getting on for a hundred to feed: it is a considerable anxiety. However, this evening, we are sending our gear back some miles on the route home, and each of us will take a prisoner who should know these parts, several boys and a couple of messengers and, going our separate ways, will see what we can bag. We know there is plenty of game in the area, but we simply cannot see it with the head-high grass and the dense, dripping undergrowth.

We are sending a boy on ahead with this mail and hope, in a couple of days, to catch up with a runner from Sesheke, who ought to have any letters that have arrived from Livingstone.

Once again, I am being called upon to act as expedition doctor. I've had several boys down with various complaints, and they have almost all been suffering with cut feet from the sharp grasses. So, they have used the skins of the very few beasts that we have shot to make moccasins, which they strap on with hide straps.

All in all, except for our success with old Kaliangula, this trip has turned out to be a bit of a disappointment. I've thoroughly enjoyed myself, and it has certainly been exciting, but we have not achieved as much as we had hoped, and have had the constant worry of where our next meal was coming from.

Sesheke
One week later
The food problem beat us. There was masses of game in the area, but it had taken to the thick bush and we could not get at it. We finally just had too many mouths to feed and, as it was, had some uncomfortable days, with no food for any of us guaranteed. You may feel I have made rather heavy weather of the food problem. Perhaps I have, but I am so totally used, throughout my life to date, to having food within reasonable reach, that it comes as something of a shock to be in the midst of a crowd of 100 humans with, literally, nothing whatsoever for any of them to eat, and not much prospect of getting any.

About a week ago, as I wrote at the time, the food problem became acute. We both duly set off with our prisoners, one each, secured to a messenger. My messenger never let up 'explaining' what dire consequences awaited him were we not to find game! I let it be, as we seriously had to have something for the whole camp.

Luck was with us, or else the prisoner knew what was required of him as, after a couple of hours, I saw two seseba. I killed one and wounded the other. I sent back for some carriers to come and collect the dead beast, while I set off with the prisoner and a messenger to try and find, and finish off, the wounded buck. But, once again, darkness intervened, and we had to turn for home. The messenger and I were at the mercy of our prisoner, as we would surely not have found our way through that forest, in the pitch dark, with no moon to help us. To ensure our guide did not lose his concentration(!), my messenger kept up a running commentary on what would happen if the great white chief was not soon in the comfort and safety of his tent! It worked, I'm happy to say and, on arrival, I found Jack had got one roan antelope and wounded another but, like me, had been beaten by darkness.

Next morning we both rose early, had a quick cup of cocoa, and went off on the track of the wounded antelope. After about two hours, we saw a stationary roan and, assuming it was the wounded one of the day before, I took my time and shot it dead at about 200 yards. When we reached it we found, to our amazement, that it was not the wounded one but another, which had obligingly stood still and allowed me to shoot it. Well, we picked up the blood trail soon after and followed it for some distance until suddenly, in a small clearing, we came upon about 25 wildebeast, feeding. Luckily, we were downwind of them and so they were not alerted. There was a small bush about 80 yards from the herd and about 400 yards from us. We set out to crawl to this bush but, halfway there, found ourselves having to slither through a ditch full of water. We managed to keep our rifles and ammunition dry, but were soaked from head to toe and covered with mud. Eventually, we got to our bush, still undetected. In a whisper, we agreed on which beast each should go for, and I chose a big male. I had brought my heaviest rifle, which throws a 440 gram bullet, so I was properly equipped. Both of us killed with our first shot, and then again with our second. But, by now, the herd was in full flight away from us. I then did the best bit of shooting I have ever done, or am ever likely to do. I slammed my sights up for 300 yards and got three more wildebeest, although they were at full gallop. I quickly reloaded – the rifle holds five shells – and chased after the herd, and we both managed to finish off all the wounded. So, our bag was nine each and, suddenly, our anxiety over food was at an end.

We were exhausted with effort and excitement, and lay down to dry, with our shirts hung over the bush which had served us so well. Each wildebeest is the size of a cow, so you can visualise the scene.

Our messengers and carriers were beside themselves with excitement, and started dancing and shouting and waving their assegais as if at some festival. When they had calmed down a bit, we sent for the camp gear, the rest of the carriers and the prisoners, and settled for the night on the battleground, beside our victims.

The natives sat up half the night chewing and gorging themselves, and recounting the day's events, whilst Jack and I had a banquet of kidney soup, brains and marrow on toast and sirloin of venison.

We now had two days store of food, and so set off for the river with a new confidence. When we reached it, we fixed for the two dugouts to take us to the spot where we had secured our boats, and off we went for Sesheke by river, leaving the carriers and prisoners to come on at their own pace overland.

Looking back, it may seem we were unduly concerned about food, but the responsibility to provide, and keep on providing, for 100 hungry male mouths, day in and day out, is considerable. At the worst moment, we came upon 15 elephants, as well as giraffe, and would, in extremis, have had to risk the law and shoot one of them but, happily, that emergency never arose.

Litia was delighted at us capturing some of Kaliangula's men. Apparently, both he and his father Lewanika had tried time and again to corner the old scoundrel and his tribe, and had consistently failed, so we were pretty popular on that score. In fact, neither of them nor any of their chiefs had ever seen the old boy himself.

I must admit it is a great relief to be dry and snug, out of the rain for a spell, we spent so much of the time simply drenched through. One evening, after torrential rain, we found our blankets and mattresses were sodden. So we had a huge fire built, and strung out our gear over it. But, as it was still raining, the undersides got dry whilst the top sides continued wet. Finally, we gave up, and turned in with thoroughly damp stuff over and under us, but we lived to tell the tale!

Suddenly all is peace and quiet, and order reigns. The daily routine starts up just as if we had not been away. But, in a few days, I shall probably hanker to be off again, as HQ and its life doesn't really suit me, but I will make the most of it while I can.

12

Our Food and Our Fun

I have been able to tell you enough of my life out on trek for you to be able to appreciate how vitally important it is for white officials to be able to shoot and fish competently, and so provide for the often considerable numbers of natives for whom they are responsible. So, the many accounts of my going out with a gun are, primarily, of excursions to bring back the food my camp needed. I shot the food we had to have, or we didn't eat. It was as simple as that.

When beside the Zambezi, especially, we had a wide assortment of birds to go after and Tolani, my cook, would prepare me delicious roast dinners from my bag. Just before the sun set, right beside the river, incredibly large numbers of duck would alight on their way to their over-night resting place. I have to admit that little skill was needed to down several, such were their numbers. Then, there would be partridges and pheasants, as well as the more exotic large birds such as crested cranes, egrets and peacocks. Needless to say, these last were always safe from our guns.

I also thoroughly enjoyed all the opportunities I had to fish, and to settle into the meals Tolani cooked with my landings. Jack and I would frequently go out in the early evenings, in a dugout with a couple of paddlers, and a native reed basket in the bottom, ready for the catch. We used spinning spool and bait, and the strong river fish fought hard and gave us much sport. Tiger fish, so called because of their rows of needle-sharp teeth, can go to 20 pounds, but I never managed one over nine. We could easily catch 30 or 40 in an evening. This was not just an outing for pleasure, as the natives, either on trek or at Sesheke, were delighted to be served up fresh fish for their evening meal. Most natives who live by the rivers are expert at catching fish with thin, pointed reeds. They stand upright in the dugout and hover, motionless, until they see their quarry, not far beneath the surface of the water, and then, like lightning, thrust the reed down through the fish. I have never come across any white man able to fish in this manner. We lack the skill and patience and, more especially, the ability to balance motionless for long periods of time.

By the river, also, we sometimes shot hippos, but only when we needed the flesh and, more particularly, the fat, which our boys rendered down. A hippopotamus will weigh anything up to four tons and, consequently, yields a huge amount of flesh and fat. It is imperative to shoot extremely accurately, otherwise the result is a wounded beast with all the cruelty, and not a little risk to life and limb for the marksman. The two crucial spots for hippos are just behind the ear, and between the eyes, and a .375 or heavier rifle is necessary. A dead hippo slides quietly beneath the water, to reappear a couple of hours later feet up, floating just below the surface. The boys then lasso the feet, tow the carcass to shore and set about cutting it up with enormous gusto.

The supplies of meat required almost daily – and a considerable quantity was needed to feed up to a hundred humans, not infrequently walking 20 miles a day, and carrying 60lb loads – came mostly from the buck, which abound in huge numbers throughout that part of the country. If that makes it sound like an easy task, it has to be remembered that all animals are equipped with the most acute sense of sight and smell, and are finely tuned in their habits and behaviour to enable them to survive in the dog-eat-dog environment.

The camouflage of wild game is superb, and is specifically designed, if one can use that word, to enable each species to blend into the landscape it especially frequents. Take zebras for instance: one might think that their black-and-white stripes would show up almost anywhere, but they often stand stock-still, especially if they scent danger, in an area of vivid light and shade, and they then become virtually invisible.

Some of the country I have to range to find food is open veldt, with little or no cover and, consequently, little chance of using the element of surprise. Other areas would be thick scrub, forest or open stretches, but with grass and bush all over 5 feet high, in which it is almost impossible to see game of any kind. All this added to the sense of enjoyable adventure except, of course, on those occasions when food was urgently needed.

I shall never forget the sheer grace and beauty of many of the buck and antelope I tracked, or came upon suddenly. Many, many times, even when I needed meat badly, I could not bring myself to shoot, such was the magnificence, or the charm, of my potential victim. I would often stalk, for what seemed hours, to end up amazed at the sight I eventually faced. Take, for instance, a herd of wildebeest. There could well be a mass of a thousand or more, almost always accompanied by their chums, the zebras. The herd – a great steaming cauldron of swishing tails and tossing heads – stirring up the dust as they grazed by, or on their way to, water would be surrounded by the biggest bulls, acting as guards. Restlessly, they watched over their charges. They would suddenly stop and freeze, scanning and scenting for any sign of danger. Strangely, perhaps, most game depend more on smell than on sight, and so I often had to make considerable detours to get down-wind of my quarry. Sometimes I had to spend hours, literally, crawling along on my elbows and knees so as to reach the position I needed to pull off a lethal shot. I strove, always, to achieve a firing point from which I stood the best chance of 'downing' my target, and not just maiming it.

The prettiest buck, for me, were impalas: they are about the size of a small donkey, reddish-brown with white bellies. They are champion jumpers, and regularly clear nine-foot obstacles, whilst not touching the ground for over 20 feet. A herd of impalas, if surprised, presents a total confusion of bodies springing, wildly, in every possible direction. It is then virtually impossible to get in a shot at the flashing forms.

Zebras are ill-tempered and dangerous, in that they fight with teeth and heels, and can be ugly customers if cornered. Their skins are widely used as chair covers throughout Africa, and very striking they are.

Letchwe, which can weigh up to 12 hundred-weight, are generally found in low-lying swampy areas; they abound on the flats by the Kafue river, where they often move about in herds of thousands. They have widely spreading horns which, in common with all water buck, curve forwards – the horns of all others curve backwards – interesting!

All the smaller buck, some no larger than a collie dog, tend to move and feed in much smaller numbers. Duiker, which stick to bushy areas for the cover they afford, oribi and reed are good examples. Of the big buck – roan, eland, sable and buffalo – the last is by far the heaviest and, by common consent, the most dangerous. They will charge and attack anything, and do so with their head in such a position, well down, that it is mighty difficult to hit the vital spot for a kill. One has to aim at the spine behind the lowered charging head. Having had one nasty experience with a water buffalo, I tried never to shoot without being sure that I was standing beside a fair-sized tree, behind which I could dodge if all did not go according to plan! The buffalo is a most unpleasant adversary.

Sables are my favourite. There is no finer sight than a proud sable bull standing as if he owned the earth, his gracefully curving horns sweeping atop his magnificent head and his beautifully proportioned body with its shining coat, the very epitome of majestic superiority.

I once found myself watching a warthog in a forest clearing. Suddenly, a magnificent sable bull walked in and strode slowly about for a bit, stamping his foot occasionally to disturb the flies, or scratching himself with the tip of his horns. I was fascinated by the sight and crouched, watching him, for quite some time. Then I slowly raised my rifle, took careful aim, and shot the warthog. As I dropped my eyes from the sights, my sable was nowhere to be seen: in that split second, and in one huge leap, he was gone. At the time, I badly needed meat for my boys, but could not bring myself to kill such a splendid creature.

I cannot let this account of some of my shooting, tracking and stalking activities pass without, as it were, going from the sublime to the ridiculous. I now write of ants: they – that is, white ants, red ants and soldier ants, not to mention the monster serni ants that sweep through practically everything in their way – are the bane of our lives. The destruction that can be caused by these tiny creatures is almost unbelievable; the house I was to occupy at Sesheke, for instance, had been made unsafe and totally uninhabitable, in practically no time, by white ants. They can, and do, quite often eat their way straight through some large wooden object without turning to right or to left and, often, in just a matter of hours.

I have told you of the loneliness, on occasions, of the evening hours out on trek, and it is then that I have often amused and interested myself by watching the antics of these exceptional creatures. I would kill a likely insect, a large beetle perhaps, and place it near a busy ant run. Along would come one inquisitive chap, and as soon as he made his discovery of a large cache of food, he would get terribly excited and rush around investigating his find from every angle and direction. Then he would try, single-handed, to move it. Finding this impossible, he would rush back and call up a few pals to help him, all this in a great panic. This bunch would now try to move the victim: more and more ants would arrive and push and pull – usually in opposite directions – until they began to break the wretched creature into pieces. Despite backing into each other, and falling over various obstacles in their path, they relentlessly and feverishly tugged and shoved to manoeuvre the pieces towards their underground home. The excitement would heighten as they got nearer and nearer to their subterranean quarters. Finally, at the entrance, each team would do its damnedest to shove its prize down below, whilst making every effort to frustrate the efforts of its colleagues. Chaos would reign, but this was nothing to the drama when, on occasions, I closed the entrance hole and smoothed sand over it. Hysteria would now be the order of the day. Rushing hither and thither, pushing, pulling and falling over each other, the ants would be in a frenzy of anxiety to find their front door.

It may be that little things please little minds, but I wanted to paint a few pictures of the life I lead, 180 miles or more from what we, laughingly, call civilization.

Sesheke
27th March 1914

Poor old Venning, he is in a proper state! His wife, down in Livingstone, is expecting their first child any time now, and he is finding the separation very hard to bear. Yesterday he regaled me, at length, with an account of his dream the previous night, in which everything went wrong with the birth, so you can imagine that I, too, shall be much relieved when he gets the news he is waiting for. A special messenger is standing by in Livingstone to bring him that news but, at this time of year, he will take at least six days to get through.

Mrs Ingram, Jack's assistant's wife, was taken ill a couple of days ago; they got some advice from the missionary but have avoided the subject with me. I am sorry, as I carry a fairly comprehensive medicine chest with me. Anyway, Jack has sent a runner to the hospital in Livingstone, describing her symptoms and asking if a doctor should come out to see her. Just imagine the delay. The runner will take six days, the doctor the same time or longer. It could easily be unnecessary or too late.

Right or wrong, I have come to be regarded as the 'doctor' in these parts. Jack and the missionary both send boys to me, but the Ingrams are an unusual pair, who seem only to believe in Epsom salts and aspirin! But it is best to keep one's own counsel: living in these circumstances, it is vital not to 'get across one another', or to quarrel.

Whilst on the subject of illness, I had my first night call 24 hours ago. At 9pm, a messenger came running to me in a great state, to say that another messenger's wife was lying dead. I went with him and found a crowd pressing in upon the prostrate wife, who had merely fainted. I sent the crowd packing, brought the woman round and settled her down. All seemed well, so I returned to my bed.

This morning, I made a visit to the patient and found her much better, but the local witch doctor was already in attendance, and about to start all sorts of weird rituals. I sent him on his way in a great sweat, as these characters know that we confiscate their 'treatments' when we come across them for fear of the harm they may do. As you can see, my medical practice is a varied one!

Natives have a confusing sense of distance and of time and so, if I ask, 'How far is it to such a place?' the boy will point to the position the sun should be in when one should arrive. I then have to do the calculation: three mph with carriers, and four mph for unloaded natives. But a spot of cunning is injected into the formula for good measure! Invariably, when I have asked this question, I have been told the sun will be lower than, in fact, it turns out to be. Native psychology runs as follows: when I arrive earlier than anticipated, I will think what fine fellows my boys are in that they will have made the journey in shorter time and will, thus, be worthy of great praise. They confirm this strategy by the huge grins they put on at our destination, inviting the congratulations they believe they so richly deserve!

The passing of time is noted in the crudest of ways. Days are recorded with notches, wherever convenient. Out on trek, a native will carry a small stick, which he regularly notches each evening. In his village, he will notch a hut upright as a form of display calendar. The months, too, will be marked with notches at each new moon. The inability of natives, even shrewd or experienced ones, to count beyond 10 (fingers of both hands) is incredible. They never feel inadequate over this, and never make the slightest effort to learn differently. I can't help feeling that I am living amongst a people, in 1914, whose behaviour one might easily be reading of in some archaeological tome.

In everyday life, they have many practical, if primitive, medical remedies. Wounds, they recognise, need to be disinfected and the flow of blood staunched, so they practise cauterising. The patient willingly submits to being spread upon the ground, and sat upon by a couple of friends. A red-hot ember is taken from the fire and the wound is cauterised, all this in front of an admiring crowd. The patient invariably makes not a sound, although the pain must be considerable. It is a fact that the native has a much lower threshold of pain. I have seen a boy step, by chance, on an upturned nail sticking through a plank of wood. At least one-and-a-half inches went into his foot, but he merely growled 'Ooooh', pulled out the nail and calmly walked on.

Much of this is psychological. The cauterising and the nail bring forth practically no reaction, but if and when I produce a scalpel to lance a boil or abscess, the din set up by the patient is appalling.

But the sight of pus, or the devil as they choose to regard it, seeping out quickly restores their good humour.

Excitement acts almost as a drug with natives, and is often able to neutralise fear and pain to a remarkable degree. When I am out inspecting herds, I always send word ahead with a messenger, that I shall need all the cattle to be rounded up, and a number caught and secured, so that I can examine them individually and, if necessary, take blood samples etc. The news is quickly broadcast on drums, and I have known natives come in from villages up to 10 or 12 miles away, on foot and often through thick bush, just for the excitement of helping with the rounding up and securing. As soon as the herd is driven in and cornered – and many of the cattle can be extremely wild – the boys start trying to catch them, by running alongside each beast and getting a hold of the horns or tail. More and more boys pile on until they, literally, drag the unfortunate animal to its knees, when they roll it over and sit on it properly. That description, however, hardly does justice to the drama of the scene. The cattle bellow and raise clouds of dust, the natives shriek and yell! But, despite the total pandemonium, the boys' cup of happiness runneth over!

I have often seen, for instance, a young bull with a native hanging on to its horns, give a mighty shake of its head and toss the boy yards. On occasions, he has been flung against a tree, but he sat up, gazed around for a moment or two, then leapt to his feet and rejoined the fray. One day, a boy came to me in the evening, after chasing after cattle for hours. He had had a nasty fall early on, and when he got to me, he had two badly cracked ribs, but the excitement had kept him going.

That gives you an insight into their attitude to physical fear and danger, but it is altogether different with fear of the unknown. Every native keeps a respectful distance from my microscope. It is regarded as the extreme example of the magician's paraphernalia. The news inexplicably spreads that I never travel without my 'devil machine' and, as usual, this news precedes me wherever I go. One day, I persuaded one of Lewanika's indunas to look through the eyepiece: he was shaking so much, with fear and apprehension, that he saw nothing, but his already considerable reputation was substantially enhanced by having been invited to examine my 'magic equipment'. Matapi bears responsibility, at all times, for the safety of my microscope, and I have heard him, on the occasions when he did not know I was near him, addressing the box in which the microscope is kept, 'Don't think that I am afraid of you, because I am not!' but his countenance says otherwise! The fact that I try and explain that it is only metal and glass means nothing.

I often send messengers off, some distance, to take blood samples. I examine these, and can easily spot if the beast is dying, or has died, from anthrax. Now the messengers, too, can readily spot anthrax when they see the beast. But the mystery, which I can never successfully explain to them, is that I can detect this disease without ever seeing the animal itself. This has to be magic of a very high order!

Quite recently, I heard that a number of cattle were dying at a village 150 miles away. The news was, inevitably, passed by drums. Not wanting to go that distance – 300-odd miles through pretty rough country – as I was busy here at HQ, I called a messenger and told him to go to the village, enquire about the deaths and bring me back some blood samples. He told me he would need eight days' meal for the journey, which I provided. Then he set off with the food, a blanket and his assegais. But, as he was leaving, I overheard him tell another messenger what a soft number he had landed! He would go from village to village asking the way, and would jog-trot every mile of the journey, averaging almost 40 miles a day! If I had decided to go myself, I would have needed about 30 carriers and a considerable amount of gear.

Monday, 30th March
Great news! Jack's wife has a daughter and all is well. A boy brought a very brief note through from Livingstone, and he is hoping that the post boys will bring more details when they arrive at about 4.00 or 6.00pm this evening.

Later
The post boys have just arrived. Jack has got his letter with full details of the birth and his little daughter, and is beside himself with

pride and excitement. I, too, got my mail, and am delighted that you are well and in good heart. As I need to catch the outgoing post with this letter, I must stop now.

John Smith had now been in Northern Rhodesia for almost a year, and at Sesheke for five months. His mood suddenly changed, as it was to from time to time. It was hardly surprising. Sesheke was a tiny outpost with three white males, two white females and a missionary, his wife and assistant a couple of miles upriver. Mrs Venning, a remarkable and charming character who clearly contributed substantially to the happiness and calm atmosphere, was away having her baby whilst the Ingrams, equally clearly something of a misfit, had their own troubles with her health. It was the end of a long, hot, wet season, and the fact that Easter seems to have taken both Jack Venning and John Smith completely by surprise shows just how out of touch they both were with what was going on in the wider world.

Smith was also suffering from all-too-frequent attacks of malaria – or fever, as he euphemistically calls it – and was being physically and emotionally weakened by them.

All in all, it seems not unreasonable that John Smith's enthusiasm for his new life should suffer a bit of a set-back.

Sesheke
3rd April
This is a nasty time of year, as the days and nights are so extreme in temperature. The river is rising rapidly and, in a few days, we expect flooding to begin: already, in places, water is over the banks.

The natives are busy reaping the harvest. The rains did, in the end, arrive in time, and the crops are good. This is about the only occasion in the year that the males do any real work, as they condescend to help bring in the harvest. But it is only fear that the floods would wash away their food supplies if they didn't make an effort that spurs them on to give their womenfolk a hand.

After the collapse of my store in that storm, the boys are building a new one. I shall be relieved when it is ready as my 'droring room' (sic) is my store, and is piled high with every kind of food and all sorts of gear.

The other day, Litia sent Jack a beautiful ebony walking stick with an ivory handle he had carved himself. Jack wrote a fulsome letter thanking him for it, and received the following reply: 'I thank you very much for the nice stick I sent you'. I sent Litia a note recently, telling him that the number of cattle in his region had proved to be greater than we had anticipated. He wrote back to say how pleased he was that the cattle were increasing 'in such mournful numbers'.

As I write, I am looking across to Jack's garden fence. It is completely covered with ipomoea, morning glory, and is one mass of flowers. As you probably know, each bloom lasts only 12 hours, to be replaced by another next morning. The effect against his 'house' is very beautiful. The building itself is covered by a wisteria-like creeper, which also is in full bloom and very striking. Poor Mrs Venning is missing the result of all her hard work, but has a much greater consolation.

All this garden colour reminds me of home. Hearing the news of your works party at Wigan, I have to say I would have given a lot to have been there. Except for Jack's rather ancient gramophone, with his extremely limited stack of well-worn records, I haven't heard any music of any kind since I was on board ship. I can't really call the Livingstone police band 'making music', even though they do their best.

The messenger who has been off collecting blood samples is back, late! I had known that he had to pass close to his own village but, striving to keep a straight face, I asked what had kept him. He replied with a most innocent look that, just as he was passing his village, a great sickness came over him, and he was forced to rest! I suspect I would have done as he did, had I been asked to make a journey past Wigan. My cook, Tolani, put the whole episode into perspective when he confided in me, in his own particular form of English, 'All people, at any time, I will like to be sick in my own village'. Tolani has a great liking for mixing singular and plural!

The upshot of his journey is that it seems a lot of cattle are dying and I shall need to go and see what appears to be the cause.

I have also had a message from Lewanika, sent via Litia, asking me to visit his territory as, apparently, a lot of cattle are dying up there also. But I can't see myself getting there before October. It's 400 miles through very difficult country, and I will need time and a big party of carriers, but I will plan to get up there as soon as is practical, as it is a journey I very much look forward to making.

Let me recount to you a charming story I have been told about Lewanika. He travelled, with a British official, to London for King Edward VII's coronation, and was introduced to the present king, George V. He later told the British resident at Lealui, his HQ far up north, that he wished King George would come and see him, as he was a great friend of his. The resident asked what they would talk about and he replied, 'Oh! We kings always have a lot to talk about'.

I am starting to plan my trip to the area my messenger visited, as I have found trypanosomes in the blood he brought back. I've sent out a call for carriers, but they will take some time to come in, as I am asking for boys from villages a good hundred or so miles away. I am doing this deliberately, as I do not want to use 'local' natives in case I need them in a hurry, in future, and they are reluctant to put themselves forward, having already earned enough for taxes etc on a previous trip.

We shall all be relieved when the floods have come and gone, as the mosquitoes are quite appalling. Litia is down with a bad attack of malaria which I am doing my best to treat. He is suffering from continuous vomiting. This is the symptom I seem to suffer from most, and I know just how debilitating it can be.

Thursday, 9th April
Only yesterday, Jack and I realised that tomorrow is Good Friday! I wish Blackpool was a bit nearer. I think I would slip away for a week. Easter won't make any difference to us here, as there is absolutely nothing to do. I can't even enjoy some fishing, as the river is too swollen and, if I was to get a decent dugout and some good paddlers to try for the duck and geese which are about in large numbers, I would only be eaten alive by mosquitoes. So, it's a matter of just mooching about to kill time, until my carriers arrive and I can get out on trek again.

The doctor Jack asked to come up and see Mrs Ingram has arrived, although she is considerably better, but we couldn't really stop him once he had started out from Livingstone. He has just remarked to me that he could not believe there could be so many mosquitoes: apparently he is shortly due for leave, and does not propose to return!

We are supposed to take Good Friday and Easter Monday off, but as there is nowhere to go and nothing to do, I suppose I shall behave as if it were just another ordinary weekend.

My patient, Litia, is getting better, but now I am treating his half-sister. She is one of goodness knows how many Lewanika offspring. None of us knows how many wives he has, or has had. So, I have a prince and a princess as patients at the same time!

I have bought a tiny monkey – a rum little beggar – hardly bigger than a rat, but great company. As I write, he is sitting on the floor eating a mealie cob about twice his size. He jumps in the air every time I make a movement, so Tolani is setting up a pole for him to perch on. I have been without a monkey companion for some time, and so am particularly glad to have this newcomer, as he helps me pass the day.

Malaria is rife: I have eight or ten patients, even though we have a doctor in our midst for a day or two. He gave me a bit of a going-over today, and has told me to increase my daily dose of quinine from 5 to 8 grains. Apparently my spleen is somewhat enlarged, but that is, it seems, common after several bouts of malaria. In Livingstone, everyone with malaria automatically goes straight to hospital!

Easter Monday
It is 11.00am, and I dearly wish I could go for a stroll down to the north pier at Wigan: how I should enjoy it. We are fed up with Easter. We have finished our reports – it's the year-end – and can't find anything to do. As we give the messengers and government-paid natives a holiday, there is nothing happening at all. The doctor is still here, and Jack has managed to dig out his old table-tennis set. The three of us have been playing all weekend.

Saturday night was the highlight of this holiday. The Rev. Roulet, the missionary, asked Jack, the doctor, McKnight, and me to dinner. The mission is on the river, about two miles north of here. We decided to go by dugout as the moon is full, in a cloudless sky. We chose a large boat as hippos are about in considerable numbers at the moment, and have a nasty habit of tipping smaller craft over.

We set off back at about 10.00pm, and it was almost as light as day, perfectly beautiful, with the moon's reflection on a near-flat river surface. The doc, who spends most of his time in Livingstone, was enraptured, but a bit apprehensive, when he saw both Jack and me carrying heavy rifles into the boat. We succeeded in convincing him that we would almost certainly have to repel a hippo attack! To his evident relief, all was quiet, although we did see a couple basking in the moonlight.

This has been a funny Easter. Today I have done nothing but just hang around. I am really looking forward to being on the go again.

13

Out on Trek and Back on Form

Maraman's Village
Lower Machile River
Barotseland
19th April 1914

I am at the end of my third day out. I had to delay my start for three days, as I had another slight attack of malaria and didn't feel up to the journey, but I'm fit again and glad to be on the move.

I am camped near water midway between three villages, and cattle from each are being brought for me to examine. I am not, of course, expected to treat individual cases – that would be impossible – but I have to report on all infectious cases and advise the natives what they should do. Specifically on this trip, I need to find out the cause of what is being called sleeping sickness, an infection confined to these parts. It killed about 50% of the herds last year, but seems to have lost some of its virulence now.

When I arrived, I sent a message to the induna to bring the usual food for my boys and milk for me. The village women have arrived with it, and are sitting in the shade. Etiquette requires that they are kept waiting by me, and I have to give the impression of being totally unaware of their presence, despite quite a large crowd sitting motionless only yards from my tent.

My carriers tried the old food trick again just after we had set out. It is fascinating how predictable they are. I gave out two days' meal at Sesheke, just before we left. On the second day, a deputation came to ask for their food. I replied that they had already received it, but they persisted that it was all gone (which it probably was). I told them the food would be distributed again the next day, and that the subject was closed. Off they went, perfectly content. They tried the trick, the white man saw through it, honour was satisfied all round!

Yesterday, I was camped near a very big village. The induna brought enough food for about six boys, although we have nearer 40 in my camp. He said he had brought a present of food. I pretended to look round for it and told him I couldn't see any. He pointed to the two small pots, and I said I had thought one of the women had brought them to give to her piccaninny. I then sat at my table and began to write. In due course, the villagers crept away and returned some time later with the proper amount of meal.

The induna is a renowned twister, and pretended he had forgotten how many cattle his village owned. I told him it was obvious to me that he was just a little boy trying to do a man's job, and that I would advise Mwana Morena (literally, the 'child of the king') as the natives call Litia, that it would be better to appoint a proper man to rule over that village. It was extraordinary how swiftly he regained his memory!

For all that I have described, my visits are real red-letter days for the villages. Gossip is exchanged between the villagers and my boys, whilst my camp and its routine provide endless interest and entertainment for old and young, male and female. They are amazed at the way my furniture folds and unfolds, and are incredulous at my 'white hut', my tent. They press in closer and closer upon poor old Tolani, preparing my meal, until he loses his temper and swears at them in his own dialect, a cause of yet more amazement and merriment. Altogether a great day, which will be talked about for weeks to come.

Samampoloso's Village
Upper Michile River
Tuesday, 21st April
We made a short march yesterday, but a long one today. We were up and off at 6.00 this morning, and now it is 4.00pm and we have just got our camp set up. Apart from a 60-minute rest, we haven't stopped. This was necessary as we had been told there was no water between the last village and this spot, a small stream just a few feet wide.

The boys knew we would come across no water throughout today – the shade temperature must have been over 100° – and their preparations were interesting. Just before we loaded up, first thing, they all went to the river and took great mouthfuls of water which they swilled round and then spat out: only a very few sips were actually swallowed. I have watched this happening before and I, too, now follow their example with great success. When we hit water again, nine hours later – and remember each native had been carrying a heavy load almost non-stop – they repeated the drill. They washed their mouths out, but swallowed nothing for a good hour.

Last Sunday night, after the ritual of the food presents, I heard a terrific racket, and asked what was going on. It seemed that one induna, who had received 6d, was quarrelling with another who had received 1/6; the latter had contributed at least three times the amount of meal. My messengers reported that the aggrieved 6d induna badly wanted to fight the 1/6 induna. So I called the former to my tent and said, 'Do you want to fight very much?' 'Yes,' he replied. 'Have you got your assegai?' 'Yes.' 'Have you got your knobkerry?' 'Yes.' It was pitch dark and we could all hear a couple of lions roaring away. 'Is your assegai very sharp?' 'Yes,' came back. 'Tsamaid ni uwana litaw' ('Then go and fight those lions') I said. His face was a picture, as were the faces of all my boys and the village men who had heard every word of this exchange. The 6d induna slunk away and a great roar went up from the onlookers. The story was obviously told and retold late into the night, as I kept on hearing the words 'uwana' (fight) and 'litaw' (lions) repeated, followed by gales of laughter.

I have had two shots at game today, both chances, but although we found plenty of blood, we couldn't find the buck, as the grass is too high, way over our heads. If we had an hour or so more daylight we ought to have got them but, as it is, the asvogels will have a feast. I feel sick at having to leave the buck, as I hate abandoning wounded beasts, and my carriers could have done with a good meat meal. I am now only a day's march from good buffalo country, and I mean to have a go at them. Although this is a glorious area for game of all sorts, shooting is well-nigh impossible because of the height of the grass – 10 to 12 feet – and the dense undergrowth. This is also a favourite spot for lions: they, too, follow the game, but we haven't been troubled so far. Yesterday, we passed a tiny pool and saw masses of lion prints: my tracker boy said five of them had been there recently, but we never saw them.

I have an excellent team of carriers, big fellows. As their loads are about 40/50lbs each, we can make good progress. I have brought three of Venning's dogs with me and they are having a great time, much appreciating the almost unlimited supply of fresh milk which arrives from each village as a present for me. My milk can is a white-enamelled slop-pail which is often used for other purposes back in England! I also carry a potty. If this seems strange, ask yourself how you would like to step out in your pyjamas, in the middle of the night, with all the unpleasant creatures that lurk in these parts waiting to pounce! One of the carriers always has my potty tied to the top of his load, and he brings it, with great ceremony, to my tent when we make camp, passing it over rather as if it were a ceremonial chalice.

I am writing this from Sikoli's village, the sixth I have visited today. At one of them, I had to dress a native's badly mauled arm. A couple of days ago a lioness, bold as brass, strolled into the village and seized the boy. His assegai was beside him, and he managed to grab it, and stabbed at the lioness as she tried to drag him off. Finally, his pals came to his rescue and despatched her, but not before she had made a pretty good mess of his arm. I had quite a time trying to put him together again. But what cheek! Sauntering into the middle of the village in broad daylight!

Mulaulie's Village
29th April
Since I last wrote, I have been to the village which was the object of this trip, and am now on my return journey along a different route so that I can take in a lot more villages. The cattle seem better, but I have come across quite a few with a disease I didn't expect to find here. The natives say they have not seen it before, so it must be something that has recently broken out.

Trading of certain cattle is to be allowed from 1st May, and I want to be back to oversee things, and make sure that any with this disease are not passed to other parts of the territory. To this end, I have already sent a runner to Sesheke to post a contagious disease notice. By law, this must be mailed up beside a magistrate's office, but as not a single native can read one word, it seems a rather pointless piece of officialdom.

I have taken in over 40 villages this trip, with an average number of about 30 inhabitants each. I have also examined a large number of cattle. I never actually go into any village, as they are incredibly dirty and unhygienic, and the smell is overpowering. The induna of a village I went to specially was a very old man, with a reputation for being a wily character. After I had camped for about an hour, I sent a message of greetings and a request for our 'present' of meal for my boys. He arrived shortly afterwards to say that all his women were away from the village and that, therefore, no meal has been prepared. He went on in this vein for some time until I cut him short. I then told him he had until 'the sun was touching the trees' (about 5 o'clock) to bring food. I also gave him a graphic account of what my carriers would do to his village, and his people, if they went hungry. Needless to say, it worked. He is the same with his tax: I carry a list of the good, bad and indifferent payers, so that I am forewarned of the reaction I can expect. Happily, I have nothing to do with tax-collection, and steer well clear of that particular business.

4th May

Back at Sesheke, and overjoyed to celebrate my 31st birthday, yesterday, in the heart of Africa, with four letters from home. What timing!

I must thank you all for your good wishes and your long letters and, of course, for the tie. (*A not-altogether-suitable present in the circumstances!*)

My trip was most enjoyable and a great success, except from the shooting point of view. Right through the next four months, until August, it will be well-nigh impossible to shoot confidently, as the grass is too high. In August, the natives set fire to the grass and scrub and, immediately, new green shoots appear and with them the game, which can move more easily and can also be spotted and tracked.

After being away, I had to settle down and deal with official papers and a good deal of red-tape. It is all rather laborious, as there is only one rather decrepit typewriter.

On this last trip I tried out, again, the native potatoes, which are very sweet, and of quite a different consistency. I also bought some honey from one village, and very good it was. It all helps to vary a diet which, at this time of year, is very samely and low on greens.

On my return journey, I had more food trouble at one village. To cut the story short, I sent a message to Litia telling him what had happened. I should reiterate that we are about 40 white officials administering a territory larger than England, and if our authority were once broken, it would be the end of the 40 officials and every other white person out here. We do not rule by fear: we cannot and would not. But we do have to impose discipline.

Venning, who is responsible for law and order, is furious with the way I was treated, and intends to make an example of this whole village to ensure that non-compliance with Lewanika's, and our, orders does not spread. These problems over food are against a background of no shortage of maize: there is plenty.

Every day I learn, or observe, some new item of interest about the Central African native. I have a new kitchen boy. He holds the pots and pans and generally runs around under Tolani's direction. He is from a tribe which has emigrated from Bechuanaland, and so speaks another language, although he does have a very slight smattering of Sekololo. Tolani couldn't really understand him at all, but has set about learning his language, and expects to be proficient in about three or four weeks. This is truly amazing when you remember that no language here has any written form, so Tolani will have to absorb a completely unknown vocabulary simply by listening to the boy and practising with him. Incidentally, Tolani has been saving his money with me. I've already sent off £8 to his brother to buy cattle, but I'm still holding £4 which I suspect he may have earmarked for another wife! The four here are all kitted out like Solomon in all his glory (wrong sex, I admit), and I've warned him I couldn't face another of his womenfolk taking up space in my compound! We shall see what happens!

Just as I was writing the words above, my messenger ran in to tell me a snake was beside my bedroom door. I grabbed my shotgun and killed it, a really big fellow, over eight feet long, and a thoroughly nasty customer. Sesheke is a notorious place for snakes: that is the fourth that has been found right by my quarters. One was actually in the bedroom when my boy spotted it. The trouble was that the outside door did not fit too well down to the ground, and these wretched creatures could squeeze through. I've tacked wire mesh along the bottom now, but we all have to keep our eyes skinned, as their bite can be lethal.

8th May
We are expecting Captain Salmon and his wife through here before long: they are to be stationed at Mongu. Salmon went home on leave a few months ago, got engaged and married within the three months, so that they could return out here together. They decided to make the journey from Livingstone, right through to Mongu, by dugout, and I am pretty apprehensive as to how they will fare. The dugout will be 24 inches wide, possibly 20 feet long, and with such little freeboard that it is impossible to stand up unless held by a paddler. They will have been a week to Sesheke, then it will take a good three weeks more to reach Mongu.

Think of the guts it needs for an English girl, in her twenties, probably from a pretty straightforward background at home, to agree to come out here with her young soldier husband. She will be 400 miles from HQ, in a small community of about a dozen white men and women, with every single item of need having to be carried or paddled all the way from Livingstone, taking weeks. The full reply-time for letters, up there, is well over three months so, if she has forgotten something, or needs something less usual, even getting it from Cape Town would take several weeks. I can only admire her spirit, and her devotion and loyalty to him.

Catastrophic news! The whisky, which the McKinnons were taking up to replenish the fast-dwindling stocks at Mongu, has been lost en route! The small white contingent sent an urgent appeal for the 'staff of life', as it is thought of out here, and the McKinnons put it aboard one of their dugouts, which was taking them back up north when he resumed his post as senior resident. The dugout, with a single paddler, carrying the whisky and a good deal of gear, was charged by a hippo, tipped over and the contents sent to the bottom of the Zambezi. The misery this has caused is boundless and, apparently, a couple of the old hands up in Mongu are in a state of deep shock!

Virtually no other alcohol is drunk here, and no 'strong' drink is ever taken, in government circles anyway, until sundown – hence the 'sundowner' – which is normally at about 6.00pm. Then just about everybody, women included, has one or, at the most, two decent measures topped high with soda. Only fools take more, as the risks, in this lonely existence, are too great. Whether the distraught officials worried as much over the poor McKinnons losing a great many of their possessions has not been related.

We got this desperate whisky news from Captain and Mrs James, who are going south for leave in England, being relieved by the Salmons. The Jameses have a five-month-old son, which they brought down in a wire-mesh meat safe! What a splendid way to carry him! But, again, just imagine over four weeks in these conditions with a tiny baby! Apparently, he has already had one bout of malaria, but seems none the worse for it. I fancy the parents can't have one moment's peace of mind, in the dugout or on the march and, probably, the meat safe wheeze has saved their sanity.

Litia's prime minister, Leashimba, is my latest patient, with a bad attack of dysentery. He is a very senior native in these parts, and goes everywhere with a considerable retinue. But I still find it disconcerting when every one of them, even Leashimba himself, drops to the ground in front of me and starts to clap, until I signal to them to stop.

I saw a native funeral the other day, a very showy and emotional affair. The body, which is carried shoulder-high on a sort of bier, is secured in a sitting position, as it is thus that it will be buried. Into the grave with the body are placed some assegais, food and water: these are for the journey into the next world, although they have no firm convictions in that direction. Except for the natives attached to, or educated by, the missions, no-one has any 'religion'. They have no gods, no idols and no beliefs, other than that a dead person needs the same material comforts and protection for the journey as the living need on earth. I would dearly love to be informed on these matters, but we have to be extremely careful and show great tact. I was conscious that I was not to be seen to be watching the funeral, and could certainly not ask questions, even of my chief messenger, for fear of embarrassing them.

Captain Salmon and his young bride have just arrived, and we will do our best to entertain them for the couple of days before their three-week-long dugout journey. She is totally enraptured with everything so far. Long may it last!

14

Egrets and Hippos

Sesheke
12th May 1914

I have never got used to my food and drinks being flavoured by all sorts of flying things. The other evening I had to leave my soup for a couple of minutes, literally, and when I got back, I counted 16 creatures floating or swimming around! Poor Mrs Salmon, she hasn't got used to it either, as I saw her give a shudder or two last evening over dinner.

My medical practice flourishes, and I'm kept busy in the mornings treating patients. I often wonder what the BMA would think of a vet having a daily surgery for humans! The missionary sends quite a few natives over to me, and I think he is grateful in more ways than one. Medicines are expensive and, within reason, I can get all I need whilst he has to buy his from limited funds.

The mission up the river has a new lady assistant who is a red-hot anti-vivisectionist, and she has been giving me a rough time, complaining about my experiments with monkeys etc. Finally, I introduced the subject of smallpox, and got her to agree that vaccination was a good thing, then added that all serum for smallpox was made under the Vivisection Act! Incidentally, there is a good deal of smallpox in this area and a great deal of leprosy. Jack has granted over 500 exemptions from tax for lepers, and there are probably hundreds more we don't know about. Much as I might wish to, there is nothing I can do for them, and I do my best, gently, to steer them away from my camps.

Litia's secretary, so-called, a young man who has been taught some English, writes us some screaming notes from time to time. The most recent started with all the usual long-winded greetings and then went on, 'I have a man who has his bed-ridden for six years. I think you will do something for him'. Another note, telling me that Litia had dealt with a village headman who had lied to me, went on, 'I have talked to him too much and have got a cow'! All these notes and letters, written for Litia, are signed by him, but this is the only writing he is capable of. He always ends, 'Your friend, Litia'. We use the same form of words to him. Lewanika, who, again, can only sign his name, uses the words 'Always, your friend', and we do the same to him. These are the only two natives, in the whole of this vast territory, who write letters to us and get written replies. All other communications to all other natives, regardless of rank or station, are by word of mouth, through a third person, or 'mouth-between'. These are native customs, not white man's rules, and we do our best to conform to the courtesies when practical.

I had a bit of luck last night. I went out in a dugout, sat in the swamps beside the river, and managed to get three egrets. Now I have nine beautiful feathers. I am trying to get a good bunch for each of you back home as their plumage is at its very best just now. But the birds are very wild and wary, and it is mighty difficult to get a shot at them. I and my two paddlers lay in the bottom of the dugout and let the boat drift into the swampy area. The snag is, one gets eaten alive by mosquitoes, as egrets only flight as the sun is going down: it was pitch dark by the time I got back.

15th May
The night before last I went down the river again to try for more egrets. We paddled quietly into a small backwater and sat still in a dugout. After a while, we heard hippos grunting and then counted eight quite near us. One rose up about 20 yards off and kept its head above water for some time. I think it must have known that I only had my shotgun and could do nothing to harm it. I looked at my two paddlers, and their faces were the picture of abject misery as they saw three tons of meat and fat escape us. Eight hippos, with a total weight of over 20 tons, splashing within 40 yards of one when sitting in a frail 15-feet dugout, is quite an experience, yet they made no attempt to molest us.

Last night, Jack and I went back to the same spot, fully armed with large-calibre rifles. We hung about for a couple of hours and then heard the hippos grunting again. Our boys silently slid the dugout towards a small pool, where we saw four of them playing about and splashing for all they were worth. We edged into the reeds and, as we would only get one shot in before they dived, we tossed for it. Jack won! Quietly, he took aim and fired at the nearest, which was only about 20 yards off. He is normally a deadly shot, but this time he missed the brain, which is about the only way to kill a hippo. To our utter surprise, at the sound of the shot, two more of these huge creatures rose right beside the dugout, splashing like mad. We lay perfectly still, with our rifles at the ready, but fortunately they cleared off in the opposite direction. We sighed with relief at our escape, but were bitterly disappointed at losing our hippo again. Just on the off-chance, we will go back tonight, but haven't much hope as the hippos will, almost certainly, have cleared off elsewhere.

I have had a busy morning in court (Venning's office), prosecuting a number of natives for a variety of offences. One of the accused was a pretty influential induna, who is also commanding officer of Litia's fighting regiment. He has obviously got a bit too big for his boots, and has been moving cattle against my instructions. The case has caused quite a stir, and Litia sent his Prime Minister to listen to the proceedings. Jack fined him and sent several of his henchmen to gaol.

The cattle trading I have recently allowed is in full swing and, yesterday, I went off to two sales – if you can call them that – to check up that no one was buying or selling cows or heifers, as only bullocks are permitted to be sold. The way natives trade is quite unbelievable. I listened to one deal, and it went like this.

Trader: 'How much?' (for three bullocks).

Native: 'I want £8, but if you won't give it to me, I want £6, and if you won't give me that, I want £5'. I asked the trader if the bullocks were cheap. 'No,' he said, 'they're damn dear, but then so are my blankets'!

I've been back in court again today, my office this time. It's all so terribly incongruous. Jack, in the most solemn manner possible, reads out the offence with such phrases as, 'upsetting the peace of our Sovereign Lord, the King, His Crown and His Dignity'. This, the interpreter manages to turn into something like, 'you opened your mouth and there came forth not words of truth. Therefore, is the Great White King angry and you will be punished greatly.'

23rd May
Another visitor this weekend, a man in the native department called Campbell, who is on his way back up north. He is a great character and has a banjo, with which he entertains us. He has just returned off leave, having not been back to England for the past 17 years! He arrived here six years ago, when the British South Africa Company was opening the country up and placing officials strategically throughout Northern Rhodesia, then he spent a year or two in Southern Rhodesia, before returning to Barotseland. He will be at his new post up north for two-and-a-half years and may, during that time, see no other white men, so he is naturally making the most of being with us both.

We told him about the whisky tragedy. He says he will stop on his way up the Zambezi and drag the river, as he claims to have an idea where the drama took place! What an optimist!

Jack is going to Livingstone early in June to meet his wife and baby daughter, who have been in Cape Town, and will bring them both back up here. There is a suggestion that I should go with him, to try and settle quite a few problems with the department, and then go straight on up to Mongu by another route. It would be interesting, but quite a journey, as I would have to do nearly 600 miles. Actually, I could do with getting to Livingstone, to replace some clothes and personal gear. The clothes are showing distinct signs of being laundered every day by my boys. They do the washing by soaping the garments, and then thrashing them against round stones at the water's edge: it cleans the clothes all right, but wreaks havoc with the material, buttons etc. If we do go south, we have decided to travel by dugout, as the current is fast-flowing at present, and in our favour. We will send the ponies overland, to meet us 20 miles from Livingstone and ride in from there. It is a perfect bore not being able to go the whole way by river, as it would save so much time.

Monday night

It's Empire Day and we have decided to have the day off, as they do in Livingstone. The three of us – Campbell is still with us – went up river by dugout, with a picnic lunch which we had under the shade of a large tree. Then we fished, and stopped on the way back for some excellent duck shooting. A very pleasant outing, and a change of routine.

I got my salary increase in December, and have now heard that when I have done a year (28 June) my pay is to increase to £475 (*this is equivalent to about £19,000*). Then it will go to £500 in another twelve months, all more than I was originally promised, so I think my Maramba work and report must have been well received.

29th May

My head messenger's father came to visit him last week and died on Wednesday. Matapi came to see me on Thursday, and asked if he could go 'to cry for him'. This is the custom. The dead are buried within a couple of hours, for obvious reasons, and then, at a more convenient time, the family and friends gather and 'cry' for the dead person. For a few hours there is a terrific shindig, and then it is all over.

The colder nights are playing havoc with the natives' health, and there have been a great number of cases of malaria. I have a long line of patients each morning. One native brought his small boy with a bad throat, and I gave him some lozenges. The next morning, there was a large and sudden epidemic of sore throats and I couldn't understand it, until I remembered that the lozenges are very like sweets! I gave the 'new' sufferers chlorate of potash, and haven't seen them since!

My most difficult patients are the prisoners. They don't have to work if they are listed as sick. Venning sends them all to me, and Dr John Smith has an awful time trying to establish if they are shamming or not. They all seem to be adept at the alarming 'short-breath technique', and it is only with a stethoscope that I can confirm trouble or otherwise. If I find it is otherwise, I give the culprit a good purgative, and that always settles his problem!

Whit Sunday

Today and Monday are the days for the rifle competition held right across Northern Rhodesia. A dozen cups and prizes are to be won and medals, also, are awarded. The competition is held in about a dozen centres, of which Sesheke is one, and five of us have entered; two of the traders are taking part. We haven't been given our handicaps, yet, as we have to send our targets in to Livingstone with the scores, and then the winners are worked out there. I can't think that I stand much of a chance, as there are some truly great shots in this country. It is a major event, as we each have to fire 200 rounds, which are supplied by the government.

We shoot at targets between 100 and 600 yards, standing, kneeling and lying. One of the targets is a cutout in the shape of a buck. A circle is drawn across its chest and we have to fire, standing, 10 shots in 22 seconds at 200 yards. I don't fancy this, as I have had hardly any practice at rapid firing. We use .303 service rifles and the competition is, basically, to ensure that standards are maintained so that, in case of major trouble, we can all be called upon to lend a hand. I have passed as 'second-class shot' but to be 'first-class' is quite another story. The test for that is to hit a 12-inch bull at 600 yards six times out of eight; a six-inch bull at 200 yards seven times out of eight and the same bull six times out of eight at 500 yards. That is real shooting!

I can manage 600 yards, and have done it twice but, for some reason, I can't do at all well at 200 yards. This target is blue, with a brown bull shaped like a man's head and shoulder, and I don't seem to be able to see it properly. Maybe I'm a bit colour-blind. The 600-yard bull is the traditional black circle on white.

Whit Monday

We have nearly finished the competition. I have done quite well, up to my usual standard, but it won't be good enough to win anything.

14th June

On Sunday, Jack and I leave for Livingstone by dugout, a large one we have borrowed from a trader, so that we can bring a good deal

Above: The United Services Club, Livingstone. The deserted look, bare flagpole and unkempt lawns suggest this was taken after 1964. (Photo: courtesy Livingstone Museum).

Left: Father and son, Livingstone. 1927.

Father and daughter, Diana, Livingstone. 1922.

F.J. (Mopane) Clarke, the legendary 'father' of white Northern Rhodesia. Believed to have been the first settler at Old Drift in about 1898. (Snapped by my mother in 1922).

Left: Drum-major Yoram of the Northern Rhodesian Police. 1930.

Below: The Naliquanda, Barotse state barge. The drum and drummer, ensuring Lewanika's safety, are to the right of the latunka (shelter). Snapped by my father in 1923.

The old veterinary department office building in 1996. On his arrival in Livingstone in 1913 my father wrote ". . . it is the envy of all the officials as it is a brand-new stone building"!

Almost certainly Mr. Dougal Malcolm (BSAC director) and Sir Lawrence Wallace (Administrator, in helmet) in one of the first cars in NR. It was this car, with Mr. Malcolm, that caused such panic at Maramba, Sept. 1913. John Smith spent his first few nights in this hotel! (Photo: courtesy Livingstone Museum).

Nanoo's Cash and Carry 1996. Built in 1905 by 'Mopane' Clarke, this was his Zambezi Trading Company store in Livingstone.

Livingstone Golf Club 1996. This colonial-era building is about the only one still used for its original purpose.

Left: Lieutenant John Smith, Army Veterinary Corps, and his fianceé, Beryl Paterson. Aldershot 1917.

Below: The site of the Maramba Camp 1996.

Left: I bid farewell to the Falls, sixty-four years after my mother and I last stood on this spot.

Below: John and Jane Smith and their family in about 1905. John, junior, is second from right.

Memorandum

12th. Maz. 1914

From . . . .

Chief Litia Eeta Lewanika,
Moandi, Sesheke,
Barotseland, N.R.

To / . . .

Mr. J. Smith
G. V. O.
Sesheke

My friend

I send you
14 Palabash. of grain
from J Mooka's Kraal
I made them to pay the grain
because they refused to bring
Some food to you when
you want it + So J
panished them for bring
grain + send it to you —
then you don't want to
pay for it. wid greetings
Your friend
L. Lewanika.

Above: The veterinary department messengers in 1922. Matapi is second from the left and Mohinda on the right.

Left: "My friend. I send you 14 Calabash (half gourd) of grain from I Mooka's Kraal. I made them to pay the grain because they refused to bring some food to you when you want it and so I punished them for bringing grain and send it to you then you don't want to pay for it. With greetings, Your friend, L. E. Lewanika." Litia meets out justice!

of our luggage back with us. Our ponies are going on ahead to meet us 20 miles from Livingstone, we then have to ride in. As the river is with us, and flowing very fast, we could do that part of the journey in about three-and-a-half days but, returning with Mrs Venning, baby and all the gear, it will be a real slog for the paddlers, up against a strong current every inch of the way. It may well take us seven days or more, going as hard as we can.

I am expecting to be in Livingstone for only three days, so will be pretty rushed, as I have a fair deal of official work to do, quite apart from my personal affairs.

15

Two Lions and Two Ponies

The office of the Chief Veterinary Officer
Livingstone
22 June 1914

I n Livingstone, and using a couple of sheets of my boss's writing paper! I arrived last Wednesday evening, and am off again in about an hour.

Mrs Venning and her baby arrived from Cape Town on Friday evening, and both seem fit and well. The plan is for us all to travel back to Sesheke by river.

I have been on the run from the moment I arrived, dining and lunching every day, paying calls in between and managing, somehow, to get through a good deal of office work. Specifically, we have made arrangements about cattle movement in the Sesheke district, and proclamations about these will be promulgated shortly. I have got some of the new equipment I asked for, but not all by any means, as budgets are especially tight.

There are a great many new faces around since I was last here: new people seem to be arriving by practically every train. The Livingstone white population, all told, is now in the region of a couple of hundred.

Sesheke
29th June

Back again, and just ahead of the post.

I had a very hectic but enjoyable time in Livingstone, being lunched and dined every day, as I was kept up until all hours, I found myself a bit short of sleep. I visited Government House, and met the Administrator's wife who was home on leave when I was last there. I had lunch and tea with Major and Mrs Stennett – he's the police chief – and found them as lively as ever. They are off on a tour of the native police in Barotseland next month and I hope to catch up with them on the way.

Most of my spare time(!) during the day, I spent cadging things I badly needed. The Treasurer and the Secretary had me in for a long meeting and tried to cut down my list of requirements, but I stuck to my guns and was backed up by my boss, Lane, so got most things.

I have got my instructions to tour right through Barotseland to the very north. I have been told, 'use your own discretion, go where you think you ought, BUT KEEP EXPENSES DOWN!'

I shouldn't be completely surprised if, when I have finished this trip, I am called back to Livingstone and promoted number two to Lane. Nothing in government is certain, but I was dropped a strong hint by a very senior person, so there may be some truth in it. A new man is due out from England any time now, bringing the department's strength up to eight.

I have managed to establish what the disease is that killed so many of the cattle in the Sesheke district last year, but I have not managed to isolate the fly that is carrying the disease. I have tried everything I know, but can't solve the riddle. Now I have to wait for next season's rain to try again. I badly needed that discovery but have failed.

Now, back to our journey down to Livingstone. Jack and I got to Katombora's village on the flood current in two days, a terrific achievement by our paddlers. We picked up our ponies and covered 22 miles, then pitched camp for the night. We left all our gear for a messenger to supervise bringing in, and rode into town. That was Wednesday; Mrs Venning arrived two days later. She was well, but very tired after that bumpy and dusty four-day train trip up from the Cape. Their daughter is a chubby little girl who, mercifully, does nothing but eat and sleep! Jack wanted to set off back at once but Mrs Venning needed a rest, so we delayed until Monday.

For the 27-mile return journey to Katombora's village, I fixed to borrow the department's buckboard and four mules for Mrs Venning and her native nurse. They were in the back with the baby; Venning sat beside the driver and I rode my pony. We reached our camp in a day, but I pitied poor Mrs Venning in a wagon without springs, bumping along a very rough track for hours on end. The next day we set off to do the 20 miles to the river. Jack wanted to rush and get it over, but at about 1.00 I could see that Mrs Venning was dead-beat, so we stopped. We had sent our boys off through the forest to the river by a short-cut and I set off, on my pony, to try and find them. I had an awful time and was away some hours. Finally, I found my cook and his kitchen gear plus food, then one tent and all our blankets. I sent these to where we had stopped, and we all arrived back there about 7 o'clock. I didn't worry about anything else after I found the food, tent and blankets. I slept rolled up in mine, and the Venning family had the tent. The boys didn't have their blankets, so lay beside a huge fire which they kept roaring away all night.

The next day we travelled to the river and caught up with the rest of our party. I must say I was relieved, as I thought it likely Mrs Venning could be quite unwell if we hit any more difficulties.

As I expected, the river trip took eight days' really hard going against strong currents, but it gave Mrs Venning time to get her strength back, even if I was bored to death sitting in a dugout day after day, with nothing I could usefully do. I was partly frustrated by never getting going until 9.30 or 10.00 each morning, and then having to stop at 4.00pm: it dragged the trip out. The paddlers, who had been expecting to do 12 hours a day pulling against the river's current, reckoned they had an easy time of it.

The little girl has been splendid, sleeping most of the time and only waking every two-and-a-half hours for her bottle. She must be one of the youngest white babies ever to make such a journey.

I will now tell you that we very nearly lost our ponies when they were going south to meet us: it could have been very serious. They had to stop one night in the middle of the forest; two lions put in an appearance and the six boys, whom we had sent with the ponies, built huge fires and piled wood on. But at some point, Venning's pony stampeded, broke loose and bolted. The two messengers grabbed flaming branches from the fire and rushed after it. But before they could get to it, one of the lions jumped on its hind quarters and tried to drag it down. At that moment, the messengers arrived and thrust the burning torches at the two lions which, fortunately, then fled: the pony was rescued, not badly clawed. But it was a near-run thing.

The boys were clearly rattled by this episode, as they refused to camp in that forest on the return trip, and did a forced march of 40 miles in one day to get through without stopping. All was well this time, and I found the party waiting for us when we arrived back by river today.

It is a year, last Saturday, since I sailed from Southampton. I have seen so much and been to so many weird places, I can hardly believe it is only 12 months!

9th July

Tax collecting started this week, and I have been in Venning's office, examining the sick and elderly natives who sought tax exemption. They come in all shapes and sizes. The day they come in to pay tax is a great yearly outing, and they are determined to make as much as possible of it. When a name is called out, a native comes forward, sits on the ground and starts clapping. Then he will untie a corner of the only bit of clothing he wears, a tiny cotton loincloth. Sometimes, he has to take it off altogether to find his money. Often his pals join in the search, with many 'oohs' and 'aahs'. Each man gets a ticket in return, as a receipt, and then the kerfuffle continues as they hunt for a safe place to keep it. It is a perfectly ordinary receipt but, as they have no knowledge of written numbers or figures, each year is distinguished by a different stamp, usually an animal. This is the year of the cock, and will always be known, to the natives, as 'Mutelo y kuhu' (tax of the fowl). They know nothing of dates, but speak of the last years, since we took over Barotseland, as the year of the lion; of the hand; of the fly; and of the duck.

We can never understand how they all get coins to pay their taxes but, as they have mostly been paying in gold, it must come from cattle sales. One old boy gave a sovereign, and was surprised to get change: he didn't know what it meant or what to do with it. It is astonishing that they know nothing of money or its value. Even Leashimba, Litia's Prime Minister, who had brought tax for his six wives (they pay for all but the first) had to put the money down in piles of ten shillings, so as not to get muddled.

One elderly native came in, and I said to Venning 'this looks like an exemption', and he agreed. Then the old boy got out a handful of coins, and we saw in the records that he always pays for five wives and had just married another young girl! He didn't get exemption!

They sit about for hours looking at their and their friend's receipts, just like a crowd of children looking at pretty pictures: the 'kuhu', cock, seems to intrigue them. I suppose tax-collection day will furnish them all with stories to tell for weeks to come. Venning took £60 the first day, but the collection will take some time to complete.

My messengers are out in the surrounding villages looking for carriers for my trip up north. I have told Litia that I want them from the same tribes as my last lot. This has surprised him and others, as they are reckoned to be the most difficult to handle in this whole area. They belong to Lewanika's old fighting impi and are a rum lot, but I doubt if they fear anything on earth. I like them better than those that are slightly more civilised, and I seem to be able to manage them better. They are all wonderful hunters, know I am keen on shooting to give as much meat to each as I can, and will do anything for me. One tablecloth has more material in it than all their clothing put together, and each has a collection of assegais and knobkerries that make it look as if they were preparing for war! Last trip, after a couple of days when they had seen me shoot and understood my routine, I came out of my tent one morning, they were all gathered in front and gave me a great deep-throated roar. I knew then that they would make a formidable party, whatever the circumstances.

I have especially sent for one boy: he stands 6'4" and is built in proportion. I gave him the job of sleeping beside the entrance to my tent, and tending the fire through the night. He interpreted this as meaning he was also my personal bodyguard and, if anyone 'unauthorised' came near, he would brandish his knobkerry, ready for anything.

I am sending some stores up the river in boats, and shall pick them up at Mongu, in about two months' time. I do hope they don't get lost en route – like the whisky – as I shall be in a nice fix for food. I just can't manage to take everything I possess with me through forests and thick bush, as I shall have a large number of carriers and will have my work cut out to shoot enough to keep us all fed. As I shall be away from Sesheke for some time, my messengers and personal boys are taking their wives with them, and I think the whole lot of them are looking forward to the journey. Getting fresh meat on a daily basis is a great attraction to all natives.

Litia has something seriously wrong with his eyes, and his father, Lewanika, has sent him money so that he can travel to Cape Town for treatment. He has never been on such a journey, and is mightily excited about it, but there is a bit of a problem about him travelling on the railway, as the carriages provided for natives are not divided into compartments and, quite naturally, Litia, who is a prince, doesn't fancy going all that way with all sorts of natives. So Venning, who agrees with him, has asked that a coach be provided, hitched to the Livingstone/Cape train, so that he can travel as befits his standing and status, and with his personal staff to look after him. As the BSAC virtually owns the railways, I can't see that there is likely to be any difficulty. Some missionary people have agreed to look after him at Cape Town, as no native is allowed in any hotel.

Jack has been keeping a record of the number of patients I have been treating in my 'clinic'! It works out at over nine a day, and he has written up my efforts in his half-yearly report. I have a lot sick at the moment, and two are pretty bad.

The administrator has just issued a proclamation prohibiting the shooting of any hippos on the Zambezi. A Greek hunter got hold of a game licence, and has been slaughtering them wholesale. The only way to stop him was to stop everyone! It is a bit severe, as hippos are the most dangerous things on the river, after crocodiles. Only this month, Jack's interpreter was out in our dugout, and was charged by one which bit a chunk out of the boat before upsetting it, chucking the poor fellow into the water. Also, hippo fat is our only source of lard to cook with: a good-sized beast can easily provide three pails of fat.

147

We were discussing this with von Frankenberg, and he at once gave us permission to shoot on his side of the river, which is regarded as German! As we have no fat at all, we are taking up his invitation, and will go off at daybreak tomorrow to try our luck.

It is jolly good of von Frankenberg to let us hunt over his side. He doesn't shoot, himself, but is always in deadly fear of hippos going for him when out on the Zambezi.

Monday, 13 July

We went after our hippos yesterday. Venning came to me, soon after dawn, for breakfast, and then away we went. First, we aimed for the large pool and saw plenty of spoor, which had been made only an hour or two earlier. But the hippos were nowhere to be seen, so we decided to go down the 'runs', after them. They make these through the thick reeds as they tramp backwards and forwards with their huge feet. But because their bodies, which are vast, are only about 12 inches from the ground, the runs are more like tunnels. One has to go through, bent almost double, as in a coal mine.

We went through these runs with our rifles at the ready, and very much on the look-out, as there was no exit if one charged. I took three boys with me and went off in one direction and, after about 15 minutes, saw a hippo standing on the bank, snoozing. I couldn't see his head, my target, so started to crawl nearer, as I needed to get him in the brain. I then found that there was water between us, and sent a native in to test the depth. It came to his armpits so there was nothing for it but to go in myself, as I was determined to get a really good shot. Off came my trousers and shirt, and I waded in with only my shoes and socks on, but I was careful to keep my rifle dry. I slowly moved to within 40 yards and got a beautiful shot. I couldn't see that he was on sloping ground, and he began to roll. I fired again, just to be sure. When we got to him he was lying, dead, at the water's edge. My first shot had got him in the brain, so there was no need for the second. I used my .404, so it was instant death.

Venning had heard the shot, and followed me with only his shoes and socks on. We must have looked a bright pair with mahogany-brown arms and faces and pale pink bodies. We nearly drowned, laughing! The messengers went in naked, also, but carried their uniforms on their heads.

The hippo was skinned, and the fat and some flesh carried to the dugout. It took four boys to carry the skin, and they had a great time getting it through the water and rushes to the boat. Then the rest of us waded back. We got home at about 8.00pm, after a 14-hour outing. As we had agreed to go 50/50 on anything we got, Venning and I should each have a good pail of fat, cheap at the price of two cartridges.

Saturday, 18th July
My carriers have arrived, and I plan to start on Tuesday. Unfortunately, I have not been able to do much this week as, for three days, my eyes have been bad. I couldn't stand the light, so stayed in a darkened room and bathed them continuously, but they are better now.

I am afraid it will be about a month before I can send another letter. It will have to travel to Sesheke, so you may be without mail for six or seven weeks. I shall send letters on every possible occasion, so you needn't worry that I am ill or that anything has happened to me if you don't get news. I have provisions, and everything I need, 600 rounds of ammunition of every sort and also my three good dogs. All my personal boys are with me, so I shall be all right. The boys have been overhauling my tents and equipment to ensure that all is in order.

My pony was bitten by a snake and was very ill indeed, but I managed to pull him through. My carriers are virtually the same crowd as before, all naked as makes no matter, and big powerful chaps: they won't have any difficulty carrying my stuff.

Sunday, 19th July
The German resident came over to pay us another visit yesterday afternoon: he really is a nice chap. I have been living off 'his' hippo meat this week, and very good it is. I have also got a good stock of rendered-down fat for my journey. Some boys told Venning that there was a hippo on the German bank, so off he went and shot

149

it. It was a large cow, and must have weighed four tons, so the natives have been having a real feast all week. The hide of my hippo was spoiled in the drying and is worthless, but if Jack's turns out all right, it could well be worth £5.

I am only taking one day's supply of food with me, and am trusting to getting what I need as I travel. When I can't shoot meat, I shall buy grain from the villages. My carriers will be fairly well loaded, and I just cannot carry food for all the gang I shall have with me. I haven't counted how many there are, but I can see we shall have a rare crowd. Three senior local natives came to me, yesterday, saying they had heard I was going to Barotse, and asking to be able to go with me. I just can't take any more, but suspect I shall find them following me after a couple of days. If I am right, I shall give them food, and they can carry for it. I find I often pick up a few stragglers like that, who join the procession for no apparent reason. They don't trouble about pay, as long as they get food. My carriers get 4d a day, and are paid at the end of the journey, when the money will seem like a fortune to them.

Monday, 20th July

What a day, and it isn't finished yet. My house is expected to collapse as soon as the rains start, so I have to vacate it and put everything into the police store. I've sent my monkey to the mission (to be educated!) and have given my chickens to Jack. So my possessions are now well and truly spread around.

Later

The post boys have arrived, and I have received the last letters I shall get for some time.

A great pile of office correspondence has just arrived too. One of the letters is from the governor of British East Africa, asking me to do some experiments for him. This is the culmination of lengthy exchanges between him and my boss in Livingstone. The upshot is that I am to inoculate 15 cattle for various diseases, and then send them to British East Africa. What a journey! On foot from Barotseland to Livingstone; by rail for eight days from Livingstone to Beira; by boat up the coast to Mombasa; by rail, again, inland from Mombasa to Nairobi and then by rail, yet again, to the Chief Veterinary Officer's camp. He is named Montgomery, a splendid chap and a fellow student of mine at Liverpool University. I really do pity the cattle all that travelling! I won't be able to do the laboratory work until I reach Mongu, but am flattered to be asked.

16

Unknowingly at War

＊

On trek
Friday, 24th July 1914

My fourth day out. I'm sitting under a tree after lunch. I started much later than I had expected, as all sorts of things kept cropping up. However, I sent my carriers and the boys on to a place about nine miles off, and rode out later in the day to join them. As the carriers had not done much work for some time, I took them quietly the second day, only doing about 12 miles. Yesterday, we did more, and today we shall manage about 15; then I shall try and average that every day.

I am stopped, mid-way between two large villages, and am waiting for the cattle to be brought in and also for food. I used every bit we had last night, when we camped far from a village.

The forest we have been travelling through, since midday yesterday, and in which we slept last night, is said to be a holy terror for lions: certainly I saw plenty of spoor. My personal boys wanted to stay at a village, but it was only noon, and my carriers said they didn't care for lions, so we walked on and camped at 3.00pm. As soon as camp was set up, I took four boys to try and shoot something to eat. We saw plenty of spoor of black sable, a beautiful buck with huge horns, but simply could not find them as the bush was awfully thick. I only got one shot at a bribi.

All afternoon we have been seeing fresh elephant spoor, and the induna of a village we passed told us there were five about which had damaged his garden. When I shot at the bribi, there was a loud trumpeting and crashing of scrub and bushes, and away went the elephants with a huge bull at their head. I must have passed within thirty yards of them, but I was downwind, and it says a good deal for the quietness with which we were moving that they didn't hear us.

If I had permission to shoot elephant I would have gone after them, but I can't afford to pay the £50 fine (*£2,000 today*). I gave up trying to shoot anything after all that noise, and got back to my tent just as the sun was setting.

We are now approaching some good game country, but the grass is still very high. I am travelling up the Loanja river, visiting all the villages along its course. I've seen 30, so far, and will go to its source before crossing to the N'joko river, and following that to where it meets the Zambezi. After that, I don't know the way at all, so will take guides from village to village.

The weather is glorious for trekking, cold in the mornings. We rest during the midday heat, so my carriers are happy with their lot. I have got about eight or nine really noisy chaps, which is a good thing as, every now and again, they start calling out and shouting, then the pace of the whole column seems to quicken. They did three-and-a-half hours this morning, without a pause, and yet were only 15 minutes behind my messengers and myself, out in front, looking for game.

As I was stretching out to start this letter, my boys drew my attention to three huge birds which had alighted about three hundred yards away, larger than pelicans and without the characteristic large beak. I shot one with my .303, and then took some photographs, as I had not seen its like before. I paced out the wingspan: it was a good 12-14 feet, so you can imagine what size the bird was. Anyway, it will provide a meal for two or three of my boys tonight.

Two days later
Sunday, 26th July
It is twelve noon and, once again, I am sitting propped up against a huge tree, wearing practically nothing. We have had to keep crossing the Loanja river, to reach villages on either bank, four times yesterday and three times today. I am on the bank and letting my clothes dry in the sun, as the last time we came over, Champagne, who was up to his belly, either slipped or stepped into a hole in the riverbed, and we both got a good ducking. So my clothes are hanging up and I am penning you a few lines.

I couldn't help laughing this morning: my cook's wife, and the wife of one of the messengers, were walking together as we came to the river. I was standing on the bank to check my stores over, when the women started to wade across, and both fell in! They were wearing the startlingly coloured skirt-blouses which were presents from their husbands when we left Livingstone. I can tell they are regarded as the last word in women's fashion from the looks they get in each village we visit. Anyway, both women were greatly alarmed at getting their clothes wet and, when they finally clambered up onto the bank, there was a good deal of teasing. After that episode, they have abandoned modesty altogether, and simply take off every stitch – one outer garment – at each river crossing, bundle it on to their heads and cross as the Good Lord made them!

I've had two days' really bad luck with my shooting. We have seen any amount of fresh spoor, and I have gone out and walked for two or three hours each evening, but without success. My messengers are convinced that somebody has been putting the 'fluence' on the game and against me. My carriers seemed to endorse this view, and I wouldn't have cared to have been anyone they suspected! I am hoping this bad-luck spell is over as, this morning, I saw four reed buck, and shot one.

We are now passing villages my carriers belong to, and there is much greeting of friends. I have had to leave two carriers behind so far: one ran a stick into his foot and the other has malaria. But I managed to pick up two replacements.

I was given a lot of food at a big village yesterday, and couldn't carry it all, so told the induna to send it on with two boys to my next camp. I gave each a handful of salt, by way of payment, and they were as pleased as punch! Fancy carrying 60lbs of grain about eight miles, and then returning, all for a handful of salt!

11.00am Tuesday, 28th July
Near the source of the Loanja river
I wish you could have a glimpse of me now and of my surroundings. As usual these days, I am sitting leaning against the trunk of a large tree, and have just finished some fried kidneys from an animal which, 90 minutes ago, was at large.

But to begin at the beginning. I camped last night at a place where we saw a tremendous amount of spoor. At about 4.00pm, my hunting boy, some others and I went out. I climbed a tree and, through my glasses, saw a large herd of zebra, sable and wildebeest, about a mile off. We went after them, and were getting quite close, when they suddenly stampeded. My boys said 'litow', lions, and I spotted three of them chasing the herd. Although it was almost useless, we went on hoping to get a lion, but darkness came on.

This morning, my hunting boy, a guide from the last village, and I started early and again saw the same herd. I decided to send my pony off to some trees near by, and he was just standing there, when my hunter said 'Fa fasi a hulu' ('on the ground a lot', lie very flat). Apparently, a big wildebeest bull had left the herd, and was standing looking at Champagne, who was about 50 yards from us. I spotted the wildebeest after a while, as he came nearer and nearer, snorting and stamping his hoofs. After about 30 minutes, I was preparing to fire, when he suddenly charged towards my pony at full gallop. He got to within 20 yards when I dropped him. I just could not make out if he was really charging Champagne, or just going for a look-see, but as he was going at top speed, I didn't think he was peaceably inclined. This is the first time I have had game come to me! He was a fine bull and, as soon as he fell, my hunter rushed to him and, thrusting his assegai into his heart, commenced his usual song and dance about what a fine fellow he was, and what fine fellows we all were, and how we would eat *ad lib.* etc, etc

The boys, at present, are covered with blood, and are eating away at the raw meat, although some of it is being cooked over a fire. As soon as it had been skinned, they were down on their hands and knees, drinking the blood and squabbling over the tit-bits, the intestines, of all things. They really are the maddest crowd I ever saw when meat is about: if the majority of normal people saw the way they are behaving, they wouldn't travel a yard with such a 'bunch of savages'! I have, quite simply, got past being disgusted at their behaviour and manners.

My hunter was amazing, as we lay waiting to shoot the wildebeest: he never moved an inch. His head was raised a bit, his eyes on the bull and his nostrils quivering. He kept whispering, 'O wata, o wata. O e swile, o e swile' ('He comes, he comes. He is dead, he is dead'). Very soon, he had a complete hind-quarter over his shoulder and was chewing a piece raw.

An amusing thing happened yesterday morning. I shot a three-parts-grown reed buck and, thinking he was dead, my messenger and I stood looking at him when, suddenly, he jumped up and, literally, 'tupped' the messenger under the chin, knocking him flying. It was the death jerk of the buck for, as soon as we had recovered, he was stone-dead on the ground. The 'tup' was a violent one, from a creature the size of a small donkey, and my messenger had a good deal to say to the buck as he stood holding his jaw. But he spoke so fluently, and so fast, that all I could grasp were the 'Ouches' and the 'Ows'!

Sifue's village
N'Joko river
Thursday, 30th July
Since writing two days ago, I have been in a bit of a muddle. I had consulted a so-called map, which is supposed to cover these parts, but all it shows are a few of the larger villages and the rough run of some of the rivers. I had been determined to go right up the Loanja river, and then cross over to the N'Joko. But I had made a mistake, and found myself going in the wrong direction. None of my boys knows these parts. I happened, by chance, to mention to the induna of a small village where I was making for, and he told me I was going wrong. He knew of a path through the forest some distance back, so we retraced our steps, slept there last night, and started at daybreak this morning. The induna had some doubts as to whether we could do this stretch in one day, but, as no water was to be had en route, we had no option but to go for it.

So we have travelled non-stop all day, through the worst conditions I have encountered in Africa. The Loanja river lies in one valley and the N'Joko in another, whilst in between is a high range of hills which makes the going doubly slow and tiring. My boys have done magnificently, as it is now 12 hours later, camp is made, and I am sitting under the fly of my tent writing this letter.

I estimate the distance we travelled to be at least 20 miles, but 20 miles of sheer slog.

I have seen spoor of game and lions before, but never anything to compare with the past two days. The lions must be numbered in scores, as we saw the spoor of absolute troops of them freshly made today. At one spot, we came upon a tremendous accumulation of spoor, and I asked the boys if they would like to camp there and try and manage without water, whilst I did my best to try and shoot plenty of meat. We didn't have a grain of food left, as I had told them to eat everything last night, to lighten the loads for today's slog and because I have three boys sick. They pointed out that it would be very hard to get game in that thick bush, as we would stand no chance of seeing it. Tough though they are, they jibbed at staying where the lions were, as they described it, 'in villages'. They said they didn't mind single lions, but if a crowd of five or six came at us, in that jungle, we would have stood no chance. I, too, decided that discretion was the better part of valour, and so we pushed on.

When, finally, we arrived here, exhausted and with our mouths and throats parched and swollen, we were greeted with the news that, last night, several lions had raided the village, killed three cows and dragged them away.

This forest extends some 80 miles, and I only crossed one corner of it. I saw the spoor of at least 40 lions, made today, so I don't think I was exaggerating when I say there must have been hundreds. Since they built the railway through British East Africa, and cleared away the habitat of a lot of lions in that part of the country, I suspect they moved west, and the N'Joko district is now, probably, home to more lions than any other part of Africa.

I am thrilled to have arrived at Sifue's village, as I have long wanted to see him. I have recounted how the Barotse, under Lewanika, first drove back the Zulus and, afterwards, nominally under Litia, Lobengula's Impis. The man really responsible for this latter was Sifue. After Lewanika, who won his throne by personal hand-to-hand combat, Sifue is said to be the finest general the Barotse have ever had. He is still a turbulent sort of chap and, only a couple of months ago, Litia had to send him a warning to calm down. Anyway he, and the whole of his village, turned out to meet me today. I said, 'Lumella, Sifue' ('Greetings, Sifue'). He replied, 'Greetings to him who healed the chief'.

This is further evidence of how John Smith's reputation as a 'medicine man' spread before him. This greeting referred to his pulling Litia out of a very severe attack of malaria from which he would, almost certainly, have died. It is interesting that Sifue used these words, as he was supposed to have no idea that his visitor was in the district, and they had never met. In truth, of course, Sifue knew very well that this white man was on his way, having been forewarned by the bush telegraph, which would have reported his progress day by day.

I have never seen such a fine specimen of a man, over 70 – a great age for a native – yet a good 5' 11", with arms and a chest on him like a prize bull. Wearing nothing except his sesiba, a loin cloth, and leg ornaments, he made a most impressive sight.

Sifue's village is a large one, he is induna of the whole N'Joko district and a member of Lewanika's inner council. He reproached me for not warning him of my visit, so that he could have called in all his people from the outlying area to give me a suitable welcome. As it was, all his women turned out immediately and made a splendid clearing for my camp, and then set to stamping meal for my boys and the rest of my entourage.

I am going to inspect his cattle in the morning, and have asked him about going out to hunt the lions which killed his cows last night, but he says the bush is too thick.

Sifue is one of a race of great native warriors, fast dying out at the approach of the white man and his civilisation. He obviously yearns for the old days, and I suspect he would like nothing better than for another Lobengula to come and try conclusions with him and his Barotse. When he and Lewanika are dead – they are both old men – the last two from the very old fighting days when the Barotse were threatened with the Bechuanas under Lobengula, T'Chaka in the south and the Mushakulunki in the north, will be gone. Between them, they overcame every invader and made their country safe for ever. If Lewanika hadn't been on the throne with Sifue loyal to him, the latter would, undoubtedly, have been paramount chief of Barotseland.

I had read of these wars and these individuals, and it seems strange to have Sifue, who was one of them, sitting on the ground at my feet, clapping his hands to me whilst I ask him all about days gone by, in his own tongue even if, as he puts it, some of my words 'come strange to him', ie my pronunciation.

Lekorongoma's village
1st August
When I arrived here an hour ago, I found a runner with my letters: how jolly glad I was to have them. Venning had to send a messenger for something or other, so told him to find me, which he did by asking at all the villages until he tracked me down. You mention having had a thunderstorm. Out here, every day during the wet season, we have thunder and lightning, and you can hardly imagine what it is like for an hour or so before each storm eventually arrives. The days are gradually getting hotter and, soon, we will be in the real heat again. I am, also, moving north all the time, nearer to the equator.

I have again changed my plan, as villages are too far apart, and water too scarce, to allow me to go as I originally intended. I have decided to take guides from village to village, and only go where I can be sure of water. My boys, and all the camp followers, take a great deal of feeding and watering, and whatever I manage to shoot seems to be gone by the time I turn round.

Sioma's village
8th August
Back on the banks of the Zambezi. A week has passed since I last wrote and, as I hope to reach Senanga in about two days, I thought I would start my letter.

I have discovered that I cannot reach another village today so, much to my disgust, I am compelled to wait here whilst the women stamp food for us. It is ten in the morning, and I am going to have to travel during the hot hours: it is now very hot indeed, during the day.

Since my last letter, quite a few things have happened. I got off track, again, and on Sunday we marched on and on and could find

159

neither village nor water. Also, I didn't have a bite for my boys. It got to 4.30 in the afternoon, and I was wondering what to do, as we were all 'knocked up' and wanted water badly. Shortly after, we struck a small stream and that settled the water problem, but I still didn't know what to do about food as, although we had all kept a good lookout, we had seen neither game nor spoor. Suddenly, one boy said he had seen something moving a long way off. On looking through my glasses, I could see that it was a large pig and a couple of warthogs. The latter are very like pigs, but have a square nose and large wart-like thing on their heads. All three have tusks, and they can be awkward beggars if they get near you when wounded. They were about 300 yards away, and I chose one boy to go with me, as well as my hunter.

There wasn't a single bit of cover the whole distance, so there was nothing for it but to go down on our tummies and start to crawl. I looked at my watch and, from the time I started to the finish was exactly an hour, so I must have taken 45 minutes to crawl 200 yards. It was simply a case of covering a few feet, keeping the rifle clear of the sand, and then lying flat and checking that our quarry was still there.

Finally, I got to within 100 yards and shot the pig, but I'm blessed if the warthogs didn't stand for a few seconds watching him kick. I got one of them and hit the other. Unfortunately, I only hit him in the leg and, although we hunted hard, we couldn't find him in the thick bush into which he had fled. I was thankful to find both water and food, I can tell you.

Next day we went on, and eventually struck a village: for the first time in Africa I was given the royal salute. This is for the paramount chief only, but this village was so far off the beaten track, that they had no idea who I was and presumed that, as I was travelling with nearly a hundred followers, I was a personage of considerable standing. So they played safe, I suppose. The salute requires that every adult claps in rhythm, starting slowly and quietly, and then gradually increasing in tempo and volume until it is almost deafening. At the climax, everyone throws his or her arms in the air together, shouting 'Oh Sho' at the top of their voices. This is repeated three times, and then the whole crowd leaps in the air and falls prostrate and silent: it is very impressive and strangely moving.

After this ceremonial, all the women ran alongside me, shouting 'Oh Sho' at the tops of their voices, then falling on their knees and clapping. This ritual they repeated over and over again.

I asked the headman if they had any sick and, a little later, was surprised to find quite a large crowd squatting outside my tent. I can stand most sights, now, but what I saw nearly turned me over. Leprosy had got a terrible hold on this village, and there were some horribly disfigured people before me. The worst of it is that nobody seems to worry, and the lepers marry and have children like any healthy couple. When NR is opened up more fully, they will have to tackle the leprosy question. There were two women with terrible abscesses and sores. I dressed these and did what I could by leaving some disinfectants etc, but it was all beyond my resources, and I cleared off from the village as quickly as I could.

There was something strangely wrong with that village. Their cattle, too, were in a bad state, but I couldn't find the cause. I will see if I can arrange for someone to go out there, isolate the lepers, burn the huts, and so contain the infection as far as possible.

I have discovered that the village was on the Lumbi, a small stream that runs into the Zambezi, and so decided to follow it up. I travelled for three days, and reached Sioma last night.

Here, there is another lot of falls, the Ngonye, which are about half the size of the Victoria, but truly magnificent. I suppose they would be nearly as big as Niagara and, as the river is getting low again, it is possible to see all the falls area, properly, without them being obscured by spray. I have camped beside them: the roar is great!

I have only struck two villages in five days but have, fortunately, had plenty of fresh meat. Two days ago I had awful luck. I am anxious to shoot an eland, the biggest buck on the veldt, bigger, but not so heavy as a good buffalo. Up to now, I have not been successful. Two days ago, about 3.00pm, we came to a place teeming with eland spoor, made that day. I decided to camp there and went out to find them. For four solid hours, we tramped in vain, and arrived back at camp in pitch dark. When only about 200 yards from my tent, there was a sudden noise, and a whole herd of eland galloped past us. But by now it was too dark to shoot. They had been grazing within sight of the boys in the camp, for a good hour before sunset, when they had been expecting us to turn up. I was mad, and dog-tired with walking all day, when I could just have sat down and shot one from my tent entrance!

Two days later
10th August

I expected to reach Senanga today but, as far as I can see, I am still two days away. I intended sticking to the Zambezi, but found this impossible. Yesterday, I hit a big forest and, as we couldn't get through, we had to go miles round. The boys had an awful time, as it was mostly deep sand underfoot and we got on very slowly. About 2.00pm, I saw it was useless trying to go any further, and there were plenty of small streams for water. I must admit I was feeling rather tired, and that may well be the reason I was shooting so badly. I missed three easy shots in succession.

I had a rest and, at 4.00pm, went off to see if I could find anything, as we hadn't a bite in camp. After an hour, we saw some impala. These are about the size of a young cow, and have most beautiful sable and white skins. They are, however, about the quickest things on their feet. We did a lovely bit of stalking and I got one. It was only a small feed for the boys but it had to do.

Whilst I was having dinner, I heard great roars from lions which had smelt the blood and had found the spot, a hundred yards away, where we had made our kill. One of my dogs, the new one Samson, is a holy terror and, as he has been fed on raw meat since I was on tour, is very fit and savage, as are all three. He kept going round and round in circles growling and barking. Normally, he sleeps in the fly of my tent and warns me of anything moving near.

Anyway, the lions made such a row that I fired two shots in their direction to try and frighten them away, and then turned in. A little later, I was awakened by some of the boys and a messenger. They said the lions were all coming nearer, and wanted me to lend them a rifle. But I refused, as I knew they would fire at absolutely anything and probably kill somebody. They asked to sleep around the fire at my tent entrance, so I put my rifles in the doorway, and assured them that I was ready for anything. They sat round my fire all night, and I'm blessed if the lions didn't keep up their racket till dawn. Samson added to the drama by prowling round, growling and barking.

This morning we moved on and, after half an hour, spotted a number of buffaloes go off into the forest. This was my first sight of buffalo, and I simply had to have a go. I stopped the boys, and three of us went after them. For three hours we went on their spoor, always near, but we just couldn't spot them. One mustn't chance things with buffalo: you must kill, or there is trouble. Finally, we had to give up and return to camp. We were all pretty sick, and I was cursing my luck when, on the edge of the forest, we came upon two beautiful roan antelope. I got in two shots, dropping them both. That settled the food question quickly, so I have camped and will have another go at the buffaloes later this evening.

The thing that is upsetting me about this trip is having to abandon all these lovely skins on the veldt and in the forest. I have six boys who have had to be left behind on the way. That means that 300lbs of load have had to be redistributed, and I couldn't possibly ask them to carry any more: these skins are surprisingly heavy. But I must have left at least 40 behind. I just wish you could have had them as they look so well on the floor. It just can't be helped, although I have to admit I was looking forward to a good collection from this trip. The roan I shot today was a magnificent specimen, full grown, about the size of a big horse with huge horns. My boys will be very full tonight!

Senanga
Wednesday, 12th or 13th August
At last I have arrived and am jolly glad to be here. I have now entered the 'thickly' populated parts of Lewanika's territory, and hope to reach Mongu in about seven days' time.

You will remember my telling you of Campbell, who plays the banjo, and came and stayed at Sesheke on his way back from leave. He is here, and I came straight to his camp. It stands up on a small hill and he saw me coming. He came down to meet me, and his first words were, 'I am glad to see you, Smith, have you got any meat? I have been living on chicken for a month'. I had brought in two hind quarters of the buck, so we were all right.

We sat talking, Campbell playing his banjo, until late last night. I am staying here tonight and, possibly, tomorrow to give my boys and myself a short rest.

I had a disappointment. I expected to get letters here, as Venning had promised to send them on, but none had arrived. Then a runner came in a few hours after me but, on opening the pouch, we found all the letters were for Campbell. I don't know where mine are. I had been looking forward to getting them here.

The last two days have been uninteresting. It has simply been walking through bush and plains, but I had a bit of luck a couple of days ago: I saw a rhinoceros. There are very, very few in this country now, and only a handful of people have seen one. It was a great thrill. One has to pay a £50 fine for a dead rhino, and it would have been an easy shot for me, but I managed to resist the temptation.

I can now put my rifles away until I reach Mongu. I shall be passing through areas preserved for Lewanika's shooting, so I can't have a go myself. As, however, there are plenty of villages, I can get grain for my boys and, as there are plenty of cattle, I shall be kept busy inspecting them.

Campbell's camp is nicely situated. On a hill, about 300 yards from the Zambezi, it overlooks the river and the large plains and hills beyond. The 'house' is corrugated iron with reeds and mud, but is comfortable. My boys are camped near at hand, and I am sleeping in a small room in the house.

It is beautiful this morning; there is a nice breeze blowing into the verandah, and I am feeling very fit, and greatly enjoying lazing about and having a few comforts, if they can really be called that! Campbell has just suggested we try a spot of fishing this evening, which I shall enjoy.

We can detect a dip in the author's mood from the lines written after he reached Senanga. He was ensconced in a house, in comparative comfort and in the company of a cheerful character he had got to know reasonably well at Sesheke. The weather was good, he could relax, enjoy a good old yarn after living on his own for some weeks, and have some fishing. Yet he wrote an extraordinarily flat letter.

I suspect this temporary fit of the blues was triggered by finding no mail waiting for him, and was compounded by seeing the runner arriving with a mail pouch which, even then, held no letters for him. We hear nothing of the companionship he must have enjoyed, with the first white man he had spoken to for some time, whilst the excitement of coming across a rhinoceros gets scant coverage. But this mood wasn't to last long.

It is worth picking up on one point he makes. He says, 'Campbell had seen me coming...' It is much more likely that one of Campbell's boys had told him that a white man was heading in their direction and that, as a consequence, he was on the lookout for him.

There is great secrecy amongst natives in connection with their message-sending by bush telegraph. We remember that Sifue remonstrated with John Smith for not having warned him of his visit. Yet, it is inconceivable that Sifue did not know that he was heading his way. He was a very senior induna and responsible for a large district. More to the point, he was a noted warrior. He would have established an intelligence system, whereby he was always informed of the movements of strangers, and of any unusual happenings. The tom-toms from outlying areas would have beaten out a warning which would have been passed from village to village, without Smith having any inkling of it. He was travelling with getting on for 100 followers; he was visiting almost every village en route and was taking guides with him to show him the way and help him find game. Sifue knew all right! But, native preoccupation with concealing how messages were flashed at such speed and over such distances required that no mention would be made of this intelligence. So, Sifue pretended that he did not know of John Smith's impending arrival, and strengthened that pretence by complaining, politely, that if only he had been given prior warning, he could have prepared a suitable reception party!

Perhaps this is, also, a suitable moment to mention what fantastic performances were put up, day in and day out, week in and week out, by the scores of runners employed by the administration to deliver mail, messages and despatches. We have already read of runners being sent out on various missions, and my father has often remarked on the astonishing achievements of some of them. We have to remember that there was, in the whole of the western province of Northern Rhodesia, an area substantially larger than the British Isles, absolutely no means of communication other than by runner or dugout.

With the outbreak of war, the importance of the runners to the very survival of some of the Europeans was crucial. Very shortly, we shall hear of a runner bringing the first firm news of the war, from Livingstone to Mongu. It was a distance of 370 miles through some of the most inhospitable country in Central Africa. There were no roads, only tracks, and the runners went from village to village, through thick bush and over open plains. Underfoot were rough forest paths with all the obstacles that suggests: deep, slow sand, mud inches thick and dangerous, slippery river banks. In the region of a dozen streams and small rivers had to be waded or swum across. Over and above all that the runner, naked except for a loincloth, holding a mail pouch and carrying his knobkerry and assegais in his free hand, had to find water, beg food from villages en route, get some sleep and be sufficiently alert to avoid being bitten by snakes, mauled by lions or grabbed and devoured by crocodiles.

The carrier of the first war message ran 370 miles in ten days. He achieved this astonishing feat simply because he was told, as he set out, that 'the Morenas need this message very, very badly'.

17

Waiting for News

Mongu
Barotseland
Monday, 17th August 1914

W hen I left home I never thought I should be writing to you under such circumstances.

I had been steadily pushing on towards Mongu when I arrived, the day before yesterday, at a mission station at Sefula. There, I learned that there was trouble between Russia and Germany. Then, just after I arrived, a runner came in with the news that war had been declared between England and Germany. It warned that supplies and provisions of all kinds may be scarce and very dear, and informing us that all travelling on the Zambezi was undertaken at people's own risk: we have German territory on one side of the river and Portuguese near us here.

I left Sefula immediately, and came through to Mongu in one day without stopping, nearly killing my carriers and the rest of us with the forced march needed to arrive before dark.

This government station is built not far from the Zambezi, to which access is gained by a short canal. It is up on a hill, and has fine views over the surrounding district and the river. Mr McKinnon, who was acting Administrator in Livingstone, is in charge of all Barotseland, and is stationed here.

Still, the only news we have is a brief note saying war is declared and that fighting has begun. This message came through in an incredibly short time from Livingstone, but we are anxiously awaiting further news, which is expected hourly. It is nearly two weeks since the outbreak of war, and yet we have no real information.

All mail has been stopped going south by river, and I just don't know when you will get this letter, or when I shall hear from you.

There should be two or three letters for me in Africa, which I should get some time. After that, goodness knows when I shall hear anything.

There is still no news from Sesheke. Venning is there and, just across the river, is the German residency with more native troops than Venning has. I simply cannot grasp that the German resident, who was dining with us both at Sesheke only a few weeks ago, is now our enemy!

We cannot realise that we are at war. It is just awful not being able to get any news. Still, special runners are out, and Mr McKinnon is sure to get all official news from Livingstone.

In Mongu there are: Mr and Mrs McKinnon; Captain and Mrs Salmon (the new bride); Lieutenant Burton; Mr and Mrs Roach (native commissioner); Warrington and Chamberlain (probationers in the native department). So, with myself, we are ten.

I came through from Senanga in five days and, in view of the situation, am keeping my carriers on as we may require them. I am going over to see Lewanika tomorrow, but what my further work will be I cannot yet say.

I do have a bit of excellent news. I heard, on arrival here, that my salary is increased by £100pa as a reward for my work at Maramba. I can't help feeling rather pleased.

25th August

Another week has passed, and still no news. A runner arrived a few days ago, saying that France, England and Russia had joined against Germany and Austria, and that a huge naval battle was going on in the North Sea. That was dated 7th August, in England: three weeks ago, and still we have no more details. It is pretty awful waiting and wondering what is going on. The runner came from Livingstone in 10 days. The distance is 370 miles, so he averaged 37 miles a day. That is good going. All of us here have contributed to give the runners extra payment if they can come through really quickly.

Venning has sent a message through from Sesheke, to say that troops have arrived there to watch the German border, and more troops are on their way here, as we are close to the German and

Portuguese borders. I am leaving here tomorrow or the next day, to go about 50 miles further north. I shall be doing my normal work, but am taking a big induna of Lewanika's with me so that he can talk to the natives, should they seem to be at all uneasy.

Lewanika has got runners out on all the borders, to bring in news if anything untoward should happen. The Portuguese and Germans never had their natives as well disciplined and under control as we have, and none of us can take any chances in times such as these. Three missionaries up here, who are on the French reserve, have received orders to join the colours and have already left. Incidentally, Venning's runner did from Sesheke to Mongu in eight days, which is wonderful travelling.

We have all got our orders from Livingstone about the Rifle Association and also the reserve. I left my service rifle at Sesheke – I never thought to bring it along with me – but there are some here. As, however, the rifle Walter (his brother) gave me is the same bore and, as I am shooting well with it, I don't need the service one. We have 80,000 rounds of ammunition and two maxim machine guns here so, if anything happens, we should be all right.

Last Friday, I paid my state visit to Lewanika. This was an occasion I had been looking forward to ever since I landed in Northern Rhodesia, as he is the Paramount Chief of all Barotseland. I have heard of him practically every day of my life since arriving at Sesheke over eight months ago, and was impatient to meet him, especially as I am now rather more able to understand the local dialect.

I took 10 messengers and 10 personal servants with me, and rode the seven miles which separate Mongu from Lewanika's state capital at Lealui. Together, we formed quite an impressive little procession. Let me try to describe the day to you: it was a considerable occasion.

When I told my boys of this impending visit, there was much hustle and bustle; uniforms were sponged, hair was cut, Champagne was groomed until his coat shone and his harness was polished and buffed until it shone. My white suit, white shirt and tie were laundered and pressed and, generally, all was made ready for the big day.

Only Matapi, of my boys, had ever seen Lewanika, as he had been a paddler in his state barge, but the thought of accompanying their white Morena (me) into the presence of their king was almost too much for some of them, and they turned that peculiar shade of grey which all frightened or anxious natives seem to achieve.

We formed up in procession at 8 o'clock. First there were two of the resident's messengers to show the way, then two of mine, then Matapi at my side, then my pony boy immediately on our flank, then four more messengers. A detail of eight askari soldiers had been ordered to escort me. Four marched, rifles at the slope, beside me, while four more brought up the rear.

This considerable procession marched across the seven miles of sandy plain separating British HQ from the native HQ, in sweltering heat, with the dust swirling and the flies buzzing. I was very far from comfortable, trussed up in starched suiting with collar and tie after months of open-necked shirt and khaki shorts. Needless to say, we were followed by a vast crowd of natives, men, women and children attracted by the excitement of an unknown white man making an official visit to their chief.

The plain we crossed is grazed by thousands of letchwe buck, which are relatively tame, as they are not allowed to be hunted by anyone. Also to be seen in vast herds are the thousands of cattle which are the personal property of Lewanika, and in which he takes great pride. Included amongst these is a herd of rare, pure white cattle which I was to see on many occasions in the future.

About a mile from Lealui, one of Lewanika's senior indunas, with the usual crowd of followers, met me. There were the customary, elaborate greetings and then they, too, joined the procession. At the outskirts of the capital, yet another induna greeted me and joined up with the procession, which was now some hundreds strong.

Lealui is the largest native township in all Barotseland: it houses the government, and all the country's leading natives live there with their considerable retinues. All told, there must be several thousand inhabitants, and it is a most impressive settlement. There are many fine examples of native buildings, and some of the huts are quite enormous. They are all built in exactly the same way. Tall, thick, wooden uprights are sunk into the ground in the required shape. Smaller uprights are then fitted in between these main supports, and the gaps are filled with reeds cut from the river's edge. These 'walls' are then plastered with a mixture of ant heap, dung and water which is worked into a fine, smooth finish. Finally, the roof is put on and thatched with more reeds. Marotsi thatching is famous, but only a limited number of craftsmen are able to achieve the delightful, and very decorative patterns, woven into the thatch, which are to be seen on all the important buildings. These huts are large and imposing, but are subject to a 'Forth Bridge' routine because of the continual havoc wrought by the white ants, which chomp their way through thatch, wood, plaster etc. Nothing is safe from these little blighters.

Our procession wound round through the town, with the population candalelling all the way, until we arrived at a special area in the centre, where stood Lewanika's 'palace'. This consists of three or four huge huts with particularly intricate thatch patterns.

I must explain about this compound, as it is built to a most unusual design. The large huts which form the parliament buildings are interspersed with smaller, but still quite substantial, living huts. Then the whole is surrounded by a series of three circular fences, which form the protective rings round the chief and his immediate entourage.

I was conducted, alone except for my personal messengers, by the indunas through the entrance in the first, outer fence. This was guarded by several huge and heavily armed men. Beside them stood a drummer, tapping away continuously on a large tom-tom. We then walked round the second fence to the entrance, which was 180° opposite the first one. This, in turn, was manned by guards and a drummer. On we walked round this fence, to the third entrance which, once again, was similarly manned and set opposite the second. All three drummers tap a continuous and unending beat, every minute of every hour, of every day, of every year, as a precaution against surprise attack. The entire population within the compound gets so used to the continuous drum taps that, were a guard to be overcome, or the drummer stealthily despatched, the ensuing silence would raise an immediate alarm. It is an impressive illustration of a simple, fail-safe protection system. Incidentally, a drummer accompanies Lewanika wherever he goes, and is never silent. The only occasion when the chief's drummers ceased their tapping was when Litia, ruling as Yeta III after his father's death, went south to Katombora, to meet the Prince of Wales, later King Edward VIII. Litia took the view that, as he was to meet a mightier prince than himself, he should not burden his ears with any unaccustomed noise.

Anyway, when we had passed through the third and final entrance, we found ourselves in a courtyard where my messengers were to remain, whilst I was conducted on by Lewanika's Prime Minister (N'gambella) named Sopi, who was a fine old man. He had originally lived much further south, near Sesheke, and had seen and spoken to David Livingstone when he had trekked through, and crossed the Zambezi on his way from Lake N'Gami in 1855. Sopi is a native with a considerable intelligence, and wields a good deal of influence in the affairs of Barotseland.

I now stood at the entrance to the khotla building, which is the largest and most imposing of all, and is the equivalent of our privy council chamber. Here, Lewanika came down the steps to greet me, while Sopi went down on his knees and started clapping his hands.

Lewanika, who is nearly 80, a very great age for a native, is a most imposing figure and, despite his years, shows off the truly massive strength with which he was credited as a young man. He was wearing a grey flannel suit, white shirt and tie, with a velvet smoking cap atop his grey, curly hair. A carefully trimmed, and pointed, grey beard gave him an air of considerable authority. A native servant held a huge umbrella over him as we shook hands and exchanged greetings in Sekololo.

'Mu lumela,' I said. 'Mu lumela, Shangive,' he replied. I was intrigued that he should know, and use, my native name which, translated literally, means 'the chief who dispenses medicine'.

The only natives with whom officials shake hands are Lewanika, his son Litia, and his sister, the Moquai.

The inside of the khotla was very impressive. The floor and walls were covered with most intricately woven rush mats, and with fine animal skins. Also, on the walls, were hung all manner of native ornaments, carved ivory, native woodwork, assegais and shields, as well as tusks, horns and trophies. Some of the ornaments were weird and wonderful, and I would have given a lot to have been the possessor of some of them. On one wall were large signed photographs of King Edward and King George, as well as one of Lewanika, taken in London at King Edward's Coronation, to which Lewanika went with Sopi. There were two large chairs at the far end of the room, carved from local wood and most beautifully inlaid with ivory. The whole effect was fascinating, as they were not dissimilar from a pair of thrones.

Lewanika led me to one, and sat on the other himself. One of his sons, who had been educated in England, finishing at Oxford, acted as interpreter, as Lewanika speaks no English. He sat on the ground between us. About twelve of the senior councillors also sat on the floor, some distance from us, as did Sopi, who sat alone.

You really cannot imagine the etiquette of a state visit like this. Every time the interpreter speaks, he claps his hands before and after his words and, if anyone else is spoken to he, and all the others in the room, clap before and after. It is one continuous clap, clap, clap and proceedings are mightily prolonged. But, as you will have realised by now, all this procedure is of supreme importance in the native code of conduct and behaviour.

This first part of the official meeting lasted a good two hours, and most of it was spent answering Lewanika's questions about the war. He wanted to know about warships, soldiers, guns and our methods of waging war. I did my best to explain about aeroplanes, armoured steel and explosives. He was fascinated by it all and demonstrated, again and again, his admiration and regard for all things British. All through my explanations I was interrupted by the old boy's 'Ohs' and 'Ahs', interspersed with 'Kauki', which is a widely-used expression of amazement. Each time he reacted in this manner, all his council echoed his sound, and then clapped. It was a most curious experience, the like of which I never dreamed I would encounter.

In due course, it was time for lunch, and I was conducted to the washroom, which was well appointed. Then I was escorted to another room for lunch. Yet again, it was a fascinating experience. The large carved table was set, European-style, for two. The main ornaments were two large silver cups and a clock, the cups from Viscount Gladstone, the clock from Lord Selbourne. Lewanika and I sat at the table, whilst all the rest, interpreter, Sopi and the council, sat on the floor in order of seniority, Sopi nearest his chief and so on. Only I and Lewanika, with Sopi and the interpreter, ate the same food: all the rest seemed to have to go hungry!

The menu consisted of soup, duck and sweet potatoes, pineapples and sour cream, coffee and bananas. Alcohol is strictly forbidden by Lewanika throughout his territory, and he has never touched it himself.

Every dish is brought to the door by servants, who place it on the floor, clapping as they leave. It is then passed from hand to hand, clapped before and after receipt, until it reached Sopi, who brought it to the table, placed it on the floor, clapped his hands and then, in a kneeling position, handed it up to Lewanika, who served me. The dishes, after we had had our helpings, went back the same way, and with the same drill. It was slow, noisy and quite extraordinary, and can be like no other custom anywhere else in the world.

After the meal, I was taken to a guest room for a siesta. It was comfortably fitted out with European furniture, and was restful, except for the drummers! In due course I was woken. I washed and dressed and was then conducted back to the chamber for more talks. Lewanika had changed from his suit and was more informally and, I should imagine, comfortably dressed in shirt and seseba, a bright cotton skirt consisting, according to one's standing, of yards and yards of cloth, wound round exactly like a kilt. Needless to say, Lewanika's was very long indeed.

We talked now of agriculture and, especially, of cattle, and my host proved himself to be extremely knowledgeable. His manner is gruff, but friendly and courteous, and his authority is undeniable. His staccato instructions were clearly intended to be executed fast and efficiently. I was flattered to notice, throughout the meetings, how much Lewanika knew about me, and to find him using my native name. This is unusual, and I hoped that it was some indication that he had formed a good impression of my work, from what had been reported to him.

After about an hour, I deemed it time to call a halt to the proceedings, and so began my thanks and goodbyes. Lewanika came to the courtyard to see me off, where my messengers, who had been fed and entertained, were waiting ready. Natives in government uniform are the only ones allowed to stand in Lewanika's presence and, instead of the royal salute, they give the more usual military one.

Before the visit, there had been much rehearsing but, as all except Matapi were almost beside themselves with excitement and apprehension, I was relieved when, at a nod from him, all my men gave a very creditable performance as he bellowed out 'slute, Morena'. They have a lingering way of saying the word 'Morena', which is only used for whites, Lewanika and Litia. I still get a shiver of excitement when, each morning, my messengers and boys greet me thus.

As I was leaving the courtyard, Lewanika said he would like to see my horse, as they are practically unknown in that part of Africa being, as I have explained, unable to survive disease. As we passed through the outer gate, the vast crowd of natives drawn by the morning's events suddenly and unexpectedly found themselves confronted by their chief. They, to a man, flung themselves to the ground and began clapping, very softly at first, then getting louder and louder, then dying down and away; then, suddenly, each one flung his or her arms in the air and shouted out 'Oh Sho' three times. This is the full royal salute and, although I, and other officials in outlying districts have been treated to it, we always discourage it so that it remains solely for Lewanika and Litia.

My pony boy, holding Champagne's head in anticipation of my return, all but fainted when he saw Lewanika, who came forward to pat my pony. Looking wildly for instructions, he decided discretion was the better part of a valour, let go of Champagne, and flung himself on the ground. Needless to say, it was Matapi who saved the day.

I said my goodbyes and, with my procession as before, set out to ride the seven miles back to Mongu. After a while, I left the rest to follow, and rode on for a good, long bath and a change into more comfortable gear. It had been a memorable day for me, and the most memorable any of my natives would ever have.

Wednesday, 26th August
I have made my arrangements and am off tomorrow. I shall send into Mongu, occasionally, for news, although I am afraid I shall not get any letters from you all.

Likopi
Barotseland
7th September
After being away from Mongu for ten days, I am steadily working my way back there. I have still not heard any news of the war, and am getting very anxious.

Three days ago I met Berringer, a native commissioner, who is in charge of the sub-district. He is touring all round to see that the natives are not getting restless. I stayed the night with him and was glad to have a chat, although we both cursed our luck at being stuck out here and not being amongst it all. He is the son of Dr Berringer the musician, and his sister, Elsie, is the well-known actress. He is an awfully nice chap, and I like him immensely. He had just heard that his wife, who is in England, had had a daughter.

I have been nearly as far as I intended to go, and having found Berringer makes it easier, as he will take in the areas I have not covered. The country here is flat, open plain: no trees or scrub, and travelling is monotonous. The tribes live on the plain in the dry season, then move away to the woods when the rains come. Then the Zambezi overflows and floods this whole vast area, bringing on wonderful grazing pasture, with abundant grass. Lewanika keeps a lot of his cattle here: I have made a count, and have seen over 15,000 head belonging to the old boy, as well as masses possessed by the villagers. This is one huge grazing area, and I have found virtually no disease.

Lewanika sent a message to the resident at Mongu, Mr McKinnon, saying he would raise a fighting force of 5000 natives in readiness against the Germans crossing over here. I haven't heard the response yet!

The day before yesterday, a runner caught up with me and the message told me to get back to Mongu if I heard of any German activity or to recross the Zambezi and trek back there. As I crossed the Zambezi four days after leaving Mongu I am, as it were, on the 'hostile' bank, as this is the side of the German territory. That crossing went well as Champagne swam quietly across. I hope he behaves as well on the return trip.

I have been very happy out here until now, but this war has made me wish I was back in England.

Mongu
10th September
I did a huge day's march yesterday, and came straight into Mongu. I knew the postboys would leave today; just after I got in, they arrived from Livingstone. They had come through in wonderful time, but we all had a big disappointment, as there was no mail from England at all. The only war news we have had, and it is five weeks since the declaration, is that an English force has gone to the continent, and that there had been huge battles.

We have just heard that the Germans in South West Africa have invaded Cape Colony, but there are no further details. All seems quiet here and, after all, I have been right up to the border.

I am paying my carriers off: they have had a long nine weeks with me, and they need to go home. I think I shall probably go south next, by boat to Senanga, where there is a vacant house on the river bank I could use for a time. But, as yet, I have no orders. My big problem will be stores. My stocks are very low, and I planned to get some up from those I left at Sesheke, but all that sort of river traffic has been stopped. I am practically out of tea, coffee and flour, so will just have to go without. My bread is being made from ground Indian corn, and is stamped out for me by the local native women. I cannot get a knife through it after a day: I simply knock a piece off! Already, I have dislodged a stopping from one tooth, and will have to persuade somebody to pull it out, as the nerve is exposed. I have sent my boys out, today, to buy fowls, native potatoes (the roots of a tree, very sweet but quite good) and bananas, which are just coming into season.

16th September

The post boys came in last night from Livingstone, but there was only one letter, written just after the outbreak of war, so it had taken six weeks. Not bad really!

I am probably leaving here in a day or so to go south to Senanga, to the administration's vacant house there. I shall be alone, but it is agreed that runners will be sent to deliver and pick up mail and any official papers for me.

I don't suppose there is any place, in any British possession, as badly off for news as we are. Other areas of NR have telegraph wires laid to government stations but, in the Barotse reserve, there are none.

We have just heard that some of the native troops, under Major Stennett who left Livingstone recently, have gone to the German border, as their troops have crossed over and cut our telegraph wires. We also hear of fighting in South Africa but, again, have no further details.

I went over and paid an unofficial visit to Lewanika yesterday, and he insisted that I had lunch with him. He is in a state of great excitement, longing to raise his army and move it against somebody, somewhere; anybody, anywhere! He is fascinated by war, and spent ages, yesterday, questioning me all about it. No wonder he has such a reputation as a warrior.

23rd September

I am still here. I've asked for boats and paddlers to take me the 60-odd miles down stream, but they haven't yet arrived.

We've had rumours that the Germans are advancing on Sesheke; if this is true, and a force is sent down from here to help, I shall join them. But they may well be sending white troops from those guarding the Victoria Falls Bridge. It is all so confusing, having so little real news.

We have a hard tennis court here, and all try and get in a couple of sets every day to keep fit, as the future could hold anything in store for us all.

I mentioned price rises the other day. A dozen small boxes of matches and three pieces of hand soap are 9/- (*£18 today*). Nice, isn't it?

Next day, 24th September
The mail arrived last night. We heard that there had been fighting in Nyasaland, on our northern border, and that Major Stennett is commanding a strong force of native troops there. We have firm news, also, that white troops have arrived at Sesheke, so I may have a chance of a smack at some Germans yet.

The runners are doing a splendid job, coming through in 12 or less days, and we are rewarding them suitably. By the way, I have just sent £5 to the Prince of Wales's war fund.

I have also had a letter from Mrs Stennett, who was with her husband on tour when things started to happen. They returned to Livingstone in a great rush, and then her husband had to try and catch his troops, who were on their way north. Stennett covered 127 miles through that tortuous country on foot in two days: incredible! I think he must have managed to pinch a pony from a farmer and have pushed on, travelling non-stop, day and night, as he averaged getting on for three miles an hour! He will also have picked up carriers, along the way, as he passed through villages, and then have dropped them off as they tired, exchanging them for fresh ones. Some march!

Two days ago, Lewanika sent me a nice fat bullock, so we have all had a great feast of fresh meat. I also had a steak-and-kidney pie. A real treat! It's such a shame that, out here, all meat goes off after 24 hours unless it's salted down.

The temperature has been climbing steadily: it is 105° or more in the shade now, and the nights, too, are very hot. It will keep getting even hotter but, soon, we shall start having short, sharp showers which will be followed by severe thunderstorms, and then the rainy season, proper, will be upon us.

In a 54' x 2' 4" dugout on the Zambezi, between Mongu and Nololo 28th September
I am writing this in one of three dugouts bringing me, my personal boys and my gear down to my next post at Senanga, towards which I am making my way very slowly. I could do the journey in about five days, as Lewanika gave me eight of his crack paddlers and one of his own dugouts, so I have just about the fastest craft in the whole

area. But I decided to take my time, visit all the villages en route, checking up on their cattle and, if and when necessary, reassuring them about the war. We all have to accept that it is always possible subversive information is being 'broadcast' by bush telegraph, originated by natives on the west bank who are in touch with the Germans. It is unlikely, but possible, so we are all going out of our way to see that calm reigns throughout Barotseland.

The rumours we had heard, of a German force moving towards Sesheke, were correct. To counter this, both white and native troops have moved up from Livingstone, and the native troops stationed at Mongu left two days ago to go south. They travelled on the Zambezi, in barges commandeered from traders, and with paddlers supplied by Lewanika. Apparently, the whole operation was organised and laid on during one night, which is pretty amazing. Major Stennett, after his incredible forced march, has been in action on our northern border, where he routed the Germans, who also got the worst of a scrap in Nyasaland. It may be that they won't try on anything else out here, as they are clearly not going to be allowed to make any headway. I tried to join our troops going to Sesheke, but Mr McKinnon vetoed it, as he said I was more valuable keeping the natives from getting restless.

The last mail brought the first newspapers covering the war: they were about six weeks old. Thank you very much.

Yesterday, I had a sharp, but happily short bout of dysentery, but felt extremely unwell. It is not a complaint I would choose to suffer from in a 2' 4" wide dugout in the middle of a river, in a shade temperature of 106°, but with no shade! I am better today, and have been able to take a little food. It is getting hotter by the day, and I only hope that I reach Senanga house before the rains start.

I hope to reach Nololo in about four days, and can stay with one of our officials who is resident there: his must be a lonely life.

I suppose that trade at the works in Wigan will be at a standstill. However, there are too many in this war for it to last long.

John Smith was no exception in thinking that 'the war would be over by Christmas'. He was also totally wrong in thinking that Smith's Progress Works were idle: they were working flat-out on war office requirements, and the cash was starting to roll in as never before.

Bindo Wina's village
Zambezi River
12th October
I was not able to get a boy through to catch last week's runners and, as no mail has caught up with me on the river, I have heard nothing of the war in Europe for some time. The German residency, across from Sesheke, has been taken by our troops, and the resident himself sent south as a prisoner of war. He is Jack's and my old friend, who let us shoot his hippos. Now, he is our enemy!

Visiting all the villages on the plain beside the river is very tiring and monotonous. There is no cover whatsoever: no trees, no shrubs and, hence, no game to give me some shooting and some fresh meat. With the temperature way over the 100° mark, it is all a bit trying. As the rains are due any day now, the humidity has risen enormously and, between two and four in the afternoon, it is simply not possible for any of us, including the natives, to do any work.

I expect to strike Senanga tomorrow or the next day. I will probably be kept up here, carrying on with my tours and visits but, as I haven't heard from my departmental boss in Livingstone for months, I cannot speculate on the future. I do find travelling on the river at this leisurely pace very boring. I have so much time on my hands, having read and re-read all my letters and newspapers. It is uncomfortably restrictive being in a dugout, only 2' 4" wide, so I have a good deal of time to reflect on events in Europe, and what my friends are doing. I suppose every decent fellow, at home, has enlisted. I should certainly be in it. I should have had no difficulty in getting a commission in the Army Veterinary Corps as they are, I know, frightfully short. However, it cannot be helped.

Not surprisingly, John Smith is in reflective mood. He was far from fit, and made light of his attack of dysentery, but it is a very debilitating affliction. One can think of few less convenient places to be, suffering from dysentery, than in a dugout on the Zambezi river! But, most of all, I believe he resented being out of the action, in Europe obviously, but also in Northern Rhodesia.

Senanga
Zambezi River
18th October

I arrived safely on Friday. The house is an extremely nice one: I am glad to be in a sheltered spot again. A few hours after my arrival a runner, who had been chasing after me all over the plain, arrived with a letter marked 'Immediate'. Inside I found instructions to proceed to Sesheke 'with all speed'.

I also got some fairly up-to-date news on what is happening in this part of Africa with the Germans. It seems that troops from the Union (South Africa) were, and probably are, driving the Bosche through their German South West African colony. That means they will be forced up to the strip of German territory, about which I have often written, across from Sesheke. This Caprivi Strip looks tiny on the map but is, in fact, over 100 miles wide. The hinterland to that strip is extremely inhospitable, with virtually no water so, if that is the military plan, it will not be easy to execute with, especially, white soldiers.

The river is not being used for transport, and ox-wagons are bringing all supplies up the so-called track from Livingstone. The track being used, and all the surrounding area, have been declared a quarantine zone, following my findings on the diseases causing so many cattle deaths. However, the military, understandably, ignore such details, and so I am to go south to oversee the operation, choose and supervise the oxen and generally do whatever is necessary.

There are seven or eight sets of major falls and rapids on the river between here and Sesheke, and the 'racing' dugouts I am using are useless in such conditions. So I have sent my boats back, pell-mell, to Mongu, and have ordered a barge as, despite the delays, going by river is so much quicker than overland. My dugouts will take four or five days, going upstream, to Mongu and then the barge a little less to get back down here, so you can see what, in practice, 'with all speed' actually means here.

I think that, having mentioned a barge and 'racing dugouts', I should explain the essential differences between the rivercraft in use on the Zambezi.

Let me start with the *Naliquanda*, the largest boat on the river by far, and the state barge of the Paramount Chief of Barotseland. Hacked out by hand with short mattock-shaped axes, the *Naliquanda* is about 70 feet long, and 10 feet wide at the centre, narrowing to a point at stem and stern. At the centre is a latunka, or shelter, enclosed at the sides and covered over with bleached and stretched hides, which had been scraped to present a smooth, white finish. The freeboard of this enormous dugout, which was constructed from a single, straight tree-trunk, is about three feet, and a pattern of checkerboard black-and-white squares decorate the sides.

As many as 35 paddlers drive the *Naliquanda* through the water, working with absolute rhythm and precision. All are hand-picked for their height and strength, both of which are essential for handling the 12-feet-long paddles. The crew wear, unusually for natives, a headdress which is made from leopard skins and tails and, when the chief is aboard, one of his drummers, of whom I have already written, is stationed centrally in the boat, tapping away continuously.

At the other end of the boat-spectrum are the privately-owned tiny dugouts, which exist in their thousands along the entire lengths of just about every river in Central Africa. They belong to a family, or an individual, and have been fashioned from a tree felled on the spot. Some are a mere 10 or 12 feet long, and only 15 or so inches wide at the centre, with a freeboard of as little as three inches. One, two or, at the most, three natives use these for fishing, for laying out and hauling in fish traps and for local river excursions. Considerable skill and an acute sense of balance are required to keep these tiny dugouts upright but, again, long paddles are used, which help.

In between these extremes, there is a multitude of rivercraft of varying length, but they all have a consistently narrow breadth and minimum freeboard: all are hollowed out from specially felled trees. I used the description 'racing dugout', because Lewanika's own dugouts have been made by master builders to ensure that, in the hands of tip-top paddlers, they are capable of considerable speed. This is not just a question of status and pride, but is of important practical consideration in that these dugouts would be used to carry urgent, secret messages when the bush telegraph, with its 360° reception area, is inappropriate.

The barge which I had sent for, to make the river journey through the rapids and falls between Senanga and Sesheke, is white-man-built and of a standard design. It is about 35 feet long with a six-feet beam at the centre, narrowing to 12 inches or so at stem and stern. The great advantage, when it comes to tackling the rapids, is the three-feet freeboard above water level and, when it comes to having to haul it across land, the flat bottom. Rough-hewn and sawn planks in local hardwood are used, reinforced with iron strips and bands, so the barge is a pretty tough, if rough, river 'work-horse'. It has a multitude of uses, and is much favoured by the traders, who need to transport considerable quantities of merchandise, such as blankets and bales of cotton, for long distances by river.

I have asked for grain to be sent down in the barge, so that I won't have to waste time picking up supplies from villages on the way. Sadly, I shall have to rush through one of the best bits of game hunting in the world, although I may have a chance to get some meat, at sundown, as we camp by the river each night.

I have been working out my travelling timetable, and reckon I can reach Sesheke in eight or nine days, about two and a half weeks from now. That would involve paddling about 12 hours each day! In this heat and humidity, the only feasible plan is to split that into two six-hour stints, one very early and one late. Even so, it is asking a lot of my boys, good as they are, to put in 12 hours really hard going, every day, for up to nine days.

There will, however, be a lot more to it than just paddling. We have to negotiate all those rapids and falls. One of the falls, Seonea Gorge, is so major that the boat has to be unloaded, and it and its contents hauled three miles overland. Oxen have to be commandeered and that, and the business of hauling a large, heavy boat through scrub, can take a good many hours. Thank goodness we will be going with, and not against, the stream. So, by the time I get back to Sesheke, I shall know several hundreds of miles of the Zambezi, as well as all the bush country I trekked through to get to Mongu.

I am seated about 100 yards from the river as I write this, and am watching a number of hippos playing near the bank. It is, of course, still illegal to shoot them, but that restriction can be pretty serious as a group of them can be a great danger to all boats and, especially, dugouts.

Thursday, 22nd October

I am still waiting for my boat. However, I had a real treat last night when a runner arrived with my letters and newspapers. There was two weeks' mail and a good bundle of papers, which are a great joy to me when I have to sit in a boat for 12 hours each day. Thank you all very much. Sometimes I find myself, literally, reading every single word on every page of each paper and, even, each and every line of all the advertisements and personal columns!

I didn't tell you of my visit to the Moquai at Nololo. I'll try to convey what an interesting experience I, once again, enjoyed.

It is curious that, in a country where women seem to be of so little account, the sisters of a Paramount Chief are chiefs, though lesser ones, in their own right. All Lewanika's sisters have the title Moquai (pronounced Mok-y). They are, of course, all subject to his ultimate authority, but are surprisingly autonomous within their own districts. The Moquai at Nololo is the eldest sister, and the senior chieftain, ruling the largest territory. In fact, 'large' is a very appropriate word to describe this lady. I had heard many tales about her, and descriptions about her size, but none came near to matching the sight that confronted me. In a land where one sees very few fat natives of either sex, the Moquai could very easily make a good living as the fat lady on a fairground! She is a real stormer! She must be all of 20 stone, with a considerable double chin and vast arms. As she is a very important personage, her seseba (coloured skirt) is made up of many, many yards of material, wound round and round, and this only serves to enlarge her already substantial girth.

I went over to her 'township' – not unlike Lewanika's Lelui, but smaller – with Stirke, the Native Commissioner stationed at Nololo, and her advisor and mentor. He has one hell of a time with her, as she can be extremely difficult to deal with.

Her 'palace' is impressive, the rooms are large and airy, and beautifully decorated with displays of native crafts. The audience chamber is a spacious room, about the size of a large village hall at home, with finely carved, ivory-inlaid chairs for the three of us.

The Moquai is, apparently, always attended by a large gaggle of giggling girls, the daughters of local chiefs, and this crowd greeted us in the now-familiar Barotse way. There was much clapping and going down on their knees.

The Moquai's husband, Ishequando, (literally 'of the house') welcomed us. He is, apparently, the latest in a long line of husbands, as with her daughter, the Little Moquai, whom I visited at Sesheke. I got to know this husband reasonably well, and found him a likeable and friendly old chap, but could only guess at what he had to put up with.

As we were conducted into the lady's presence, I had my work cut out to refrain from laughing outright. She was truly massive, and would have been totally incapable of going through an ordinary door. A nice story is told of her visit, a year or two earlier, to Livingstone, which she reached by river. She had heard that white people travelled by a 'house on metal wheels' (a train), and asked to be shown one. She was taken to the railway station and, after gazing in amazement at the engine and carriages, asked to be allowed to see inside one of them. She was helped up the coach steps, but could not get through the door. 'Push,' she shouted at her attending servants, but to no avail! Despite threatening them with all sorts of dire consequences if they failed, the Moquai had, finally, to admit defeat, and was helped back down to firm ground.

Anyway, the two of us were conducted to our seats and the usual, long palaver started as to the state of our health etc etc. At this stage, the fat, wheezing and coughing chieftain insisted on showing me her repulsive, ulcerated leg, having heard, I suppose, of my reputation as something of a curer of ills which had, by now, spread through most of Barotseland. But I managed to refrain from offering to treat her as a patient.

Beside the Moquai, there were present at this interview, her husband – I heard later he was thought to be her eighth – her two chief ministers and Lewanika's son, Lubassi who, again, acted as interpreter. This was the same son who had interpreted for Lewanika and who had, obviously, been sent for in a hurry when the Moquai heard I would be paying her a 'state visit'. Lubassi had gone to Oxford, and to a number of weekend country house parties whilst in England. I often wondered how he appreciated having to sit on the floor and candalella to a veterinary surgeon in his father's country!

I had resolved to speak my mind about the state of some of the cattle I had inspected within the Moquai's territory, of my opinion of some of her indunas and the way they carried out or, rather, failed to carry out instructions I had passed on. On hearing my forthright views, the old lady looked considerably surprised, but took it all in and I fancy that when I had departed, no-one was left in much doubt as to the pain she had suffered at the hands of this new, young Morena, who seemed to know a good deal about all their herds and animal husbandry practices.

She gave us tea and cakes, and was courteous and interesting and, again, I had a fascinating insight into the way the ruling family of Barotseland held this vast country under absolute control.

The Native Commissioner, Strike, who took me on this visit, explained that many tales could be told of the eccentricity of this large lady. I particularly liked one. It seemed she had visited the District Commissioner at Mongu, and had been shown round his house. Some months later, he paid a return call upon her at Nololo, as she had asked him to come and see what she had done to one of her rooms. Over the walls were hung all manner of pots and pans and jugs and similar objects. But, in the greatest number and variety, were hung china and metal articles more usually kept under the bed!

Somewhat taken aback, the DC asked, 'Why have you done this?' 'Well,' replied the Moquai, 'I saw that you had many of our things on the walls of your house, so I sent to Livingstone, for English things to hang on mine'.

After about a couple of hours we left, with the usual courtesies and ceremonial. I wasn't quite sure what was the reaction to my visit but, the next day, I was sent a young bullock, which provided some welcome fresh meat!

In preparation for my return to HQ by river, I have sent Champagne on overland as he, and the boys with him, will have a 300-mile walk, and will need the extra time so as to be waiting for me when I land from the Zambezi, to do the final 27 miles into Livingstone. I also sent my two big dogs with this party, to act as guards when the pony is tethered at night.

Senanga
27th October
I am still waiting, and finding it awfully monotonous. There's nothing to do and no shooting. I have also had another letter telling me to hurry back to Livingstone. But, without river transport, I can do nothing. My boats should have arrived a good week ago so, goodness knows, they should reach me any time now.

18

A Nightmare Journey

Sesheke
19th November 1914

Back at Sesheke, five lots of letters were awaiting me, a great pleasure. From what you say in them and from the dates, I think several are missing, chasing me around Barotseland. When I arrived, I found that Jack Venning had instructions to swear me in as a justice of the peace. As a JP can act all over Northern Rhodesia, this gives me authority which I can exercise as and when necessary.

My barge arrived at Senanga nine days ago, but I found that they had sent a small one into which I could fit hardly any of my gear. Fortunately, I found that a trader's barge was also coming down at the same time, so I was able to 'commandeer' this to take my extra stuff.

I had heard that Captain and Mrs Downs were a day and a half ahead of me on the river. He was a member of the Anglo-Portuguese boundary commission, examining territorial queries, and had his wife with him. When he heard the news of the war, they left their colleagues and trekked about 200 miles across country to reach the Zambezi, so as to get down to Livingstone and then try and get a liner home, as he is determined to rejoin his regiment as quickly as possible. He had discovered, somehow, that in the early days of the war, this regiment had been in heavy action and that over half the officers were casualties. So he felt an obligation to do his best to get to France.

I set my boys the challenge of catching the Downs and, by the third day, we found them beside the first major rapids. To achieve this, we set off at 5.30 each morning and, except for a 35-minute stop by the bank for some food, my boys paddled flat out until 7.00pm, by which time it was virtually dark. It was tremendous travelling.

189

At the Sioma Falls, we had to pull the barge about two-and-a-half miles overland, with oxen we were able to rustle up from nearby villages. It was impossible to negotiate these very steep falls any other way, but it was hard work and took a good deal of time. About two hours paddling below the falls, we struck the Kali rapids which, again, are too fierce to tackle with a barge. No oxen were to be had, so there was nothing for it but to unload the boat yet again and drag it, by human effort, over the stones and riverside scrub to calmer waters lower down. This, too, took some doing.

From Kali, we had to face up to two more lots of big rapids, but we negotiated these quite easily and then, two days later, hit the N'whwi rapids, which we found impassable. Once again, we went through the whole rigmarole of unloading, and then dragging the boats across land. My catching up with the Downses was particularly fortunate as, between us, we had over 60 paddlers, and so were able to put the combined team to work on each boat, when it came to the hauling bit.

But we still had three more lots of rapids to negotiate and, by now, I was increasingly concerned lest I lose any of my precious gear which, in wartime, would be irreplaceable. All went well with the first two but, when we hit the Katima Mulilo rapids (the ones I described going up about a year ago), we had problems. The usual route, via a small and relatively quiet tributary, was impossible, as it had dried up. So there was nothing for it but to go for the main river. My boat went faster and faster until, right in the middle, a cross current caught us and span us broadside on. In those few terrifying moments − it seemed like hours − I was sure all was lost but, unaccountably, the boat span back on course and we lost neither gear nor humans! It would have been tremendously exhilarating, had it not been for the almost certain feeling that all my precious belongings were about to go to the bottom of the Zambezi.

I reached Sesheke in eight days, and would have done it in seven and a half, except that the Downses were not quite as fast as I was. I believe that is probably a record for a barge on that trip. The Downses stayed here just one night, and then pressed on south.

I heard that, locally, a good number of cattle were dying so went, immediately, to visit Litia, and he seemed delighted to see me.

Will you, please, go and see Mr Woods and ask if they are still giving commissions in the AVC, and if I could get one. If I could, please send me a cable at Livingstone. I shall be making enquiries there to see if, as I believe, I can be given indefinite leave to join up, with my job being held open for me when the war is over. I have just heard that Chambers, from our department, has done just that. He sailed last week. I want to join the regulars, not the territorials. Please follow this up as quickly as possible.

John Smith suddenly switches subject, asking his family to help him get into the army. Mr Woods is the man who, 18 months earlier, had told him about the job with the bulls.

Captain Easton arrived in Sesheke, yesterday, and took command of the Caprivi Strip. All our native troops in the German territory have been ordered back over here, as the 300 miles of country between them and the enemy is a virtual desert with no water, and there is little likelihood of any hostile move in that direction.

The telegraph line, which was ordered to be installed from Livingstone at the outbreak of war, is now only 15 miles away. Apparently, it consists of baling wire, as the proper copper stuff is not available. Still, it's quite a feat to get it this far in just a matter of weeks.

Sesheke
29th November
I am still here, 10 days later. I am waiting for news that a wagon has been sent from Livingstone to meet my boats. I am hoping to get this news by telegraph, as the layers are only a 100 yards from the office, and we hope to be connected in two or three hours.

I expect this letter will reach you around Christmas time, and so I wish you all a very happy Christmas. I feel it will be a strange season for everyone, as so many people have friends and relatives who have been killed or wounded. I expect to spend Christmas in Livingstone, unless I am sent off somewhere at short notice.

Quite a lot seems to have been happening here this week. Our men, under Captain Easton, are evacuating the Caprivi Strip and are returning. There are about 250 native troops with five white officers. They are camped outside our HQ, whilst the white troops have gone back to Southern Rhodesia to help out there. Captain Salmon and Lieutenant Burton are the two who were at Mongu, and they have with them their CO, Captain O'Sullivan, and Lieutenants Hornsby and Castle.

News has just come in that the Germans have cut our telegraph wire on our northern border and the administrator, the commandant general and Colonel Hodson have gone up there. A mobile column is being enlisted in Livingstone to meet them, whilst the native troops here, are hourly expecting orders to join in the expedition.

Amongst the 'spoils of war' brought over from the German residency, is their motor boat, but no-one seemed able to get her going. The engine was drowned in oil which somebody had pumped in. I decided to have a go and, eventually, managed to get her going. We then put in a river trip – we called it a defensive patrol – with a crowd of us on board, including Mrs Venning and her 12-month-old daughter! Some patrol! Jack steered and I acted as stoker. O'Sullivan, who, as you might guess, is an Irishman, 6' 4" and 16 stone, took command, shouting orders at all and sundry. We posted two messengers in the bows as look-outs to warn us of sandbanks, but they were frightened to death at the whole thing. When we turned back downstream, I gave the throttle all she had and we got up a topping speed!

On Saturday, I took a dugout over to the ex-German side and shot a hippo in the pool there. I also saw about 200 letchwe feeding on the plain, but could get no closer than 600 yards, as there was no cover. So I missed.

All the 'inhabitants' of Sesheke dined at the Vennings' last Thursday. My boy did the cooking, and my personal boys helped out with the waiting etc. There were 12 of us. We killed a calf, and so had a delicious meal of veal. The native troops, too, had a feast on the hippo I had shot, and which was towed back to this bank.

I've been kept busy, as we have a serious outbreak of cattle disease in the district, so it will be a comfort to have the telegraph installed. The engineers brought it through from Livingstone in five weeks which, considering they had to cross the Simalaha Flats, was an outstanding feat. On these flats, there are no trees, and they had to fell them 15 miles away, cut and trim them, and then carry or drag them back to support the wires. This is the first telegraph line in Barotseland. It takes a war to establish anything like modern means of communication. I can see the final few yards being completed from my office window. As there is a team of 70 natives, there is no shortage of manpower to carry poles, dig holes and stamp the poles in. The white engineers have, of course, fixed the wiring. It's really quite an achievement.

I have lost another tooth stopping, so now I have the nerve exposed in two of them. It is giving me gyp, and I will have to have something done about it in Livingstone.

Perhaps I should have told you that I have been promoted to second-in-command of the veterinary department. I must say that I never, in my wildest dreams, considered that this could have happened a year and a half after landing here, raw, from England. I do have to feel encouraged.

Sesheke
5th December
Just a short note. I leave for Livingstone at daybreak: two days in my barge, and then an ox-wagon will take me most of the way into Livingstone. I hope to get into town on Tuesday morning, having ridden the last 15 or so miles during the night. It is just too hot to consider doing that bit in daylight hours.

There is a general exodus from Sesheke. 200 troops leave tonight, arriving in Livingstone a couple of days after me. Then Jack and his wife will be on their own again, with just some native troops as guards and sentries.

I'm glad I don't have to go overland like the troops, in this heat and with the constant threat of the rains starting. I have been able to fix for our department wagon and oxen to come out for me at Katombora and so, with Champagne waiting to take me into Livingstone, I should travel in rather more comfort than usual.

John Smith never wrote nine words which were to turn out to be so far from the truth. His next letter was written from his hospital bed in Livingstone, 16 days later. That letter only told a part of what happened but, in the draft of his book, he sets down many more details of this episode which was so nearly fatal. I have pieced together as full a story as possible from these two sources, as well as from what my father told me himself.

Following the sharp attack of dysentery in Lewanika's dugout on the Zambezi, a couple of weeks earlier, John Smith increasingly felt 'under the weather'. He assumed this meant he was to suffer another bout of malaria, so he took the appropriate action, doubling up the dose of quinine he religiously took every single day. But the malaria never materialised, and so he left for Livingstone, by barge as planned, but feeling far from fit.

Fate now played its hand, with the rains breaking a few hours after he set off.

The first days and weeks of every rainy season always produced storms of especial severity, accompanied by almost hurricane-force winds. Thunder and lightning added a full measure of drama to a scene quite outside the experience of those who have never lived in the tropics. Several inches of rain could, and often did, fall in a matter of hours, and escape was virtually impossible.

On the river there was no protection whatsoever, whilst the gusts of wind flung the craft this way and that, despite the efforts of the most experienced of paddlers. On the bank, things were not much better. The ground became awash in minutes, and torrents of rainwater swept through the camp, which the natives would be doing their best to prepare. Fires were out of the question, and no-one would risk opening food containers for fear of the entire contents being spoiled.

All in all, it was a frightening and traumatic experience.

It was against this sort of background that John Smith found himself heading south on the Zambezi, on what he had envisaged as an orderly and relatively comfortable return to 'civilisation'.

So, let us pick up on his own account of what happened next.

I left Sesheke, as planned, nearly three weeks ago. For several days I had not been feeling at all fit, I was sure that my double dose of quinine would stifle whatever it was that was pulling me down.

The first day, paddling with the stream, we were making really good progress. Then, quite suddenly and without warning, at about 4.00pm, the sky blackened and the humidity soared. It was plain we were in for 'the father and mother' of all storms, but, as luck would have it, there was no possible way we could land on that particular stretch of river. There was nothing for it but to push on, with all speed, to a part lower down which, from my previous trips, I knew was suitable for a camp site.

But, before we could reach this site, the storm broke with a fury I had never experienced in all my 18 months in the tropics. My boys, somehow, got the barge to the bank; we secured it to some trees and unloaded only the absolute essentials, which included the smallest of the tents and Tolani's shelter. Matapi, helped by every available native, tried again and again to erect the tent and secure the shelter, but it was just impossible. The wind tore through the site, ripping away everything in its path. By now, the whole area was a sea of mud, with water squelching underfoot, inches deep.

For the first time since he joined me, Tolani failed to get a fire going. At about midnight, with the storm no less severe, I found a piece of canvas and, rolling myself in it in the mud tried, unsuccessfully, to get some sleep. We had not dared to open any of our food boxes, so went hungry.

The next morning the rain stopped and the wind dropped. We now managed to get a fire going, cooked some food, and did our best to restore some semblance of order to our belongings and the gear in the boat, which was inches deep in water. But, by now, I was feeling extremely unwell, and could only sip some milk that Matapi had found at a village an unexpectedly short distance away.

As soon as we could we took to the barge, having baled most of the water from it, and paddled furiously for Katombora. My wagon, with its well-rested oxen would, I was confident, very speedily whisk me to where Champagne was waiting, so I expected to be tucked up in bed in Livingstone in a matter of days.

However, before we could reach our destination and the wagon, the storm struck again. If anything, it was even more violent than last night's, and I found my boys, usually only mildly put out by such conditions, seriously unnerved and frightened. Somehow we managed to land, as it was quite out of the question to make any progress on the river and this time, by Herculean effort, Matapi managed to secure a piece of canvas as some sort of shelter for me. A fire was, again, impossible, and so we all went foodless for the second time, but I couldn't have managed anything anyhow.

I had a high temperature, was somewhat light-headed and lay, shivering and shaking, wrapped in some sodden bedding. All I could focus on was the obsessive need to get to the oxen, and some degree of cover and protection from the rain. When the storm again ceased at dawn, I had spent another sleepless night and had eaten nothing.

We took to the river, paddled as before and, to my eternal relief, found the wagon and rested team ready for us at Katombora.

There, once again in a storm, we managed a camp of sorts and, in my befuddled state of mind, I decided that a good wash might make me feel better. When I peeled off my clothes and mud-caked shirt, I found my stomach covered with yellowish-brown spots, and realised I had a nasty attack of enteritis. No wonder I felt so ill!

The boys transferred all our gear to the wagon and, to my utter relief, we set off on the last-but-one leg of our journey to Livingstone. Uncomfortable as it was, being thrown about in the spring-less wagon, I was at least in the dry, and could wrap myself in some not-entirely-sodden blankets to try and stop myself shivering and shaking, despite the intense heat.

When I had planned this trip, I had reckoned on travelling by wagon through two nights, doing about eight or ten miles a night, whilst camping and resting during the heat of the day. I would then spend the third night riding Champagne along the track to Livingstone, reaching the Club in time for a bath and change, and some well-earned breakfast. It was all to be so simple and straightforward!

We started, that first evening, confidently enough even though it was pouring with rain with the usual thunder, lightning and tearing wind. All went well, with us making reasonably good progress through the mud with our double span of 30 oxen. That is, until we struck the so-called Livingstone road. In reality this is simply a track cut through the bush. In normal times, the surface was reasonably flat and was passable – just – in most weathers. But the passage of, literally, hundreds of laden wagons with their long spans of 30 or more oxen each, going to and from the war zones up north, had turned this rough trail into a nightmare track of deep ruts and ridges, now churned up into thick mud.

Once on this 'road' we began to run into real trouble. We would go a few yards and then either the oxen would sink, almost to their bellies, in the mud, or the wagon would 'drop' a wheel into a deep rut and stick fast. Again and again we dug animals or the wagon out, and then tried to coax the team forward to some surer footing.

For two days we struggled on like this. I gave what help I could, but I was now terribly weak, and becoming delirious with phases of unconsciousness.

Finally we stuck. Nothing we all did could move either the beasts or the wagon. I was lying in the wagon, not able to think sufficiently coherently to formulate any plan at all but, thank God, Matapi kept his head.

There were still about 18 miles to go to reach Champagne, and so he improvised a hammock (machili) out of a piece of tent canvas and two poles cut from the bush. He chose the three strongest natives to take a corner each, with himself, and then lifted me gently down from the wagon and into the machili. I was now only vaguely aware of what was happening. I had had no food and practically no sleep for four days, and had a raging temperature. I shook from head to toe, and could produce no intelligent thoughts except to recognise that, unless I could get some medical help, I was in a fair amount of trouble.

My faithful Matapi and the three boys now set out to carry me, through torrential rain and great heat, the 18 miles or so to meet up with Champagne.

I remember nothing of that journey, which must have taken those natives, even with their massive strength, at least 10 hours, and probably a good deal longer. They, too, had to struggle through the same deep mud, and to negotiate the ruts and ridges which had beaten our oxen.

I came to, in a dazed sort of way, to find myself once again in Matapi's arms, being lifted onto Champagne. With utter devotion, those four natives had carried me, non-stop, to our rendezvous, to find my pony and my pony boy patiently waiting to take me the last miles into Livingstone. The latter was expecting his familiar 'Morena': instead, he was presented with a crumpled, delirious and sodden heap.

Matapi now cut some thongs from reeds at the river's edge, and lashed my feet to the stirrups, and myself to the saddle. He then led Champagne to the water, and drove him headlong into the

Sindi river. Shrewdly, he calculated that the pony would travel faster alone with his load than he would with either my pony boy or himself leading him. It must also be a fact that, strong as Matapi is, helping to carry me all those miles in such terrible conditions must just about have finished him off.

The torrential rain had caused the Sindi to rise appreciably, and it was already in near-flood, so Champagne, faithful creature that he is, had no alternative but to swim across with his 'sack of potatoes' slumped across his back.

Having made that journey a good number of times, the pony knew his way at night as well as by day. So, having crossed the river, he struggled up the other bank and struck out for Livingstone, still in the pouring rain and through the pitch-black night.

I write all these details, but it was some time before I was able to question my boys and learn exactly what had happened. The only facts of which I was aware were being lifted into the saddle, and of being almost completely submerged as my pony swam the Sindi. I was, and remain, oblivious of all else.

The next thing I knew was that a pretty white nurse was bending over me as I lay, clean and in pyjamas, between cool cotton sheets, in a darkened room with an electric fan swinging back and forth, playing warm air at me. I was in Livingstone Hospital.

I was later to learn what had happened.

Mr Nightingale, head of the Transport Department, was driving his mule cart along the track from the railway station and towards the town centre early in the morning when, to his amazement, he saw a weary, mud-caked pony plodding towards him. He then realised that the pony had a body slumped over its neck, with feet tied to the stirrups.

He managed to haul me, unconscious, down from Champagne's back and into his buckboard, and drove straight to the hospital, where I was washed and put to bed, still unconscious. The Deputy Principal Medical Officer was called, diagnosed a severe attack of enteritis and exhaustion, and gave his instructions.

Having told the story of his nightmare return to Livingstone as it happened, rather than as he felt was suitable for his family back in England, we can now let John Smith take up the tale in his next letter.

Livingstone Hospital
21st December

This is rather a strange place to write from. It's my eleventh day here, and I'm sitting up in bed. I'm all right now, and only need bucking up, as I've had nothing but barley water and milk for a week or so, although I'm now allowed eggs and a light diet. Thank goodness my constitution seems to be quite strong, as it had to stand up to a fair old knocking about. I must have started the enteritis at Sesheke and the wet and wind, and lack of sleep and food, fuelled it up into a nasty attack.

I shall not forget in a hurry the feeling I had when I came to, washed and between clean sheets, after five days in that rain. Fortunately, I can remember nothing of the ride, other than Champagne swimming the Sindi, with the swollen waters swirling over the saddle. Had it not been for my faithful boys, and my gallant pony, things would probably have turned out rather differently.

My wagon was brought in eight days later, but only after an extra span of thirty fresh oxen had been taken out. So it took 60 beasts to shift the load out of the mud and along the so-called road.

I learned when I started to recover that I was recalled here urgently to accompany a force of 100 native troops who left last Saturday to go two days up the railway line, and then cut across country to our northern border, to reinforce the contingent already there. They were using ox-wagons, and the month's hard marching it will take them will involve cutting right through the 'fly belt', where a lot of the oxen will undoubtedly sicken. I was to be the vet-in-attendance.

Instead of that interesting and demanding assignment, I am still confined to bed, feeding on slops and, frankly, only too happy to do as I am told. Each day the rain falls in the afternoon and the evening, in the torrents I experienced recently. The old hands here all seem to agree that they never remember such a beginning to the wet season.

The hospital is quite small, consisting of a general ward of 10 beds and four private rooms. I am in one of the latter, and get all medical attention free, but have to pay between £1 and 25 shillings a day for the room and food. There are three nurses at present, as one is on leave, but they are all very nice and have looked after me beautifully.

I can hardly grasp that Christmas is only two days away. I never expected to be spending it in hospital. I am now beginning to get to the hungry stage and hope, soon, to be allowed some proper food. All my pals have visited me and have been most kind. My somewhat dramatic return to HQ has obviously caused a bit of a stir but, as I am so deeply brown, I suspect some of them may think it was all a put-up job!

Livingstone Hospital
28th December 1914

Still in hospital, but going on splendidly. I am now able to sit on the verandah and, I am glad to be able to report, eat solid food. I still feel pretty weak and my legs don't quite know their work yet, but I am getting on quickly.

Christmas has been a very quiet time, but the nurses have been awfully good. When I awakened on Christmas morning, I found a stocking on the end of my bed with a rattle, tin trumpet and other toys! I sat up and blew the trumpet until the night-nurse came round. My Christmas dinner consisted of rice, onion and a glass of champagne, not exactly the traditional feast! During the day I had half a dozen visitors. Lane, my boss, has been three or four times each week.

I had planned to move into my original camp at Maramba, but the doctor says that, while the rains continue, I must stop in Livingstone and get my strength back. It is still pouring every day.

I was thinking of you all on Christmas day, and wondering what you were all doing. I went to sleep at about 7.00pm, when I suppose you would have been having your tea. The nurses had their Christmas dinner on Boxing Day: their dining room is close beside my room, so I crawled round and joined them for a short time.

The Judge and Lady Beaufort gave a Christmas dance which, of course, I missed, but the acting matron went, and gave me all the news and gossip. Matron is on leave, and has left her parrot (needless to say, called Joey) behind. He has taken a great fancy to me, and sits at the end of my bed. In fact, he is on my knee as I write!

I keep thinking of our troops, slogging north in this dreadful rain. I should have been with them. I can't think they had much to celebrate on Christmas day.

Livingstone Hospital
1st January 1915
Happy New Year, and may 1915 bring peace, and an end to all this wretchedness in Europe.

This is my twenty-first day in hospital and, although I am going on splendidly and eating everything that is put in front of me – I had my first bit of meat yesterday – my legs are still rather rubbery and I'm terribly thin.

The hospital has filled up this past month. Apparently, it always does at this time of the year, because of the effects of the endless rains. All four private rooms are full – Captain Salmon has been brought down into one – and there are five serious cases of malaria in the general ward.

I am being a real little devil. I've ordered the departmental buckboard, so that I can have a short drive this afternoon, before the evening downpour begins. It will be a change from looking at these four walls.

Livingstone Hospital
4th January
You will be surprised at my next news. Doctor May, the PMO, has said I must have complete change, and go to the Cape. He said it would take me a long time to get fit here, at this time of the year especially, and that I should quickly get well down there. It seems a pity to have to go five days in the train to get to the sea, doesn't it? I will be four-and-a-half days getting to Cape Town, then I have to go 20 miles on to Muizenberg, which is judged to be the best place for me to convalesce. The administration has given me four weeks sick leave and a concession ticket on the railway.

John Smith spent 26 days in hospital. His illnesses, dysentery and enteritis, together with the dramatic events on his journey from Sesheke to Livingstone, had taken his weight down from ten stone to six and, to use one of his own favourite phrases, 'it had knocked the stuffing out of him'.

Just before he set out for Livingstone, he had written to his family to try and get some help in enlisting in the Army Veterinary Corps in France, but his prolonged stay in hospital left him less impatient to get back to England. As with all able-bodied young men, he wanted to do his bit but, at a distance of many thousands of miles and with letters taking four weeks, it was difficult for him and his colonial colleagues to set their feelings in proper perspective and balance.

He had also found himself, suddenly and unexpectedly, second-in-command of a large department, at a time when problems were multiplying and as the available manpower dwindled. His promotion had, it is true, been accelerated by two veterinary surgeons going back to the UK, but one of his previous letters had hinted that he was likely to get this position regardless. His success, over his 18 months' service, had undoubtedly made an impact on his seniors, who badly needed someone with his skills, experience and resourcefulness. Yet he was still aged only 32.

We leave him 'doing splendidly' (his words) but obviously far from fit, waiting to be discharged from hospital so that he could either argue his release to go home to enlist, or pick up the reins of substantially greater responsibility in Livingstone.

But, for a time, he was to find himself doing neither.

On the train
Mafeking
7th January 1915

It isn't easy to write as these trains rock so. This is my third day and still two to go!

As I was leaving the hospital to get to the station, your cable arrived, saying I could have a commission in the Army Veterinary Corps. So I rushed off to see Lane, my boss, and we both then went to see Sir Lawrence Wallace, the administrator, to check if I could get permanent leave to enlist.

When we got to his office, he told us that he had just had cables from the Colonial Office, in London, saying he was not to let any of our department leave NR. There is a lot of rinderpest in German East Africa, and the authorities are afraid of it getting here. If it were to do so, we would be in a real mess. HE was very nice, but said he couldn't possibly let me go. Lane, too, said he couldn't manage without me. HE said that, with all my recent experience, I would be fully up to handling any such situation.

It is a great disappointment not to come home and join the war, but I realise that I may be badly wanted here.

Friday 6.00pm
We have travelled for 48 hours, and I'm awfully tired of it all. I can't help thinking of having to do the whole journey over again in only a couple of weeks. We are due at Cape Town in the morning, and I shall then go on the 20-odd miles to Muizenberg.

Park Hotel
Muizenberg
13th January 1915
At last I am by the sea. We were due in Cape Town last Saturday at 8.00am, but did not arrive until 12.00 noon. We are about 15 miles from Cape Town on the east coast, so the sea here is the Indian Ocean. (*The author's geography is at fault here, as Cape Town is on the south west tip of Africa and beside the Atlantic Ocean.*)

Muizenberg, itself, is quite small. The only attractions are the mild summer weather and the wonderful bathing and surfing. I have been forbidden to bathe.

Each morning, I go down to the beach and sit on the sand watching the surfers. After lunch, I rest for a couple of hours, and then repeat the dose on the beach. I turn in soon after dinner, as I still feel pretty feeble at the end of the day, but I am really much better, and can notice the improvement all the time. Fruit here is delicious, and I have been spoiling myself with huge juicy peaches.

14th January
I have just seen in the paper that Major Gordon and Captain Dixon are due in Cape Town today, so I am off to see if I can find them. Poor Dixon has lost both his brothers in France, and now he is off there as well.

21st January

I went for a bathe on Monday and felt all right but, on Tuesday, having stayed in too long surfing on the vast rollers, I got a touch of fever again and retired to bed. I dosed myself up with quinine, and have been feeling fine since Thursday morning. I bathed again yesterday, but was careful not to get cold.

Mafeking
28th January

I am on my way back, although my leave is not up until Tuesday next. We arrived at Kimberley yesterday. There we learned there had been torrential rain up north, and the railway line was washed away in six places. We are going on from Mafeking at midnight, as far as some place where a bridge has been washed away. A train is stuck on the other side of that bridge, and we are to trans-ship to it. That train will take us to the next wash-away, where we shall trans-ship again, and so on all the way! I can see we are going to have a great time carting ourselves and our gear, not to mention the children, from one train to another in pretty awful conditions, especially with the bridges down. How we get on from Bulawayo to Livingstone, goodness alone knows!

Fancy having 28 days' leave and having to spend 15 of them in a train! Most of all, when I get back, I am looking forward to having my mail. It seems, and is, ages since I received any.

John Smith's convalescence had been a disaster. He arrived back in Livingstone stronger in body, but noticeably frail in spirit. No doubt the doctors gave their advice in good faith, but circumstances conspired to spoil what could have been a reasonable plan.

19

Dancing the Fever Away

————⟫•◦•⟨————

Maramba
8th February 1915

Twenty months after first arriving at the camp, just ahead of the bulls, I'm back again. In the end, the train was three-and-a-half days late(!) We reached Livingstone at 8.00pm on Tuesday. I last wrote from Mafeking, where we stuck for a day, and then we stuck again for 24 hours at Gabarones. Then we made it to Bulawayo. On that stretch, we had to negotiate the six washouts I mentioned. This took hours, and the train had to crawl over hastily relaid track, sometimes supported on boughs of trees cut from the rail-side, where the ballast had disappeared in the floods. Much of the track was under water, so our progress was not unlike that of a motorboat!

I am to be stationed here for a time, anyway, with a newly equipped laboratory so that I can get to work immediately if the anticipated rinderpest attack occurs.

This rainy season has been exceptional, and the old hands, who have lived here for years, say they can remember nothing like it. The whole country is flooded and sodden and, in consequence, mosquitoes are around in clouds.

On Saturday, I went 20 miles up-country to inspect some cattle on a ranch there. The owner and I took a passenger train up, the weekly one seven days after mine, and planned to complete our inspection and catch the goods train back at 3.00pm that same afternoon. There is no station, the train simply pulls up beside a broken name board at the side of the track, so we found a gangers' hut some hundreds of yards off to get some shelter. We waited and waited and, eventually, the goods crawled to a halt at 1.00am on Sunday, 10 hours late. We were very wet, very hungry and thirsty, and pretty much put out.

So, at 2.30am on Sunday, I had to knock up a friend of mine who lived reasonably near the station, and beg a bed off him for the remainder of the night. I came on down here, had a nap, then gave tea to Mrs Clark and Miss Beaufort, the judge's daughter, who'd both just walked five miles down the railway track to Maramba from Livingstone. I saw them most of the way back, a walk of eight miles, fell into bed and slept for 11 hours!

I am much better, but am still plagued by feeling unreasonably tired, a real nuisance.

While Lane is away, I have to ride five miles into Livingstone each day to attend to the paperwork etc, and it's hard going. Poor old Champagne often sinks up to his knees in water and mud, and we make slow progress. So I don't really have much time, or opportunity, to catch up with all my Livingstone friends.

15th February
It's still raining. One and three-quarter inches fell in two hours last Saturday. Now I have to go to Livingstone along the railway line, as even Champagne cannot manage the waterlogged track up through the trees and scrub.

The outlook for our market in cattle is rapidly getting worse. Yesterday, movements of cattle were stopped from Northern Rhodesia to the south, whilst the Congo market is almost non-existent, as most of the Belgians have left to go back to Europe, and those remaining are almost bankrupt. So the outlook for our traders is grim. Despite this, the paperwork grows: last Saturday morning I was dictating letters, in Livingstone, for two-and-a-half hours to our new clerk. He's just out of Oxford, and I'm not sure he is too happy with his lot!

I have not seen many people in Livingstone yet. The usual calling time is 6.00 to 7.30pm, which means riding back in the dark. With all this water lying about, it is nearly impossible and very dangerous, so I'm not keen to do much of that yet.

22nd February
After the wettest weather on record, I fear we may now be facing a famine! The ground has been so wet that the mealies that have

been planted have either died or been washed away. The whole countryside is one long sodden mass.

As Lane is still away, I rode up along the railway line and had dinner with Mrs Lane. I told you the government printer was in hospital when I was laid up. Well, we arranged to give our nurses dinner when we got out, so we fixed for last Saturday. Crowther, the printer, who is a bachelor of about 40, has a very nice house in which he takes great pride. I sent my bed up on a wagon, so that I could spend the night there. We had a nice dinner party: caviar, soup, fish, fowl, sweet, cheese and fruit; the latter we'd ordered to be sent up from Bulawayo! I think the nurses enjoyed it. My cook handled the food, and Crowther's and my boy waited. I'd got a four-mule cart from the department stables, and collected and returned them. I stayed the night and came back here on Sunday.

With all my belongings being out in the rain for so long on my trip south from Mongu, I have an awful lot spoiled. I had a box of curios, carvings, egret feathers, marabou tails and photographs, all rotten with green mould. A lot of other bits of my gear suffered the same fate but, as you rightly say, it was a good job I was on my way home, and not further out and alone.

28th February

This is a weird country. Ten days ago here, in Maramba, we were squelching through over a foot of water and mud. Today, with no rain for that time and a blazing sun, the ground is like iron, and has started to crack! It's hard to believe!

We have had some more cases of rabies up the line and, unfortunately, two people have been bitten, one the wife of a sergeant-major in the police. The dog's brains were sent down to me to examine, and I have reported my findings to the principal medical officer.

I am expecting some horse-sickness serum which Lane should have brought back. Several horses were brought up here a few months ago, but every one of them is now dead. So, I am expecting to do inoculations on any more that arrive.

8th March
As we are getting reports of more rabies outbreaks, I am writing a paper on how much it would cost for me to keep a strain going in rabbits here in Maramba, so that we could treat people who had been bitten: it is the Louis Pasteur treatment. If it is agreed, it will mean a lot of work and, possibly, that I would be stuck down here for ever.

22nd March
I have sad news about the McKinnons. They both arrived from Mongu in a terrible state and were unable to walk. They travelled with Palmer, the native commissioner who, too, is seriously ill. All three were carried in by their boys. Just about every official, and several wives, from Barotseland have been casualties of this rainy season. The McKinnons' messengers and two of the indunas who travelled with them, came yesterday to greet me, as they'd heard where I was. I gave them salt, and told them to take my greetings to all their people when they got back.

Three more cases of rabies this week, and I have the brains to examine again. All dogs have to be kept tied up, and all loose ones are shot on sight: it's the only answer. The Administrator has decided against the Pasteur treatment, and I can't say I'm sorry.

I have just seen the account of the expedition I was due to accompany when I fell ill. The contingent had to abandon its wagons and oxen at Kasama, as over 200 of the beasts were, by then, unfit for work. Woods and Hornby, two of our vets who are patrolling the border watching for rinderpest, moved down to meet the troops, and I believe they had a really rough time. HE, whom I saw on Thursday, said he was relieved that the situation had not been worse, with even more oxen being lost.

I am expecting a lot of horses up from South Africa, and will keep them here and inoculate them against horse-sickness. I have a big store of serum ready.

29th March
It started to rain midday yesterday, and it is still pouring down. We have been having rain on and off for a week and, odd as it may

sound, it is a splendid thing for all of us. It looked as if the wet season had ended a week or so ago, and this was followed by extreme heat and continuous sunshine, so the land dried much too fast and began to crack. Had we not got some wet weather to follow, the crops would have failed completely and the grazing would have been extremely poor. With a bit of luck, things have righted themselves.

I fear you all think I am obsessed with the weather, particularly the rain. But the survival of the people, the crops and the cattle depends, literally and critically, upon the seasons behaving reasonably to a pattern and timetable. But if it all falls out of kilter, the whole territory, and hundreds of thousands of natives and many more head of cattle, are put at risk. So, I suppose, that explains my telling you, in letter after letter, about the weather.

I'm off up to Livingstone after tea as the Judge and Lady Beaufort are giving a dance on their verandah tonight. It's only a small affair, as there is another at Government House next week, to which I am also invited. I am staying overnight in Livingstone, and will send my evening clothes ahead this afternoon and ride up, or rather swim up, later! I believe we have a gramophone for the music, as the humidity has proved too much for the piano, and it has warped so as to be unplayable! The native police band is doing guard duty to release regulars for other activities, but I expect they'll turn up for next week's do.

3rd April
Easter Weekend
Last Tuesday, the Judge and Lady Beaufort gave a dance which I was really looking forward to. Then the rain began again on Monday night, and never let up. About 2.00pm on Tuesday afternoon, I began to feel very unwell with fever and a high temperature but, as I was determined to get to the dance, I took 15 grains of quinine and some zaxa. I set off on Champagne at 4 o'clock and got to Livingstone, through the floods, and changed into a stiff dress shirt and white tie. It was a great evening and I thoroughly enjoyed myself, although I was sweating profusely all the time. I said to Dr May, 'This is my latest treatment for malaria'.

'Is that it,' he replied, 'I thought you were just an advertisement for a damned bad laundry!'

Tomorrow, I'm having an Easter Day picnic down here. I have had shelters built and covered with leaves at a perfectly beautiful spot overlooking the Zambezi, and in the midst of a palm glade. The very high palms are interspersed with lower ones, which make it a most unusual and attractive setting. My guests are: the judge, Lady and Miss Beaufort; Mr and Mrs Lane; Mr and Mrs 'Dinkie' Jalland and a couple of bachelors.

Did I tell you of an official named Davis, whom I saw in Barotseland some months ago? He had been badly savaged by a leopard out in the bush: both his arms were broken and he was mauled all over. His boys carried him for three-and-a-half days, covering 150 miles, to get him to Mongu, which he reached delirious and raving with pain and infection. Goodness alone knows how he survived. We managed to patch him up there, and then got him to Livingstone. In due course, he was sent back to England, joined the Norfolk Regiment and was killed in France. I just can't think what I can say of such a terrible story.

This frightful episode is a stark example of John Smith censoring his own story. Firstly, he was at that time trekking exactly as was Davis, and will not have wanted to alarm his family with the fear that he might have the same sort of experience. Secondly, the 'we' of 'we managed to patch him up', was undoubtedly himself. There were less than a dozen white men and women at Mongu, and certainly no doctor. Our vet was, almost daily, called upon to treat humans (remember the native boy mauled by the lion) and he will have done the 'patching up'. Thirdly, there is no account of poor Davis's terrible ordeal, being taken by dugout through, over and round the rapids and falls between Mongu and Livingstone, a river journey of about two weeks. It is an amazing, tragic story of native devotion, human suffering and medical improvisation. But it is not at all untypical of colonial life at that time.

12th April

I have a rotten trip before me in the next two days. A lot of cattle, some thousands, have come down from Barotseland to go to farms near the railway, about 20 miles away. There's a train up tomorrow night. However, there isn't one back until Friday. So I am sending my pony up by road, shall take a couple of blankets and sleep on the veldt, then ride back. It is awfully hot to do 20 miles at a stretch, for both of us.

The dance at Government House was splendid, and I thoroughly enjoyed myself. There is another on 4th May and so, if all goes well, I shall be having a bit of a kick-up on my birthday.

This next weekend, Mr and Mrs Lane are coming to spend two days with me here. Thomas is still away, and I don't want him back this week as I shall need his room for the Lanes.

16th April

I have typed out the two menus for the dinners I have planned for the Lanes. I have managed to get an assortment with only three tinned things in it, pears, caviar and asparagus. I am sending a boy out tomorrow morning to catch fish: the bream in the river are quite good, and Tolani serves them up beautifully. I've grown the French beans myself, and the paw-paw (fruit very like melons) I can get from a local native. I have a plum pudding left over from those you sent me last year. I was saving it for Christmas, but I was in hospital, so it will come in handy now. The boys are busy ironing table cloths and napkins.

Thomas arrived back unexpectedly, last Tuesday, so he will help in the feasting. The Lanes will have his room and he'll have a tent close by.

There was a cricket match last week, and they got the Victoria Falls Hotel people to bring lunch to the ground. About 50 of us were there, and it was very jolly. Major Byas suddenly called on me for a speech, and I managed to dream up something suitable, I hope!

I wrote and asked Mrs Lane to make a cake for us, as the ones my cook makes are dangerous. They never seem to rise, and are like putty in the centre! Funny thing is that he makes splendid bread, so I told him to let the cake rise in the same way. He always says, 'This cake I will not rise'!

Yesterday, one of my messengers asked to go to town as he wanted to 'laugh at his brother'! I asked him what he wanted to do that for, and he replied that his brother had just arrived from Barotseland. After a lot of questioning, I discovered that the verb 'to laugh' is used in connection with a particular greeting, when they are very pleased to see each other, so he really wanted to greet him! I'm always finding fresh uses for words like that.

19th April

The Lanes have just gone and I have enjoyed their visit. They came to lunch on Saturday and, after tea, we went for a walk. We did the same yesterday morning and again after tea. I think they slept all afternoon. Mrs Lane is a good sort, and very jolly.

22nd April

There has been an outbreak of disease on a farm up country, and I'm going to see it. I go by train on Saturday morning and arrive at the sidings at about 9.00pm the same evening. The farm appears to be about 12 miles from the railway, and they're sending a mule for me to ride in on! So I shall have Sunday afternoon and Monday morning on the farm, before I ride again to catch the train back at 1.00am on Tuesday morning. It's a pity the trains reach the siding at such unearthly hours! I shan't take any boys, just a couple of blankets and a gun.

The Lanes had a dinner party last night, and asked me. I got a cart and two mules to go in, and returned at about 11.30pm. It was pitch dark and very difficult to see 'the road', just a cutting through the bush. It's much easier to find one's way on horseback, but it makes such a mess of one's evening suit.

There's another cricket match this weekend, but I shall miss it as I may have to go to a big farmers' meeting at Kafue, about 200 miles north up the railway line.

29th April

I left here on Saturday morning early, and arrived at Choma station at 9.00pm the same day. I enquired if anyone was waiting for me, but there was no one. The station is like all the others, simply a signboard at the side of the track. I slept the night in my blanket in a hut belonging to a storekeeper, beside the track, and on Sunday morning started to walk to the farm, thinking I should meet something for me to ride in on. Only then did I discover that the farm is 24, not 12, miles away! Well, I walked on and on, with a piccaninny to carry my bag, and met nothing. Eventually, after walking until 4 o'clock, I arrived at the farm and found about half-a-dozen Europeans from neighbouring farms, all gathered together and gawping at a dishevelled and exhausted self, traipsing up the path. It appears that Lane hadn't sent the letter early enough, and I got there before it did. The gathering was waiting for letters from the very train I had travelled on! I was good and mad, as well as being tired out. It's a good long while since I walked 24 miles through the heat of the day!

Next morning, I examined the cattle and started back, riding an old mule. I broke four sticks knocking that old slow-coach along: it was nearly as tiring as walking! When I got to Choma 'station', I discovered the storekeeper's wife had appendicitis. I arranged to bring her with me on the train to Livingstone, and she had a four-month-old baby! We carried the mother to the train at 1.00am, and I nursed her baby and fooled about with it all night. The hospital cart was at the station to take them both, and another to take me. There was a message, with my driver, to see Lane urgently. So I drove to Maramba, had a quick breakfast and bath, and drove back into Livingstone. There I found a message from Venning, at Sesheke, saying that cattle were dying wholesale in Barotseland, and asking for help. Also, another from Lewanika, saying the same thing. Both had come in at great speed by special runners. Sounds as though pleuro-pneumonia might have broken out and, if that is so, it is really serious, as it could make a clean sweep of everything throughout the territory. I could see myself chasing back up to Barotseland as hard as I could.

The administrator sent for Lane and myself, and we dispatched runners to stop all movements of cattle, everywhere. It was arranged that I should go off, as I know the country etc. There were other messages on the way, so I stayed up all night, in Livingstone, just in case they arrived.

I was tired, I can tell you, after my weekend's experiences!

Yesterday, we saw Sir Lawrence again, and he had changed his mind and decided that I should stay here, so we have arranged for Jones to go and send word back, as quickly as possible, if it is pleuro-pneumonia. If it is, I am to go and take some others with me. In the meantime, I have to make arrangements for drawing a sort of quarantine line between Barotseland and here, and the farmers. I rather think I shall go to Sesheke and start there, moving cattle for many miles around.

I sent Thomas off last night, with a small cart and six oxen, to try and find about 3000 head of cattle which are fairly near here, on their way down from Barotseland to the farmers. He is to stop and quarantine them all. I think I will then go and make an examination as soon as he can find them. We wired Sesheke to stop all trading due to start 1st May, just as we had to last year. The traders will have got all their stocks together, and it will give them a nasty knock. I only hope the natives will keep quiet if they start shooting their cattle.

Poor old Jones has to travel 250 miles overland with carriers back to Livingstone, then 450 miles up to Barotseland by river, and off into the bush again with carriers. As I know the route he must take, I am sending to all the big indunas to have food ready for him. He doesn't speak a word of the language, and I estimate it will be at least 10 weeks before we can get any definite news from him. Such is the speed of dealing with emergencies in this country.

So far, only five of us at HQ know anything of this emergency, and it is a dead secret. If the two diseases, rinderpest and pleuro-pneumonia run through this country, it means virtual ruin. We could easily do with 30 vets at a time like this, and we have six, with no chance of more as the War Office in London are snapping up every available qualified, or partially qualified, man there is.

Both Venning and Lewanika were expecting me to go north. I only hope Jones hits it off with the natives, as he will have to be very tactful.

3rd May

Our arrangements have been altered yet again. Lane, himself, is going up river to Barotseland this weekend, and Jones is to follow him as soon as he can. Lane will only stay a short while to see what the trouble is, and will then return. If his paddlers do well, he could make the round trip in three months. I'm going on the cattle road beyond Sesheke, then back to Sesheke, then down here again. I am going to be as quick as possible, as there will be no-one here, and I will have to do Lane's work as well. I think I can get round in four weeks. If anything really important happens, I will be contacted by special runners, and will have to chase back to base as fast as possible. It's awkward being short-handed, but it can't be helped.

I'm getting my carriers together with all speed, but I look like having a rough time finding food for them. The grass is far too long for shooting, and the only hope of getting game is a chance shot. There are very few villages, but we'll get through somehow, as usual.

Lane is not looking forward to this trip as he's not done much trekking, but at least he won't be troubled over the food question, as he can carry it in the boats.

Tomorrow is my birthday, and I got four letters for it two days ago: that was good timing. It's the dance tomorrow and, if my carriers haven't arrived, I'll celebrate my birthday there.

7th May

One more letter before starting off: I go tomorrow morning. This has been a most peculiar week. I was planning to start on Wednesday, and had got all my gear together. I was to go to the dance as a birthday treat but, that morning, I began to vomit and knew I was in for a dose of malaria. I lay down until my temperature dropped to 102 and then piled on the blankets and had a four-hour sweat. It was a jolly sharp attack, and I felt wretched: what a nice way to spend one's birthday! So the dance didn't see me.

The packet of books arrived this week, with more letters. Many thanks. It was very nice to get a birthday present again.

Lane got away yesterday and, at the last minute, Mrs Lane decided to go with him. He'll leave her with Mrs Venning at Mongu, while he tours around. Mrs Lane has never been out on tour before. I hope she manages to keep fit and well.

There are such a lot of carriers needed just now, that everyone has to put up with any that can be found. We have some thousands continually carrying supplies to the troops. Mine are a scraggy lot. Apparently they thought I was a new man, going out for the first time! One said something to his neighbour and I heard it. It is the first time I have had boys from the Baloka tribe. They are a slave race of the Barotse, and pay tribute to Lewanika. I overheard Matapi telling them that he and I had been all over Barotseland and that we were just about the bee's knees at touring!

Again, thanks for my presents.

Senkobo
16th May
I eventually got away from Livingstone on Saturday last, eight days ago, and only went eight miles. The next day I came on to Senkobo, where I found Thomas. We are at a railway siding around 22 miles from Livingstone. 20 miles away, Thomas had stopped over 2,000 cattle, and was waiting for another 1,500 expected daily, so I decided to stay a day or so. Next morning, two cattle were dead and another sick. I killed the latter, and decided it was lung-sickness (pleuro-pneumonia).

This is very, very serious.

The next day was when the trains pass here, one to Livingstone in the morning and one back at night. So I went back and saw the Administrator. I had two interviews with him, and he gave me the power to do anything I liked. We stopped all movement in the whole country, and quarantined everything. I have never sent out so many telegrams and dictated so many letters as I did in those two hours. My office was besieged with worried traders. We have a new clerk, named Wardroper, who is just down from Oxford, and the only man left in our department in Livingstone, and he tackled everything splendidly. I simply gave him an outline, and he composed the letters and telegrams, as well as the statements.

Then in came the butcher to say he had nothing to kill and, if we stopped all cattle, Livingstone would starve for meat. Southern Rhodesia has 'east coast fever' in its cattle, so nothing could come up from the south. I saw HE about this meat question and he said 'very well, we'll do without meat'. I passed this on to the butcher, and then told him to send me a last roasting joint for the trip: how is that for insider trading!

To cut a long story short, I was driven to the station by mule cart, and just managed to catch the train.

The railway company have their own telegraph wire along the line. HE ordered them to give me a key to their private phono-phone, so that I could keep in touch with him in Livingstone.

When I got to Senkobo, I heard that 1500 cattle we were expecting were on the Michili river, 130 miles away. 60-odd were dead and over 100 sick. I packed Thomas off with my carriers, as fast as I could, to get to them and start inoculating. I had never seen lung disease before, but was sure I was right in my diagnosis. Thomas, of course, doesn't know much about the disease, but he saw my case here. I told him that if he found the same symptoms, to inoculate from the lungs of a dead beast. I showed him how it was done, and told him to pretend he knew all about it! Off he went, but he has to travel through 10 miles of 'fly' (sleeping sickness) country, and I'm afraid his horse will die, but it can't be helped. Jones, who is coming from Namwold, is going to join Thomas as soon as possible, on his way to Barotseland.

The traders whose cattle have been stopped are in a bad way, and I feel very sorry for them. They buy all their supplies 'on tick' and depend on selling their cattle as soon as they arrive down south, to pay these bills. Now, the cattle are stopped and many may die, so there will be no funds to meet these commitments. Two of these chaps arrived here without food. Thomas was also short, so I gave him some and have been helping all the others as best I can. I have had to send down to Livingstone for more for myself.

Another 5,000 cattle were due to go 300 miles up the line, so I wired our new young vet, Armfield, to find and stop them. On Friday, he came down on the goods train with some lungs. I was meeting the train, to see if there was anything for me. Fortunately, I spotted him just as the train was leaving and he tossed the lungs to me. There is no doubt they have got the disease up there and news from Barotseland says, 'cattle are dying like flies'.

It is a job trying to get round the cattle, here, as they are in a 20-mile area, and I am at one end of it. So I've been on the go all the hours there are. Our next problem is to find grass and water for all the cattle in quarantine, as it takes about two acres to carry one beast at this season. I keep sending out to look for fresh grass, and hardly know what to do for the best.

A number of traders are camped here, and they're terribly down in the mouth. This is a very serious situation for the whole country. Things were bad enough as it was.

We've just heard of the sinking of the Lusitania: terrible!

20

Blushing Beneath His Tan

————⇒•◦◄⇐————

Livingstone
21st May 1915

A note only. Have just arrived, having been sent for, and a special car on the railway provided. I am going as hard as possible, am very fit but rather tired. I have to assist with a letter to the London board, per this mail, and it goes in three quarters of an hour! Hope you are all well. More next week.

The Hospital
Livingstone
31st May

You'll be surprised to be receiving a letter with the above address on it once more!

A few hours after I sent you that hurried note last week, I saw the Administrator. He told me a man had brought two horses to Livingstone, and asked me to look them over and buy them, as we wanted horses badly for this cattle trouble.

I jumped on one and had just put it to the gallop, when I found the saddle slipping. I came down between the forelegs, the pony fell over me and then kicked out, hitting me in the back. I was brought to the hospital and found, after an hour or so, that I couldn't walk for pain, so I was put to bed. The muscles in my back were torn, but nothing was broken and my spine seemed intact. I must say it gave me gyp for three or four days, but is much better now and I can sit propped up in bed. The doctor says I shall be all right in a week. It's a bit of bad luck, just when I'm so sorely needed elsewhere. The outbreak is very serious, and cattle are dying everywhere.

The week before the accident, I came back to Livingstone twice to see Sir Lawrence, and each time chased back to Senkobo on the

219

rail coach put at my disposal. I was also riding 40 or more miles a day examining cattle.

HE told me to find, and engage, twenty men to help with cattle examinations. So I sent wires up the line to every available and suitable European. I was out riding round the herds on Sunday and Monday, before getting the rail coach back to Livingstone that evening. I went in to see the secretary, had a long chat with him, then went out to try the two horses and here I am!

I feel quite fit, except I have pain whenever I move, but I'm doing a lot of paperwork, as the typist comes here and takes down the letters etc. Most of the messages I am getting tell of the disease spreading and of the alarm of the native population.

I hope you can read this. I cut my hand rather badly in my fall and it's heavily bandaged.

We have sent up country to all the senior indunas to come down to Livingstone, and as soon as I am fit enough to move, I and the Secretary for Native Affairs who is the senior official here, will see them all together to explain exactly what is happening and why. Litia will be among them. Not unreasonably, they cannot understand us shooting their cattle. Their herds are being quarantined, but it is a huge job.

Since writing the above, my clerk has been in to report another outbreak in a new area. I can tell you that I am not popular, as I've issued such stringent regulations. You will judge the seriousness of it all when I tell you that the penalty for acting contrary to these regulations is a fine of £100, or six months in jail, for each beast involved!

I must stop, but will write to catch the next mail.

The Hospital
Livingstone
7th June
I am still in here, but up and able to get about. I have to use a stick, and am strapped right round my middle.

Whilst here, I have had to write and cable to Southern Rhodesia, the Union of South Africa and the Belgian Congo, so perhaps it was something of a blessing that I could deal with it all in the calm of the ward. It has been good experience for me, having control of the whole country as far as cattle are concerned, and it has brought me to the attention of just about everybody. But I didn't quite realise what it all meant when I first discovered what was happening. HE, naturally, seeks advice from whomever is in charge of the department. I have had to devise the whole scheme, and if it doesn't work, I know who has to take the blame! Up till now, it seems to be going all right, but I know I have taken a risk. We haven't had one case outside the quarantine area I drew up and, although cattle are dying and are being shot in those areas, I am hoping we have got the problem cut off.

Although I'm so busy, and I suppose we're doing good work at the present, I'd give all I possess to get amongst things in France.

Livingstone
15th June
I left hospital on Saturday and came to live at The Bungalow, the government guest accommodation I stayed at before I first left for Sesheke. My back is greatly improved, and I can walk about, but I have it bound up, still.

The lung disease has broken out here, in Livingstone, and all this weekend I have been busy arranging transport for troops to Sesheke. I have so much to do, I don't know whether I am on my head or my heels!

21st June
I am now nearly all right again. I am still wearing a broad belt and whalebone support, but I am driving myself in a mule cart and doing a good many miles each day.

I have never hated this job so much as this afternoon, when I had to order a whole span of oxen to be shot. They belonged to an old man earning his living carrying goods to and from the station. His wagon was his whole life, and I don't know what he'll do. HE is going to help him I think, as I went to see him about it before dinner.

No word has yet reached us from Lane; I expect he's having a rough time up the river. Handling the natives over this affair is a big problem, and I hope things go well.

28th June
My last two or three letters have, I'm afraid, not been very interesting.

This disease is still a worrying problem. My advice was to shoot all infected cattle and also those which had recovered, as they remain a source of infection. There is no compensation paid here and, whilst the majority agree with the shooting of infected animals, many do not agree to shooting those that have recovered. It will run to many thousands, and will ruin a few people. You can imagine how I'm being criticised. However, I'm sticking to it as it's the only way to stamp out this disease. I also advised the stopping of all movement, and the formation of quarantine areas. Almost all transport, here, is by ox-wagon, and so everything is at a standstill.

I have never in my life before seen this disease. The last outbreak in England was 30 years ago, so it was a hellish job having to diagnose on one case at the first, but I knew I was right. I think the problem has come from Portuguese Africa. When we have got it cleared from the ranches, we shall have to start on the whole of Barotseland. How we shall manage things I just don't know. We can't go killing cattle wholesale, or we shall have the natives rising against us. The great Matabele rising followed an outbreak of cattle disease. Right up to Sesheke, then on up to Lewanika's place, the whole country is affected. Whole herds are being wiped out. We have just heard that Lane has arrived and found things in an awful mess. By not hesitating to shoot white men's cattle, we have given the natives a good example, but it won't be enough.

We're prosecuting everyone who breaks the regulations, and big fines are being imposed. Luckily, my new clerk Wardroper is first class, and he shields me from most who try to buttonhole me here. I see HE every day, and he's followed my advice on everything. Of course, he signs the orders.

I've been driving about the whole area: it's a rotten job shooting, and ordering cattle to be shot and burned, but is has to be done.

5th July
It's been a busy time and a worrying one. The police, themselves, were the first to be summoned, for letting their transport oxen stray,

and were fined £25. Last week, a trader was summoned and, as it was the first case here where cattle are concerned, a lot of interest was aroused. The defending solicitor is a farmer himself, and a bit of a prominent person. Jones and I both had to give evidence and, between us, were in the witness box for a day and a half. A good deal of mud was slung at me and at our department but, finally, the verdict was a £100 fine or six months in prison. As the man hadn't the money, off he went to jail. He is an elderly man, over 60, and there is, naturally, a good deal of feeling over the case.

I have dined with Colonel and Mrs Stennett twice lately and yesterday, with a friend from Salisbury, they joined me combining a little pleasure with business. I had to inspect some transport oxen, so we all drove out to see them, and then had a lunchtime picnic on the veldt. I am dining with the PMO (Dr May) tonight. I often go to them *en famille*, but tonight it's a real spread!

I have to change into dinner clothes every evening, as I never know when I shall be called to see HE, and after 7.30pm one is expected to be in that gear in Government House. (*War or no war, cattle crisis or not, the colonial routine never lets up!*)

12th July

Today and tomorrow, Rhodes' day and Founder's day, are holidays here, but the secretaries and our departments are still at work, as we are every Saturday and Sunday.

The Germans in West Africa have surrendered, but Maritz the Boer, with his rebels, has come right through close to Sesheke. Troops arrived yesterday by train to go after him. These are the men I was called in to help over transport. They couldn't use oxen because of the quarantine, so they've brought their own mules. They unloaded at my camp siding at Maramba, and are still getting their guns off. Col. Stennett, Major Gordon and five other of our officers are to go with them.

Lung disease rages and we estimate a loss, so far, of 11,000 cattle, but I feel another 50,000 native cattle will go in the future. It's a real problem.

I am trying to find time to get in a few drills with the volunteers, who are guarding the Falls Bridge to release the regulars for active service. The bridge is a vital Central African link, and is heavily guarded night and day.

I rode, yesterday, for the first time in seven weeks and felt none the worse for it, although I'm still in corset supports.

19th July 1915

Another week has gone and I am still here. The troops went off on Wednesday, but the chief decided I must stay. I fixed them up with medicines etc, and went out each day for three days to inspect their transport. Then I rode a few miles out with Col. Stennett and the Major and one of the medical officers who went with them. When I left them, I could have cried, I was so disappointed. I would have been useful to them in so many ways. I know the country so well. Major Murray, the senior staff officer, said, 'I do wish you could come, Smith'. They were an awfully good lot of officers and very nice fellows.

That night I dined with Mrs Stennett and her house guest, Mrs Lazard, to cheer them up, and again on Thursday I dined there. Mrs Lazard left by train to Salisbury on Friday, and I drove her and Mrs Stennett to the station and, afterwards, drove Mrs Stennett to the Drews (the Treasurer) with whom she is staying whilst her husband is away.

I have, today, found this lung disease amongst our own cattle here at Maramba. Thank goodness our new man, Brogan, is good at his work and a nice fellow.

The reports coming down from Lane, in Barotseland, are very bad. The disease is raging everywhere, and I shouldn't be surprised if they withdrew Lane and sent me. I know the language, which he doesn't, and the people, whilst he really should be at HQ, and not five weeks away by post.

26th July

This disease has been got under control in our European settler areas, but in the native parts it is raging furiously. A rumour, which seems to have some truth in it, says that it has broken out in the Musakubumbere country. This is another large native area with many thousands of cattle. The problem of the disease in the native parts of the country is causing a bit of unease and, if this district is affected, it will get a lot worse.

Our new man Brogan has gone up to Kalomo, beside the railway line, and Jones is about 20 miles in from the line, with about 2000 sick cattle. I have a lot of sickness here, in Livingstone, and have had to send for more mules from South Africa to do the transport.

I have been giving evidence in another prosecution this morning. This is the fourth, and Selby, the magistrate, said I was getting quite a frequent visitor! I hate running these people in, but it just has to be done. I fear this whole outbreak will ruin quite a number.

2nd August

It is August bank holiday, but I am still at the office. What with fighting on our northern border, the Germans so strong in German East Africa, the cattle sickness and all the distress over the war in Europe, people here are very worried, but most don't realise just how serious things are. HE is looking awfully ill, and has aged tremendously in the last three months.

Lady Wallace (HE's wife) has her sister staying, and she came riding with me on Saturday. She is French, and speaks very little English, so we had to use what few bits of each other's language we knew! She is an awfully good sort and very pretty. I am going to play tennis at the Beauforts this afternoon.

9th Aguust

The war news is none too good here. There are rumours that we are being pushed back from our borders. We are sending out reinforcements, and I have been told to arrange transport this morning. It's a five-to-six week journey for them, through a lot of tsetse-fly country. The campaign in German South West was a triumph of transport: the way they carried water and other supplies through that vast desert, was wonderful.

I was sworn in as a private of the Northern Rhodesia Rifles last week, and have to put in three drills a week. If I go off with any troops I shall be given a commission as a veterinary officer, but if it comes to a sudden scrap, I don't want to be shot as a civilian! The Secretary and the Treasurer are both privates and are being shouted at and drilled by a sergeant, who is a clerk in the Treasury Office!

I got a wire from Stennett at Sesheke, where he is using my old house as his HQ, asking me to send some 'Vitelizo': guess what that is? It begins with a 'w'... whisky! I sent if off by runner without delay!

17th August

Things are very glum on our border. The Germans were reinforced and gave our men a right going over. Major O'Sullivan, the 6'4" Irishman who 'commanded' our captured German motorboat at Sesheke on our picnic/river patrol, has been wounded. One hundred and fifty white troops are being rushed up tomorrow, and another 150 next week, together with the native police, who have been recruited and trained since war started. It will take them five weeks, hard going, as they have some field guns with them. Stennett and his men arrived back from Sesheke on Sunday. I have been expecting all their horses, and will then send them back to Southern Rhodesia, as they'll not live on our northern border because of tsetse-flies. Wardroper, my new clerk, has been made a second lieutenant and is going with 80 native police, and a number of other men from the administration who can be spared. They have been told to make forced marches all the way north.

23rd August

I leave here on Saturday for Kafue, to go to the Farmers' Association meeting. HE is going as well, and I shall be able to travel in his special coach. It's rather nice, as it is put in a siding, and we can sleep and eat in it. We arrive at Kafue on Sunday, go to the meeting on Monday, have our dinner at 8.00pm and train back at 10.00pm, arriving some time on Tuesday. I expect I shall get a hot reception, as the transport of all grain has been stopped, and the farmers cannot get their mealies away.

Lane is expected back in about a month, and I have just had a letter from Thomas, who is in charge of cattle near Sesheke. Over

500 have died, or been killed, and all the lions for miles around have put in an appearance. Thomas got a big male ten yards from his tent, and Henry Dillon, a native commissioner, had an awful time with three of them at once, four days ago.

3rd September
No chance to write last week.

It was jolly comfy in the special coach, with a dining and a sitting room. I had a wee bedroom, and a dressing room to myself. In the siding, our telegraphist was busy sending and receiving messages and, as the secretary couldn't be spared from Livingstone, I acted as a bit of a dogsbody. We had our own servants, and I had a valet!

The senior officials came to see us off, also Lady Wallace and her sister. I think I told you they are French. At the station, her sister gave me a bunch of roses, and I nearly had a fit. Quite a few of the officials were there, and I haven't heard the end of that by a long chalk, I'm sure!

John Smith has dropped his guard for just a moment in relating this charming, and typically French, episode. He has always written of his social life in pretty bland phrases but increasingly, we are hearing of the only two eligible young ladies in the area. One was the Beaufort daughter, who rides with him and attends his picnics; the other has recently appeared, his chief's sister-in-law. The latter, suddenly, presents him with a bunch of roses on the very public railway platform, as he sets out on his first official trip with his chief, and in front of a crowd of officials and their wives gathered to see them off. One can imagine the delight of the onlookers at this unexpected diversion! Livingstone's social climate was heady and rarefied: everyone knew everything about everybody! John Smith, still only 32 and unmarried, was good company and popular, and had managed a not-altogether-undramatic couple of years' service. It would have been strange if he had not found favour with one or more of the unattached ladies. But, oh! How he must have blushed!

When we arrived at Kafue on Sunday, HE told me not to go to the meeting, as they would badger me with too many questions. So I put in a report, and then the association committee came for a meeting with HE and myself afterwards. There was a dinner, with dancing, and we managed to stay until 11.30pm. All Monday I acted as secretary, as various deputations came to the coach for meetings. We were eventually hitched up to the passenger train at 10.00pm and arrived back at Livingstone at 8.00am on Tuesday. We were met by the same crowd of officials, plus wives, as saw us off. (*And what did our hero say to his French admirer this time, again in front of the whole administration hierachy?!*)

On the train was a district officer named Bellis. He has sleeping sickness, and there is no hope for him. Poor chap, he's convinced he will get better, but he won't. HE made a point of going down the train to comfort him.

The High Commissioner for Southern Rhodesia, Lord Buxton, and Lady Buxton should have come on an official visit this weekend, but he's not well enough. Their son and daughter arrived this morning in their place. Lady Wallace is giving a small picnic for eight, in the launch on the Zambezi, and has asked me. I shall, therefore, give myself a day's holiday. There is a dinner in the evening, and the Buxton children leave on Tuesday.

HE is awfully good company when not on official business, and we had some long chats. He came stalking into my room on the coach, in his pyjamas, at about 6.00am on Tuesday, to ask me about something or other. He's always addressed as 'Sir' but, when alone, likes you to drop that.

Another batch of native troops has left for the front this morning; they've trekked all the way from Barotseland, and now face another 600-mile tramp. One of the officers, Graham, said it was like being a Cook's tourist!

20th September
Sorry to have sent you such a short note last week. I had a busy time and then, on Sunday, a party of us went to the Zambezi. We canoed over to one of the islands, had lunch and slacked about until 5.00pm, when we had tea and came home. Mrs May, the PMO's wife, gave the lunch. It may seem funny to you to have picnics on Sunday, but the men cannot get away on any other day, and it isn't good to stay indoors in this climate. Church service doesn't start until 8.30pm.

This is an interesting couple of lines. John Smith is suddenly conscious that his family might think he was not 'keeping the sabbath' as he should. So he invents the health angle and adds that he would have been back in time to go to church which, in all fairness, he almost certainly did.

On Monday, I went to dinner at Government House, and there was a small dance afterwards. On Tuesday, Wednesday and Thursday, I was riding around inspecting cattle in the afternoons, after mornings in the office. Mrs May, who gave the picnic, has a girl from Jo'burg staying, and either she or Mademoiselle Duboc (*his admirer*) rode with me. On Friday and Saturday, I played tennis and, on the latter evening, I went to a dance at the Beauforts (*his other admirer*). So, you see, I had a good week.

The women are all beginning to feel the heat now, and will soon be off to the Cape to avoid the worst of it. Lane should be back, and I hope to get in a short tour before the rains, proper, begin again.

I wish to goodness I could get away home to join up. I mentioned it to HE again, on the train, and he said, 'you will just stay where you are, Smith'.

11th October

Lane is expected back today, or tomorrow, and I have sent a mule cart to meet him on the road. Mrs Lane will be glad to get back as, apparently, she has been miserable on tour.

Things are very unsettled in the Sesheke district. Litia refused to have his cattle touched, after he promised me to have them inoculated. Venning is at Mongu, and Ingram has no hold over Litia. Lane telegraphed from Sesheke, on his way down, to say that Litia now wanted his cattle inoculated in a hurry!

On Saturday night, we had a very lively evening at Government House. About 25 of us went to dinner, and had some singing and dancing. At midnight, we had to stop (it being Sunday) and so about eight of us went back to the Stennetts, and stayed until about 2.00am. It was a treat to be out in the cool of the night.

25th October

I am going to live at Maramba for a week or two, to inoculate some new mules against horse-sickness. After that I am going on tour in the Sesheke district.

Lady Wallace, her sister (*Mademoiselle Duboc*), and two or three others of the ladies are away to the Cape today. We're going to see them off at the station; Mrs May and three others left last week, and they'll be away, now, until after Christmas. Lady Beaufort and her daughter also leave today, so Livingstone really will be empty.

We had a jolly outing last Saturday. It was full moon, and fourteen of us went to the river by the rail trolley, after dinner. There was the Government House party, four of the young married couples, Dr Ellacombe and me. We got to the Zambezi at 9.15pm and then went upstream by dugouts. My boys paddled us (I never engage a boy unless he's a good paddler). We had a topping supper on the bank and arrived back at the landing stage at 12.30am, then home by trolley. It was a nice outing, and ends everything for some months now, as all the womenfolk will be away.

21

Death of the Chief

Back again. I shall probably be here for about three weeks to inoculate these mules. Weather has been stifling: on Thursday, however, at about 10.30pm, a very violent storm sprang up with the most awful thunder and lightning. It was really terrible, and I thought something must give. Suddenly came the rain, and it poured for 20 minutes. That, and two showers since, have greatly helped things.

On Saturday, I woke with a splitting headache, and the sharpest bout of malaria I've had for some time. I got blankets piled over me, had a three-hour sweat and then took a big dose of quinine. I slept nearly all night, and awakened better yesterday. Then I slept eleven-and-a-half hours last night, and am practically myself today.

9th November

I have to go to the Rhodesian Cattle Company's place, to see about an outbreak of disease. I leave by goods train at 8.00pm tonight and should arrive at the siding at 6.00am tomorrow. So, it's a nice night in a rocky guards van! Then it's 27 miles from the railway to the homestead. I expect to be there for a couple of days, and shall then try to get the goods train back on Friday, as there's only one passenger train a week.

Yesterday, the Lanes came to lunch with me, and I think it was one of the hottest days I can ever remember, 113° in the shade at 10.30am, and goodness knows what it got to at about 3.00pm.

15th November
I left here by goods train on Monday at 8.30 in the evening. It was a rotten 14-hour journey, with no sleep. They have a car at that ranch and it met me at the station. As all the rivers are dry, we could motor the whole 27 miles to the ranch, but it was jolly bumpy crossing the river beds, down and up the banks! On arrival, we got horses and rode out about 30 miles. The next day we did 40 miles in the saddle, and then on Thursday, I started inoculating. The trouble was anthrax, and quite a few beasts were dead.

I've never seen such a place for game: there were thousands about. It's also a great place for lions. We ran into a lioness and two cubs, and she bolted off as fast as the cubs could run. I left the ranch at 4.00pm on Thursday, got to the siding, slept in a shed wrapped in my blanket until 7.00am the next morning, and caught the passenger train back.

At the ranch, I saw some of the bulls I inoculated two-and-a-half years ago, also two of the boys who worked with me then. They spoke to me in the language I first learned, here at Maramba. It seemed strange, as I seldom use it, being very much better in Sekololo. The mules I have been inoculating are now reacting and some are pretty sick. I just hope they won't die.

22nd November
The rains have come to cool things down a bit, and the grass will soon begin to sprout. It is badly wanted as the cattle are nearly starving. In quite a few places the natives have very little food, but it's their own fault for not planting enough.

6th December
We're all rather worried about this proposed amalgamation of Northern and Southern Rhodesia. Sir Starr Jameson has come out to order economies, and we hear that the amalgamation is likely to be effected on 1st April next year. There would be one administration, one headquarters at Salisbury and we, up here, would be swamped. The senior officials would have to be compensated or pensioned, and the junior ones would get absolutely nowhere. There are 30,000 whites in Southern Rhodesia, whereas there are

not over 2000 in the whole of Northern Rhodesia. I am supposed to be second-in-command of the Veterinary Department here, but would be thirty-second there!

13th December
I've only been to Livingstone in the evening once in five weeks. I went to dine with the Lanes, and then on to the annual meeting of the Club afterwards. Then I rode home in the dark.

Horse-sickness, which arrives every rainy season, is here again. I had a new horse, as well as Champagne. He was perfectly all right at 5.00pm yesterday, but was dead at 8.00pm. That shows how sudden it can be.

20th December
I can hardly believe it's Christmas week. I suppose I shall have my Christmas dinner all on my lonesome at Maramba!

On Wednesday, we had a terrific storm, and two inches of rain fell in two-and-a-half hours, the first inch in 22 minutes!

I am going, this morning, to Livingstone to see Mrs Venning. She arrived yesterday with her baby, Norah, and Mrs Berringer. All the women in Barotseland have been ill, and will have to leave the country. I believe the Venning's baby is really bad and nearly a skeleton.

Livingstone
10th January 1916
Last week I was in Lusaka, where I had been called to see a sick horse. Back here, I was told to stay in Livingstone until the BSAC directors' visit was over. They all arrived last week, Sir Starr Jameson, Mr Malcolm, General Northy and his suite, General Edwards and all the secretaries etc.

Saturday was the annual dinner at the Club, and we had all this crowd there. Jameson spoke, and there seems little doubt that amalgamation is coming. Today, there are deputations about it, and, tomorrow, the Farmers' Association come to complain about their treatment over the cattle disease. As I was in charge here during the worst of the outbreak, I suppose I shall get it hot as, last week, the newspapers went for the Veterinary Department and, up the line, I encountered nothing else. I saw HE on Friday, and prepared him for all I had heard. Lane and I are going to the meeting.

Yesterday, Sunday, all Livingstone and his wife were at the parade ground. HE and the two generals reviewed our corps. For the first time we wore tunics and full kit. By gum, it was hot! We paraded at 10.00am with the band, and were reviewed at 10.30, which meant standing to attention for 20 minutes. At the march-past, I found myself left-hand marker. It wasn't too easy to march dead straight whilst doing 'eyes right' but, with a bit of squinting, it went off all right. We were told we had done well. The rush on cold drinks afterwards was a thing to see!

The horse I went to see in Lusaka has been destroyed.

17th January
The directors left on Friday evening. They've been receiving deputations all the time. The farmers and the traders came on Thursday, and the meeting lasted all day. Lane and I were present. They had a lawyer as spokesman, and he cross-examined us about everything, and called us all sorts of names. I had to answer for the action taken at HQ and, as it was the first time I'd had the chance to defend myself, I made the most of it. A lot of their allegations were absolute lies and, in others, the truth was twisted. A report in the local paper, the *Livingstone Mail*, said I gave 'a lengthy and cogent explanation of what was done and why'. As compensation has been refused, I understand a test case is to be heard in the High Court in the UK. Anyway, we've received a letter from the directors complimenting our department on the way we'd handled the disease outbreak.

John Smith, a young man of only 32, had been in the territory for just two-and-a-half-years. Many of the ranchers affected by his actions were old enough to be his father, and had been in Northern Rhodesia for up to 20 years. It is not surprising that he was the object of their wrath. It is also obvious that Lane, who did not have the depth of knowledge needed for this situation, was deliberately sent off to Barotseland, so that our vet could be available for the Administrator at HQ. John Smith was the obvious choice to go north — both

Venning and Lewanika expected him – but he was considered too valuable in Livingstone to be allowed to be out of touch for all those weeks.

27th January

We are expecting some big fighting here when the British East Africa advance starts. A naval contingent went through here some months ago, with small gunboats. They walked 600 miles from the railhead, with their dismantled boats on ox wagons, and reached Lake Tanganyika. They assembled their boats, and have already beaten the largest of the German gunboats on the lake, and will soon have command of it. In consequence, our land forces will be more mobile.

The transport question is most difficult. They are now going to try and get through with motors, but I doubt whether that will be managed. Thousands of carriers have been going through, and there isn't a bit of food left on the road. (*At the height of the military activity, there were in the region of 260,000 carriers working for the army.*) A native boy can carry a load of 60lbs, but his provisions for the journey amount to a load of 65lbs. Most of the going is through tsetse fly country. We have sent thousands of oxen with wagons. Many died from trypanosomiasis; the remainder were eaten by native troops on arrival, and the wagons left stranded on the border.

31st January

Yesterday, I went to the river and pulled about a mile-and-a-half up the Zambezi with a man who owns a nice little boat. We found a shady spot on an island, had tea, and pulled back just before sundown. Miss Beaufort came with us.

7th February

We have been without any mail for a month but, last Saturday, three lots arrived at once.

Prices are jumping at an alarming rate: tea is now 7/- per pound, coffee 5/-, eggs 3/6 per dozen. So I sent my messenger to buy some fowls at 1/- each, and am now getting six-to-eight eggs a week.

We have now lost nine of our horses through sleeping sickness and only have three left, including Champagne, my old pony, who seems able to stick anything.

There was a church parade of the volunteers at 8.30am yesterday. The church is at the top of the hill, and we were in a right state marching in tunics and full equipment. We sang 'Onward Christian Soldiers' and Hornby, next to me, whispered, 'They didn't have to march in 115° in the shade'!

14th February

News arrived, yesterday, that old Lewanika died eight days ago. I feel very sad, as he was a nice old boy, and a real native gentleman. He's had great influence on the Barotse people, as he realised that the white relationship was for their good. His death couldn't have come at a worse time: famine, cattle disease and war, all at once. What will happen now is impossible to say as Litia, who succeeds him, is not the same type at all. I suppose he will leave Sesheke and go to Lealui. I do wish I had been in Barotseland just now.

I shall never forget my meetings with Lewanika: only a month ago he sent me greetings. I think I shall give my Barotse boys – my senior messenger, Matapi, is the son of a big induna up there – an ox to kill for him, as they have none of their own down here.

Although busy at the office, I still get tennis and riding in the afternoons. Mademoiselle Duboc is back from the Cape, and we ride together. All the ladies are back and, after the cool down there, they are feeling the heat.

21st February

The cattle sickness has become very bad around Sesheke; Litia has been sending urgent messages about it, and the vet who relieved Venning has been worried to death, sending telegrams daily. HE decided, on Friday, that Lane must manage here for a bit, and that I must go and see what I can do, as I know the people and the language. The trouble is, now, to get there and tour afterwards, as no rain has fallen and the people are practically starving. I am trying to arrange to get a lot of food to the river, 27 miles away, and then get a barge and take it up to Sesheke. I shall have to take every bit of food for my carriers, as not a grain can be had from the villages I shall pass through. I hope to get good shooting and that will help me out a lot.

I am looking forward to going on tour again, but am rather worried about the food problem. However, I've been in a tight spot for food before and shall get through somehow. I've been told to go for a month, but it will take me much longer. I expect it will be a three-month affair, depending entirely on how I find things.

I hear that old Lewanika's funeral rites and ceremonies will last two or three months. Of course, the old chap will be buried by now: they have some primitive embalming process.

On Thursday last, it was Mademoiselle Duboc's birthday and we had a dinner at Government House, quite a lively affair. Yesterday, I went to the Falls on a picnic with Mr and Mrs Marshall – he is acting Administrator whilst Sir Lawrence and Lady Wallace are away in Southern Rhodesia – Mademoiselle Duboc, Miss Beaufort and Dr Ellacombe. We had a mule cart and I drove four-in-hand. The Falls people sent over lunch. I have never seen the Falls look so well before. There is a large amount of water going over, but not sufficient to cause too much spray. Sometimes, it is impossible to see anything because of the spray. It was really a magnificent sight, and we had lunch overlooking the Eastern Cataract.

We have to smile at the innocence with which John Smith writes of his picnic party. He makes a point of explaining that he 'drove four-in-hand'. This means working the eight reins leading back from all four mules. The more usual drill is for only the two leading mules to be steered by rein, the other pair, the wheelers, just following. It is obvious, with both his admirers on board (and with the Marshalls as chaperones) he was showing off his prowess as a driver of mules.

There can have been no case of 'how happy could I be with either, t'were other dear charmer away' as, so often, he has both of Livingstone's eligible young ladies (Duboc and Beaufort) in tow at the same time, and in the same place. Poor John Smith, no sooner had his lady friends returned from the Cape, than he is ordered away for some weeks. Having previously told us how he longed to be able to go north, he is now surprisingly unenthusiastic. It isn't hard to guess the reason!

On the Zambezi
28th February
In my last letter I told you I was ordered to Sesheke. I meant to write another, but was prevented.

We suddenly heard, by runner, that Mr McKinnon, the resident in Barotseland, had been taken very ill and was coming down the Zambezi to return to England. He asked for a doctor to go north to meet him. I had arranged with the transport people for a boat to be on the river, ready for me, so I was asked to take the doctor with me. This meant setting off immediately. I got hold of an ox-wagon, loaded it with my gear, and started out to get to my boat with all speed. I left that same evening, travelled all night, rested men and beasts during the heat of the day, and travelled all through the second night. I got to the river at the same time as the doctor, he having come through, in one day, with a buckboard and six mules.

They had to get paddlers for me in a great hurry and, when I saw them, I nearly had a fit. There wasn't a proper paddler amongst them. When I first told them to lift my gear on board, they took no notice. However, I had a few words with them, as did my messengers, and now they jump to it if I so much as whisper. It has taken me three-and-a-half days to get to this point. I should have done it in two. If I hadn't had two really good paddlers in my messengers, I should have been in a right old mess. You should just hear Matapi telling them what he thinks of them. I dare not tell you what he said, but I quite agree with him!

The doctor and I met McKinnon and his wife the first day out, and we camped together. He is awfully ill. He lies on a mattress, under an awning in the boat, and has to be lifted out onto the bank. We all had dinner together, and Mrs McKinnon produced a magnum of champagne. I don't know what they had to celebrate, perhaps it was just the relief at being in good hands that prompted it.

I'm afraid this letter is badly typed, but the boat is rocking and it is some time since I used my machine.

I had a weird experience two days ago. We came to the Mambova rapids, and I decided to walk round, whilst the boat was being taken through, to try and shoot a pheasant. Matapi and I set off and, after going about 100 yards, I turned towards a patch of grass. Just as I walked into it, a leopard jumped up right under my feet. It stared at me, snarling and spitting, and I was so surprised I couldn't move. It was exactly as if we were acting out a tableau for a couple of seconds, then the leopard turned and bolted into the bush. Fortunately, I had stood stock-still — with fright! — and just gaped in horror. I had sense enough to let it get away without firing, as I only had a shotgun, and that would have made it mad!

As the leopard made off, I turned to look at Matapi and he, too, was standing stock-still, with his mouth open. He looked at me and then whispered, rather than said, 'mawei'! This is quite untranslatable, but is the expression used to convey utter amazement and incredulity. It is in the saying that the effect lies: the sounds seem to fall reluctantly, and very slowly from the mouth, ending with a jerk on the last vowel. It can be quite dramatic.

After this, I felt quite shaky for a minute or two. It had all been so sudden. Then I recovered and, sending for my heavy rifle, set off after the leopard. But I never found him. I do wish I could have got him, as he was a real beauty. I suppose he was asleep, and was just as surprised as I was. One more step, and I would have landed well and truly on top of him!

Later that day, when we were camped, I heard Matapi recounting this episode with much dramatic effect and excitement. He told his amazed and admiring audience, 'The leopard was as big as a donkey, but the Morena (that's me) simply spoke to it, and it ran away'.

And so, yet another instance of my, supposedly, powers of magic was broadcast and taken on board by my boys!

This episode cannot be allowed to pass without the author being taken to task for not heeding his own advice. In one of his earlier letters, he recounted the alarming experience the Paris Evangelical Mission team, with poor M Arnot, had when M Ellenberger, having shot a guinea fowl, found it snatched from under his feet by a lion. John Smith wrote, 'He disobeyed one of the rules of survival in that he did not take a rifle as well as a shotgun, and did not take some natives, armed with assegais, with him. In similar circumstances, I would expect to take one, or perhaps two, messengers and a couple of natives, all with assegais.' Well, well, well!

Mention in the leopard story, of the powers of magic with which John Smith was supposedly endowed leads, naturally, to a yarn he wrote of later. On one of his river trips, he was using a large dugout lent to him by Lewanika; it had 12 paddlers.

We had pulled up to the water's edge, and were all resting on the bank when the induna, or chief of the district, who was with the party, asked for permission for all the natives to 'go to greet Mwana Bingi' (literally, Son of Bingi). I agreed they could go, although I had no idea to what they referred. Off they all went, except Tolani and my personal boys, none of whom was from the Barotse tribe.

I was intrigued by this sudden and unexpected request. Why should my natives wish to meet this unknown character and why, in the normal custom of the country, did he not come to greet me? I determined to find out for myself and so followed my boys, keeping a safe distance from them, and well out of sight.

Eventually I caught up, still unseen, and found them all sitting round a large hole, rhythmically clapping their hands and staring intently into the depths. In due course, the session came to an end, and they returned quietly and, apparently, in a spirit of great contentment, to our camp. I lingered on, behind some bushes, and when the coast was clear had a good look at the hole. It was nothing unusual, just an old hole, dug into the earth, a good many yards across and 20 or so feet deep. It was considerably overgrown with grass and scrub.

Getting back to my tent, I called up one of my senior boys and asked why they had wanted to go and greet Mwana Bingi.

This was his reply.

Long ago, the valley we are in was inhabited by Mwana Bingi and his people. They were prosperous and owned many cattle. One day, word came that an enemy, in very large numbers, was quite close. Realising that they had little or no hope of surviving, Mwana Bingi and his followers decided to go down the large hole, over there, until the danger passed. Every living human, men, women and children, all went down and took all their belongings with them. Suddenly, they remembered that they had left their cattle 'up top'; they clambered out and tried to drive the beasts down the hole, but they stampeded. Mwana Bingi decided to change the cattle into birds, into egrets.

The enemy appeared but, finding a deserted village without people or cattle, proceeded on its way. The villagers then felt it would be safe to climb out of their hiding place but this time, inexplicably, they were unable to scale the sides of the hole.

The Marotsi, (the local tribe from whom my paddlers came) believe the villagers are still down there below. They say they can hear the women stamping grain, and the others going about their daily tasks. It seems that, each evening, the egrets fly down the hole, change back into cattle, are milked and then fly out again. As proof of this story, I was told to notice how the egrets continually circled the area, and flew over the plain, now safely grazed by large herds of healthy cattle.

The last part of this charming tale is certainly true as, wherever there are cattle in Central Africa, there are lesser egrets, the explanation being that the birds feed on the ticks brushed from the cattle by the scrub and grasses.

But the story is gospel to the Marotsi, and all passing the hole call and greet Mwana Bingi and his subterranean people.

I'm going to make a big effort to reach Sesheke today, but the current is very strong against us. The McKinnons had the most magnificent set of paddlers I have ever seen. They had two barges with 20 in each. Litia will have provided them with his own state barge paddlers.

The news of Lewanika's death reached Livingstone in a most extraordinarily short time, by boat. Four boys, in a fast dugout, did the 370 miles in four days! That sounds impossible, but it's true. They paddled, virtually non-stop, for 20 hours; that included shooting the rapids and walking round the falls with their dugout. Then they had to run the last 30-odd miles. It's an astonishing feat! By comparison, the McKinnons, with 40 picked paddlers, took nine days on the river.

Sesheke
5th March

I arrived here on Wednesday last, having come right through after typing the first part of this letter to you. We paddled all day and two hours after sunset, to arrive at 9.00pm. I was really glad to be here; it hasn't altered one bit. Palmer has taken Venning's place and Ingram is out on tour, so there are just the two of us, and I expect to start touring, myself, in a day or two. Hundreds of his retinue have gone north with Litia, so the area is quite deserted.

This seems an appropriate place to describe what happened at Lewanika's death. John Smith pieced together the details and wrote the whole story up later.

On Lewanika's death, a vast multitude of natives from Lealui dug an enormously deep and wide hole, just outside the township. Natives don't use spades as we know them, but a kind of long-handled drag hoe. The spoils will have been carried up in wicker baskets, and spread around the surrounding area. The size of the hole can be appreciated, when I say that a large sort of house was then built in it. On completion, Lewanika's body was placed inside the 'house', together with every single one of his possessions bar one, the uniform he had worn at the coronation of King Edward VII, as this is probably regarded as being a state robe. Into the house, with the body, went all his ivory, carvings, trophies, clothes and the presents he had collected over a very long and eventful life. Having seen many of Lewanika's priceless possessions around his buildings, I can only feel deeply sad that they will have been left to rot and be devoured by white ants. They will stay there, as it is inconceivable that anyone would dare to try and steal any of them: death, and an extremely unpleasant one at that, would be the reward.

When one considers the heat in this country, one can imagine the speed with which this whole operation was conducted; it will have taken some hours rather than some days.

As soon as every single one of the old man's possessions had been taken down into the hole, it was thatched over with an enormous and elaborate roof built by the most skilled of the Barotse reed-workers.

Whilst all this was being rushed along, other of his people were rounding up his thousands of cattle, many of them extremely rare and valuable, and slaughtering them. Likewise, all his rivercraft were sunk in the Zambezi. Only the *Naliquanda*, the Barotse state barge, was saved.

The ceremonies and mourning, extending throughout Barotseland, lasted for two months, and until Litia moved up to Lealui to pick up the reins as Paramount Chief, taking the title, Yeta III.

Lewanika seized the throne in 1884 as a young man, and killed everyone who did not support him. He trained his people to be a wonderful fighting nation, and conquered all the tribes as far away as the Congo, and up to the borders of Tanganyika. They all paid tribute to him. 'The tusk that touches the ground', that is the tusk of the biggest elephant, or leader of the herd, was given to him.

When Lewanika grew more mature, and began to have contact with the handful of Britons who ventured up to that part of Africa, he decided to ask for British supervision and protection. And so Barotseland became a protectorate, under the chartered company, which arrangement continued until Northern Rhodesia became a crown colony.

I had a great liking and respect for Lewanika which, I am conceited enough to think, was reciprocated. On a number of occasions, after completing our official business, I would stay on and chat to him about this and that. I, by then, knew enough of the local dialect to be able to converse directly with him and, as the occasions were then private, we dispensed with the interpreter and the rest of the formalities and etiquette. I also felt I could ask him questions which it would have been inappropriate to bring up with a third person present.

He would tell me of the fights he had been in, as well as of the battles he had commanded. He would speak slowly, and use words he was sure I would have learned. He told me he had two rules in war: never fight when the other side wants to, in other words, always try to spring a surprise; do everything to terrorise the non-combatants, burn villages and crops etc, so that the women and old men, left behind, will do their best to persuade the fighting men to make peace.

When I received orders to leave Mongu, I went to Lealui to bid farewell to the old man. I had an inexplicable feeling that we would not meet again. I hoped to be allowed to return to England to join up, and Lewanika was already of an age when he could slip away at any time.

We had a long conversation, quite alone, and he then went out for a moment and returned with a flyswitch with a beautifully carved ebony handle, inset with ivory. It was my parting present as, it seemed, he had feelings similar to mine. It so happened, I had one for him too. I had, some months earlier, felt I would like to give him something, but could not think what on earth I could get, as it would have to come up from South Africa or from England. For some reason, I settled on a compass, which I ordered from a catalogue sent up from the Cape. It was rather a handsome job in silver.

So, as he gave me the switch, I was ready with the compass. He studied it for ages and then asked what it was. I explained that the 'indunas' of the big ships which sailed to England (like the Union Castle boat he had sailed in to go to King Edward's coronation) all had compasses to find the way. One needle, wherever they were, always pointed to England (may the Astronomer Royal forgive me!), and so they followed the pointer and arrived safely. He was delighted. It seemed he had always wondered, since his voyage, just how they found their way when out of sight of land, and now all was clear! I heard, later, that the compass went everywhere with him, and that on the Zambezi, in the *Naliquanda*, he ordered that it be set up before him.

On this rather sad occasion, Lewanika insisted on accompanying me to the outer gates of his compound. There we shook hands and said, 'Saila fo', which is the special farewell only used when it is suspected the parting will be for a very long time, or forever.

I mounted Champagne and rode away. Some little way off, I turned and waved, and he waved back. He continued to stand there, amongst hundreds of his people prostrate on the ground, until I could see him no more. We had, indeed, parted for ever.

Lewanika, as a younger man, did many deeds which we should regard as terribly cruel, and anyone who opposed him was removed by extremely unpleasant means. His own brother, in the early years of his reign, had plotted against him to seize the throne.

He was then put in a small enclosure, just outside Lewanika's living hut, and left to starve in the great heat. It was, no doubt, a dramatic deterrent to others who might have had thoughts along the same lines. It was, also, an example of the cruelty practised only a few years before the times of which I am writing.

There had, too, been a most barbaric practice which had ended when the British gained control of Barotseland. Until then, on the death of a chief, his wives had been trussed up and secured in the 'funeral house', together with the rest of his chattels, and left there to die. This seems an unimaginably cruel way to demonstrate respect. Happily, this was no longer the custom when Lewanika died in 1916, but he had known times when it was. Barbarism of this order was in the only-too-recent past.

Lewanika had fought, literally, for his throne, and had to hold it. He ruled, at first, over a country of lawless and savage people, and had no option than to do so by fear: that was the only rule his people knew. At the same time, he did everything in his power to better the way of life for all. He truly had their welfare at heart. He never unduly taxed his subjects, and brought about many changes, in custom and culture, which were for the good. As he grew older, his position was established, and it was not so much by power that he ruled. He became their 'Morena', and was something quite apart from the ordinary man. To say that he was looked upon as some sort of god would not be correct, for the Barotse would not understand such a term; but there is no doubt that he was seen as something more than mortal. He was honest, straightforward and utterly fearless.

Central Africa has witnessed the end of an era.

Sesheke
8th March 1916
I am waiting for carriers from the district I got them from before. I expect them any day.

I am afraid it is going to be a hard tour for water and food. The countryside is all parched and burnt up, and the pools and streams quite dry. Goodness alone knows what will happen to the natives and their cattle for the next eight months, until the rains are due again. I am cutting down my kit, so as to have as few carriers as possible because of the shortage of food, but will still have about 24.

I told you we stopped all movement of cattle out here, but we're going to have to relax these restrictions, or the herds will die of thirst. That, in turn, will almost certainly undo much of the good we have achieved in cutting down the disease.

I really can't decide what to do about my future. If I say I'm going in June, they can't stop me, as my agreement will have run out. I really want a change. The doctors will, ordinarily, only allow men to stay two-and-a-half years at a time. I've been here nearly three. I've had a good deal of malaria and other things and, were I to agree to stay on, it would mean another year at least.

I simply don't know what to do for the best.

I hope you are all keeping well.

From your loving son,

John.

Those were the last words John Smith was to write from Africa for several years. They were to prove highly prophetic, as we shall shortly see.

22

The Mosquito Has the Last Bite

John Smith was not to put pen to paper again in letters from Africa to his family in Wigan for over five years. The proboscis of the female mosquito saw to that. As my father wrote, years later, 'I was, by now, thoroughly soaked with malaria'.

No contemporary account of what happened to him after he sealed up his letter dated 8th March 1916 exists, so we must rely on the account he wrote later, and on the explanation he gave in answers to questions I put to him over the years.

It seems that, in the second week of March, at Sesheke, he was again struck down with a particularly virulent attack of malaria, having recovered from his last sharp attack only four months earlier. Palmer, the district officer then at Sesheke, became thoroughly alarmed and decided my father could not possibly recover, properly, without medical attention. So he fixed for Matapi, the two other messengers and some paddlers to take him back to Livingstone.

Runners were sent off to arrange for their barge to be met by an ox-wagon and a doctor at Katombora. And so, for the second time, our extremely-unwell veterinary officer was paddled and carried back to the hospital at HQ. There, he was given a thorough going-over by two doctors, who declared him unfit for any further service in the territory. He was to be sent back to the UK as fast as possible, to be treated by specialists to clear his system of malaria and to rebuild his health, generally, after the effects of the tropical diseases he had suffered from over the past three years.

Judge Beaufort, his mentor and local champion was, by fortunate chance, called back urgently to England, and volunteered to escort John Smith down to the Cape and onto the Union Castle liner *Saxon*, for the voyage home. The judge, with characteristic kindness and generosity, 'nursed' my father through another horrendous four days on the train, and then 21 more at sea. He was so weak and debilitated that he had to spend most of the time in his bunk, but the judge went to all lengths to help him get what benefit he could from the sea voyage.

In April, RMS *Saxon* docked at Southampton. John Smith senior met his son and took him straight into the care of the Liverpool School of Tropical Medicine, in whose hands he was to remain for the next four months.

23

'Doing His Bit'

J ohn Smith, out in Africa, had fretted that he was not able to
join in the war and 'do his bit'. Although he could acknow-
ledge he was making a useful contribution, like most 30-year-
olds, he believed he should be in France with the rest of his
generation. Now, it looked as if he would be.

But he was still a sick man, soaked with malaria, seriously under-
weight and with a system thoroughly poisoned by tropical disease,
he needed to be tended by medical specialists for some months.
The Liverpool School of Tropical Medicine set about getting him
fit, while he impatiently cooled his heels and badgered medical
and army authorities alike. By the summer of 1916, he had
persuaded both that he could get into uniform, and was
commissioned as a lieutenant in the Army Veterinary Corps. His
medical board, however, restricted him to home service for at least
six months.

He was now appointed adjutant of the Army remount depot at
Aldershot, the largest reception unit for army horses in the UK.
Teams of veterinary surgeons scoured the land for horses to buy,
suitable for the needs of the army on all its fronts and, having made
the purchase, dispatched them to Aldershot for acclimatisation and
basic training. The depot also took in hundreds of sick and
wounded horses from France and rehabilitated them, prior to
sending them back for further service.

This job might have been made for him: he had a great deal
of experience of horses and, very recently, had been involved in a
major administrative operation with animals.

It is difficult to appreciate, in our world today, that motors were
only just being introduced to the army and that horses were
needed, in tens of thousands, to pull guns, ammunition litters,
supply wagons, ambulances, in short, any and every wheeled

vehicle. Hundreds could be lost in a day, and the need for reinforcements was always pressing.

John Smith, as was his wont, set about his new responsibilities with great enthusiasm and commitment. Being in Aldershot, the traditional home of the British army, he also joined in, and contributed to, the hectic social life which, in those times of long, daily casualty lists and endless slaughter, helped to keep people sane. The life expectancy of an artillery second lieutenant, once he had reached the front line, was four days. It is little wonder that in England everyone was determined to fill those 'unforgiving minutes' of leave, in an attempt to blot out memories, and deaden the dread of what tomorrow might hold in store.

It was on just such an occasion, at a dance at the officers' mess in the depot one Saturday in the late summer of 1916, that John Smith met Beryl, the middle daughter of Charles and Maud Paterson. Charles was a much-loved GP in Farnborough, and their daughter was a VAD in one of the local hospitals taking wounded from the front.

In an interval in the programme of dances that evening, my father and his nurse had taken a stroll, as the young do, which had brought them to the stable buildings. Suddenly, my father heard one of the horses gasping for breath, in a manner which instantly made him realise it was suffering from acute tracheitis. He rushed into the stall, saw the horse was moments from death and, seizing a milk bottle which, fortuitously, was in a corner of the yard, broke off the neck and used the jagged edge to make an incision in the horse's throat. He then thrust in the bottle neck to allow it to breath again. In the meanwhile, the nurse had been dispatched to find help. The horse lived, and John Smith's reputation as a resourceful and fearless vet was further enhanced.

Gaining strength but still suffering, periodically, from recurrent bouts of malaria, my father was at Aldershot until the following summer when, on 3rd June 1917, he and Beryl Paterson were married.

Almost immediately, Lieutenant J. Smith was posted to France, and into the third battle of Ypres which finally, on 6th November, resulted in the capture of Passchendaele, but only after 245,000 British casualties.

Veterinary surgeons accompanied the columns of horse-drawn transport, as, day and night, supplies were taken up to the front and wounded men and, sadly much less often, wounded horses were brought back. Endless processions of wagons, drawn by teams of two, four, or even six terrified beasts, were driven by their human minders into, and through, this hell that was trench warfare in those years. Almost continuously shelled, in all weathers and along so-called roads, men and animals strove to serve the troops at the front.

Nineteen years later, in 1936, my father took his family to Belgium for a summer holiday. One day, he suggested we should tour the Great War battlefields. With a map, he directed our driver to that Ypres battle area.

Soon, we began to pass farmhouses and church towers still unrepaired, and to see walls pockmarked with bullet holes. The trees – and there were still not many of them – were all uniform in height, every single one having been planted over the past few years. Remnants of trenches and pill-boxes were beginning to appear when, suddenly, like a pointer sensing an unseen quarry, my father stopped the car, got out and stood quietly searching the landscape, and his memory. Then he called us over, and calmly described a remembered night along the very road we stopped upon.

He had set out at dusk, from the back area, escorting a long column of guns and ammunition litters being taken up to the rear of the infantry lines for a dawn barrage. As it grew dark, and in pouring rain, the enemy shelling began. By now the 'road' was a sea of mud, potholed with ruts and edged with craters. As the gunners found their range, casualties amongst men and animals began; guns were blown into shell holes, ammunition litters exploded and horses, crazed with fear, bolted or fought to escape their harness. Stores, guns, gear and bodies were strewn around, as so much rubbish dumped on a tip.

The vets with the column, my father included, with their revolvers in their hands, did what they had to. Wounded men could be carried, dragged or lifted by colleagues and ambulance men, wounded horses could only be put out of their pain and panic with a bullet. There was no time, no equipment, no hope of saving any but the least seriously hurt creatures. All the rest were hauled or levered onto the verges or into the craters. The carnage was indescribable, the loss unmentionable. Fresh horses were led up the same wreckage-strewn road, to be hitched to righted wagons and rescued guns, only to be driven on through the same barrage, with the same odds-on chance of a similar fate.

As I, aged eleven, stood beside my father that day, looking at what had been Hill 60 and at Passchendaele, I saw the recollected horror and agony in his eyes, for veterinary surgeons had also, then, to be veterinary executioners.

Years later, seeing him wearing his medals – I fancy it was at an armistice day parade – I noticed he had twice been mentioned in despatches. His answer to my questions about them ran something like this, 'Oh! I've no idea, unless one was for writing, producing and directing a mammoth pantomime, called *Babes in Delville Wood* at 48th Division HQ in France, to keep the troops happy over Christmas 1918'.

He seldom spoke of that war or of his experiences. His inability to save life, to mend the broken, to heal the hurt scarred him deeply and, like countless others who survived, he preferred for history to tell their story.

In the summer of 1919, Captain J. Smith was demobilised. That November, my sister, Diana, was born, and the Smith family had to face the future, in what was optimistically described as 'a fit country for heroes to live in'!

But the health card was played again, this time against my mother and sister who, in turn, were both seriously ill. Whilst they recovered, my father cast about and tried to plan his future.

There is no doubt he wanted to go back to Northern Rhodesia. His heart was there, but he couldn't contemplate taking a young bride in her early twenties, and a daughter of a few months, out to the conditions he had left three years previously. He would, most likely, have been posted to one of the outstations he knew so well. He had seen the health of too many women broken, and the death of too many of their children, to consider such a life for his new family.

He turned once again to the idea of farming. He had quite substantial savings, and his father was prepared to help him but, as soon as he began to study the proposition in detail, he realised that post-war farming costs were such, that it would not have been possible for him to make it pay.

Over the next months, the Colonial Office and the British South Africa Company three times asked John Smith to return to Northern Rhodesia, picking up where he had left off, but he adamantly refused. Then, out of the blue, he was made an offer he found impossible not to accept. He was asked to return as head of veterinary services, at a considerably increased salary and with an agreement that all his past service, together with his war years, would count for pension. He would be stationed at Livingstone, would have one of the houses built in 1910 for senior officials, and rank amongst the territory's government hierachy.

So, the Smiths again began to draw up lists and to scour the Army and Navy Stores for their needs. This time, however, it was a much more formidable task. Apart from their personal belongings, they had to provide absolutely everything for the house and sufficient of everything to last the two-and-a-half years before they would get any leave. Furniture was, normally, provided by the government, but my parents had other ideas, and planned to buy all the furniture and furnishings they would need. This was especially difficult for my mother, who had little idea of what she was going to, or of the life she would be living.

The vet was on his way back to Africa, still only 38 but much matured, from his previous experiences, from his wartime service and from his marriage and fatherhood. The gods had smiled on him – at long last he may have felt – by providing the opportunity he must, secretly, have been longing for. He was returning to the country he loved, to a way of life he knew and understood, to a job he was confident he could do well, and which allowed him the scope he sought. He must have thought that he was, after all, going to be able to fulfil the ambitions he had, for so long, harboured.

John Smith, during those days and nights alone at Maramba, out on trek, in a dugout on the Zambezi or on horseback under a scorching sun, had dreamed of how he could consolidate and develop the agricultural potential of Northern Rhodesia. He had dreamed of how he could educate the natives in modern animal hygiene and husbandry; of how he could establish research stations to improve the quality of all their stock. But, most of all, he had dreamed of a meticulously crafted, and scientifically implemented campaign to combat cattle and horse disease, so that the undeniable potential of that vast area of Central Africa might be realised.

We are now to read something of how he went about trying to realise those dreams, as well as of a Northern Rhodesia quite materially changed since he was last there in 1916.

24

My New Life and My Old

——◆◇◆——

T here were several reasons for the marked change I found in Northern Rhodesia when I returned. Following the end of the Great War, a number of young men moved out there as settlers and ranchers. Activity in the copper mines was stepped up as the administration tried to broaden the base of the territory's economy, and the inevitable changes in every aspect of life which always follow major wars, were making themselves felt throughout the land.

It was positive and exciting. After four years of misery and devastating destruction in Europe everyone, even far away on the African continent, seemed conscious of the urgent need to rebuild and to expand.

In Livingstone, one of the largest and most comfortable government houses was made available to us. Although it was, of course, a bungalow – they all were – it stood in over an acre of land and occupied a corner position, with virtually no other building in sight. Brick-built, and standing on piers to try and put it beyond the reach of marauding white ants, it had the regulation corrugated 'tin' roof, which ensured that no sleep could be enjoyed by anyone during the heavy storms of the wet season. Even now, I can recall the rattle, as of shingle being flung down from a great height.

The house consisted of three bedrooms, a bathroom, a dining room and a central reception area. The statutory front verandah ran the length of the building, and was about 12 feet deep. It was here that the whole family (and visitors!) slept, in a row, during the worst of the hot weather. It was netted in with anti-mosquito mesh and had a cool, tiled floor. A second, open verandah ran along the back of the house, acting as a passageway to all the accommodation.

Sir Drummond Chaplin, whom I first met at my initial interview in London in 1913, was now Administrator of both

Northern and Southern Rhodesia. He called me down to Salisbury soon after I arrived, to discuss my plans.

He was enthusiastic about my proposals and, surprisingly, readily agreed to my request for a substantially increased budget for my department. At the same time, he authorised the building of some additional rooms to our house, which I had told him would make a great difference to the comfort of our growing family.

Back in Livingstone, living temporarily at Government House with my old friend Sir Richard Goode, the acting Administrator, I set about making all ready for my wife and daughter, due to arrive during February. I needed to replan the garden which, apart from anything else, was badly overgrown. With almost unlimited native labour immediately available, it was possible to transport trees of considerable size, and this I proceeded to do. We moved orange and lemon trees; we thinned out the mangoes which bordered both sides of the main pathway up to the house, and we repositioned some palms and papaws. I then had flowerbeds dug and manured for roses and annuals, and generally landscaped the whole area to my satisfaction. All the rain water and, for that matter, domestic water was carried away from the house in brick gullies which ran down to deep ditches surrounding every property, and which were dug alongside the town's roads and tracks. I did my best to plan our garden so that these were concealed, yet could provide irrigation to the fruit and ornamental trees.

In the far corner of the plot, behind the house, stood a brick 'privy', 'the little grey home in the west' as we used to call it. This was equipped with a large bucket, a constant supply of fine sand and a 'tin' roof which made it, especially in the hot season, a place to visit for the shortest possible time! A squad of natives nightly made their round clearing the buckets, using an alley known as the 'sanitary lane', which ran behind all the plots. So much for the more personal side of life!

Our family was served, for just about all the years we were there, by the same team of senior servants, and in this we were most fortunate. We were, I believe, considered good employers. I had moved amongst natives for three years and understood their ways; I spoke several languages, and had managed to acquire a reputation as a good man to work for. Beryl was a fair, consistent and methodical manager, and quickly established a reputation for treating her boys well. Consequently, our domestic arrangements were the envy of many of our friends.

Masange was our head boy, and in charge of the domestic team. I shall always remember his never-failing, Cheshire-cat grin. He was totally honest, slow as a tortoise and a thoroughly faithful retainer. He took a proprietorial interest in everything connected with the family and was known to, and highly regarded by, all our friends. If my wife and I happened to be out at sundowner time and friends arrived, which they quite often did, Masange would insist that they wait a while so that he could pour and serve drinks exactly as he would have, had we been at home. He always collected the mail from the box on the road and, if he found any letters with English stamps, would wait so that he might be told the latest news from 'home'. He was jealous of his standing with the three (and later four) of us, and only Jackson, my personal boy, was allowed near us without his permission.

Masange had been Major Dickinson's servant during the fighting on the Tanganyika border a few years earlier. One morning, when the Germans had launched an attack against their camp, the major was lying prone on the ground trying to co-ordinate a counter attack, when up wandered Masange, at his usual slow pace, with a tray with silver teapot, milk jug, cup and saucer. Battle or not, it was eleven o'clock and time for B'wana's tea!

Despite his exemplary behaviour, Masange was always capable, as are all natives, of losing his wits to an almost extraordinary degree. My wife, soon after her arrival, was giving a rather special, large dinner party for the senior officials and their wives. To ensure that the drinks and puddings would remain really cold (it was still the hot season), she had ordered extra supplies of ice for the cold chest which stood on the very hot back verandah. Just before her guests were due, she decided to make a quick tour of inspection to see that all was well. To her horror, she found the drinks and food laid on the scorching floor. Calling Masange, she demanded to know what was going on. He explained, with a devastating display of basic logic that, as the B'wana (my wife) had ordered so much ice, there wasn't room for anything else in the chest!

Sufu was our cook, tall, handsome and cheerful. He was master in a small kitchen with a huge open range which was alight from dawn to late evening. The temperature in which he worked, usually singing away to himself, must have been getting on for 130° at times but he, too, grinned his way cheerfully through life. He was a considerable chef, and readily learnt new recipes under Beryl's tuition. On a number of occasions, I was more than a little suspicious that Sufu 'had the drink taken', but never seemed able, or perhaps chose not to be able, to nail him on it!

The third of our senior and long-serving team was Jake, the garden boy. We had had a succession of unsatisfactory garden boys from local tribes, so I telephoned 'Dinkie' Jalland, the resident District Commissioner, and asked if he could find me a Marotse native, who might be visiting or had moved south. 'Dinkie' replied that there was a naked, murderous-looking native, well over six feet tall and built with it, squatting outside his office at that very moment, and he would send him along. So Jake joined us and stayed. He was huge: mostly he wore nothing except a wisp of cloth intended to satisfy decorum but, after I gave him an old overcoat, he insisted on wearing it, buttoned up to the neck, regardless of the heat. It became a treasured possession, to be shown off as often as possible.

In the dry season, Jake had to water the garden for six hours every day, from 5.00 to 8.00am and from 4.00 to 7.00pm. This involved carrying two eight-gallon drums of water from the tap beside the kitchen, down to the garden which was laid out in front of the bungalow. To this day, I can see and hear the slurp, slurp of the water as he carried this considerable weight in the rhythmic, almost sensual walk so typical of natives carrying loads. Somehow, white men and women never achieve such grace in the execution of hard labour. The spilt water patterned his progress round the flower beds, shrubs and trees; every living thing needed to be watered, if it were to survive and serve us with fruit and colour.

Jake spoke not a word of English, young Tony not a word of his language, yet they spent hours together, in the garden, chattering away! Rather, Tony did the chattering while Jake grunted. When Beryl and Tony left Livingstone for the last time in 1932, Jake was seen standing by the station platform, huge and seemingly menacing, with tears streaming down his strong black face, wearing his overcoat!

The houseboys, so called because they were the only ones to step foot inside the bungalow, all wore long kansas – shapeless 'nighties' – in heavy white calico which were laundered until they seemed to shine. On their heads they wore matching round caps in the same material. They always went barefoot. This could be quite unnerving as they moved noiselessly around the house. When we had dinner parties, which was at least once and usually twice a week, these boys waited and served, and wore brightly coloured shoulder sashes, each household having its own distinctive colour. With the vases of exotic flowers, and the gay prints of the ladies' dresses, it made a colourful setting for what was a major Livingstone social pastime.

With so many servants – four houseboys, a cook and a gardener – there was precious little for the Europeans to do in the way of household chores. But one weekly routine was never-changing: cleaning the car. Every Sunday, I would get the car from the garage, which was at the end of our garden. Jake would start delivering the water, and I would sponge off the dust and dirt. The houseboys, excluding Masange, who held himself to be above such menial tasks, each took a chamois leather and wiped off my efforts before there was time for the sun to dry and spot the surface. Then I took a tin of Simoniz polish and applied it to the large open Maxwell tourer we ran, small areas at a time. The three boys followed me round, polishing the waxy surface. The ritual was solemnly continued until I, having made a minute inspection of every inch of the car, declared myself satisfied. The team then dispersed with enormous relief as, working with me, they were required to be at least three times as speedy as was their wont.

At least one of our natives accompanied us whenever we went anywhere by car. He, or they, would perch on the wide running boards and hang onto the large sidelights, roaring with laughter, and loving every moment of the precarious ride. Sometimes there would be as many as four boys, all travelling in this manner, along roads which consisted more of potholes than of flat surfaces. Wagons being drawn by spans of up to 30 oxen, and buckboards with two, four, or even six spirited mules raised clouds of dust. It was this dust, which found its way into everything, that dispirited us most. Hot, sweating and dusty humanity is very unchic.

By 1921, there was quite a number more of stores and offices, and the roads in Livingstone itself were somewhat improved.

Our daily routine varied little, although I, as head of a large department responsible for, and to, settlers and ranchers as well as native cattle owners throughout Northern Rhodesia, did a fair amount of travelling. A typical day at HQ went something like this: I would drive to my office, only about a half a mile away, and start work at 8 o'clock. Three or four messengers would stand, all day, outside my door to take messages, run errands and generally look after me. Matapi supervised this, and controlled the team with a rod of iron. At midday, I would return home for lunch – always a light meal – after which I would make a complete change of clothing. Jackson would immediately take the discarded gear and launder it, whilst laying out the next lot ready for later. I would return to the office at 2.00 until 4.30pm, when I would go straight off to play tennis or golf. Virtually everyone took this sort of exercise every day, regardless of temperature, as regular hard exertion is essential in such climates.

There was an 18-hole golf course, the excellence of which was due almost entirely to the enthusiasm of Dick Gordon Smith, one of my closest friends and a considerable golfer. The greens were made of very fine, grey grit dredged from the Zambezi bed and rolled to a hard, flat surface. The tennis club had eight hard courts, and these were seldom vacant from early afternoon onwards.

At 6 o'clock, the sundowner ritual began. This is a time-honoured social routine in all tropical, colonial territories and is, in many ways, the activity that provides cohesion to a life which, by almost any standards, is exceptional. Every European on the 'circuit', which means the government, military and associated communities, would have drinks (little was drunk besides whisky) glasses, soda, ice and a circle of chairs laid out, ready, on their verandahs from 6 o'clock sharp each evening. They and their friends, having changed their clothes yet again would, in a relaxed and unstructured way, call round. Groups of up to a couple of dozen would visit each other for a drink, to gossip and exchange eagerly sought news from home.

In a rarefied and enclosed community such as that in Livingstone in those days, the traditional sundowner hour acted as tonic, morale booster and safety valve all at once. Petty quarrels, jealousies, moral issues and such-like would surface, and be dissipated in the daily presence of a bunch of changing faces. Cliques were frowned upon, routine dispensed with, and a social Paul-Jones between 6.00 and 8.00pm kept the colonials on the straight and narrow, more or less!

As the sun set, parties fragmented, more often than not to go home and change into dinner dress, to dine at one or other of their houses.

Life in Livingstone in that forward-looking, optimistic 1920s was fun. It was relaxed and congenial. We worked hard, considering the climate, and we certainly played hard. With leave coming round only every 30 months, and with no amenities or entertainment beyond what we created ourselves, everyone was required to be a 'doer' and to contribute to the emotional and physical wellbeing of his or her friends, neighbours and colleagues.

Writing this brief account of how our days were spent in Livingstone in the 1920s, I find myself making comparisons with my life before the war, five short years before. So much had changed since I, a 30-year-old bachelor vet, first arrived to take charge of a hundred pedigree bulls being shipped out from England. Almost against my will, I find myself reliving some of those times, most of them gone for ever, and remembering the pattern of my days and nights out on tour or in one of the tiny, lonely government stations along the Zambezi.

Matapi would be standing in the middle of my camp as it was being dismantled, early in the morning, watching each carrier pick up his load and checking it was properly secured, shouting the while, 'comoni, comoni, comoni', this being what he fancied were the English words I would use! Then he would 'encourage' the whole assembly in their own tongue! A strict disciplinarian, he was liked and respected by all. In his blue tunic, khaki shorts, black fez with silver crested-crane badge and bare feet and legs, always with his knobkerry and bunch of assegais in his hand, he looked a difficult customer to tackle. Had it not been for Matapi, this tale would never have been written: he saved my life several times.

My second messenger, Mohenda, was quite different. Very tall and massively built, he had a wonderful capacity for walking or jogging. I once had a very urgent message to be taken from Sesheke to Livingstone and gave it to Mohenda, telling him to whom it was to be delivered. He went to his hut, picked up three assegais and set off at a slow trot. It was exactly 9.00 in the morning. He delivered the letter at 7.00 the following evening. He had covered 180 miles across every kind of country, much of it full of lions; had swum or waded several rivers, and had kept going, through forest and bush, in the total darkness. He told me afterwards that he only stopped three times to eat a little and take some water.

My other senior native was Tolani, who so nearly died of malaria at Sesheke. He had been a cook at Government House, but much preferred to be out on tour. He was, also, responsible for my personal staff. He had found the boy who looked after my clothes and my bedding and who might, I suppose, be described as a valet! I had a curious and unnerving experience with the latter in Barotseland, when I noticed a large, strange mark on his side. I examined it more closely and found it was leprosy. I obviously could not have him handling all my things, and tried my hardest to persuade him to go to one of or government centres for treatment, but he refused, and set off for his village. He was only one of many lepers I was to see on my tours.

My camp was at the centre of my life out on tour, and I had worked at making it as comfortable as possible. My main tent was 16 feet by 14 feet, with a fly stretching across the front, acting as a verandah. This was my dining room! Behind this was an eight feet by six feet bathroom tent, where perishable loads and my personal gear were stowed, out of the wet. The floors were covered with Barotse rush mats, and my bed was properly made up with linen sheets under a carefully tucked-in mosquito net. My folding table had a cloth over it with my toiletry gear and my photographs. I had a small folding chair against which my guns were always leant, ready for any emergency. On the 'verandah', I had another folding table complete with linen cloth, napkin and everything laid for dinner. I also had an easy chair to relax in. Then, out in front, a large fire burned continuously, not an ordinary fire but a huge blaze. It was all very cosy.

About 10 yards to the side, Tolani set up his kitchen: two big tree trunks, cut green, formed the range and, balanced on these, were his cooking pots. A very hot fire was built between these trunks but away from the pots. Tolani would draw the hot ashes under his pots as necessary to provide the heat he needed. I never saw him cooking over the flames. I would see him taking his bread from his 'oven', a large, iron cooking pot on a tripod. He used hops to raise the dough. This was a precious part of his larder, and something he worried about constantly. Each day, he would wet a few hops, ready for bread-making the next.

Beyond the kitchen was the messengers' shelter, a large, strong canvas sheet. Two forked trees were cut and set up in the ground, a long sapling was then cut and laid through the forks, and the sheet spread over and pegged down.

Right round the camp was a ring of fires used by the carriers for their own cooking, and beside which they slept. Just inside this ring, and clearly visible from my tent, was Champagne's stable, at least what passed for a stable. He was secured by his halter to a post or tree trunk, and seemed perfectly happy with his lot.

After a day's trek, at about 6.00pm, I would have my bath. Then, in my pyjamas, I would have my sundowner, two fingers of whisky to the brim with soda. My sparklet bottle would have been wrapped in a wet towel as soon as we made camp, and lodged in the fork of a tree; the breeze caused the bottle to cool remarkably. Then dinner: soup, river bream caught at sunset in the nearest stream, or meat shot during the day. Tolani never failed, even in the pouring rain, to provide me with an excellent hot meal. If I had shot any birds I would have soup, roast partridge and a sweet, usually rice pudding. If I had shot a buck, I would have soup, a joint and a savoury of brains or kidneys on toast. Vegetables would be sweet potatoes when I could get them, boiled rice, boiled nuts mashed in milk or, perhaps, boiled melon, pumpkin or papaw. Often, I had fresh bananas or papaw cut from trees as we passed. After dinner, I had coffee and a pipe, sitting as close as possible to the fire to keep away from mosquitoes. Then to bed at about 8.30 to be ready for another early start.

Sitting by the fire after a long day's march was a great luxury. It could also be very lonely. The camp was quietening; weird sounds were growing from the dark bush; and England seemed a long way away. There was no-one to chat to, or with whom to exchange ideas or worries. That is the time the wise man pours himself one long, decent-sized sundowner, and has the bottle and the soda packed away. Too many have, sadly, tried to beat that loneliness with 'just one more drop' of the hard stuff, and have found themselves on the slippery slope to real trouble. I always drank water at meals and, sometimes, pretty bad water at that.

In lion country, we surrounded ourselves with huge fires and these, together with those of the village a little way off, made a fine sight. After my dinner, I would sometimes sit outside my tent and watch my people gradually drifting away to the village, leaving a few to look after the fires. Soon, I would hear the drums, and a dance would begin which would go on for hours. Occasionally, I would go quietly across, always with Matapi beside me, and hide in the trees to watch. Natives get embarrassed if a European is looking on, and the dance loses its vigour. Usually, two lines are formed, and all begin a sort of humming whilst swaying and clapping their hands. Gradually, they begin to warm up, and one or two will jump into the middle and perform all sorts of fantastic gyrations. They would then retire to the lines and others would take their place, everyone getting more and more excited. Women, with tiny babies shawled to their backs, would twist and turn until one is certain the children will be crushed. This pace of performance can be kept up for several hours, until all are too exhausted to go on. It was a gripping and strangely emotional sight.

Natives have an extremely keen sense of rhythm and balance and move, especially the women, with a grace that is truly remarkable. All family and household belongings are carried, with the babies, by the women. It was by no means unusual to see one, straight as a rod, with a hand on her hips for balance, a baby in a shawl on her back, and up to 100lbs of goods and chattels, all wrapped up in a huge piece of gaudy cotton, balanced on her head. To walk with such a load necessitated a movement that was flowing, rhythmic and bewitchingly graceful. It would be equally likely that the next woman would glide by with a single item, such as a precious umbrella, laid longways on her head. Nothing ever fell, such was the deportment of these women who were, for the most part, utterly subservient to their idle husbands.

My visit to a village would occasion great interest, especially if it had hardly, if ever, been visited by a white official. My tent would amaze the onlookers. As the canvas was stretched out the villagers would gasp, 'Ah, Ki numba fina', 'It is a big hut'. My pony, too, was always an object of great interest and, in the deep hinterland, they were terrified of this strange animal completely unknown to them. They could not imagine anyone riding 'a zebra'.

My impending arrival at a village would have been announced to the chief by one of my trusted boys, who would have gone on ahead. On arrival, and while my camp was being set up, I would inspect all the cattle which would have been collected outside the village. Then I usually went out after game before settling down for the rest of the day. In the evening, a procession would wind down from the village. First would come the chief, then the senior men, then the other men and finally the women, many of them with children. They would come inside the ring of fires and sit down, on their haunches, in the same order. Not a soul in my camp would take a blind bit of notice. I would go on with my writing, or pretend to do so, even though up to a hundred natives were sitting a few feet from me. After a time, depending on what he thought proper, Matapi would come up, salute, and tell me that the chief and his people had come to visit me. I would look up and pretend I had no idea they were there! The other messengers would stand beside my chair, and the carriers would close in to witness the inevitable ritual.

After the initial pantomime, I would say 'Mu Luenelie', 'Greetings'. At this, all the villagers would clap (candalella), my carriers would join in and sometimes it could be deafening. The chief would then come forward, bent almost double, and hand Matapi a couple of fowl, some sweet potatoes, eggs or such delicacies as he could muster as a present for me. Through Matapi ('the mouth between'), I would thank the chief. Then all the women would creep forward with the mukekes (wooden bowls) full of mealie meal. Each placed her bowl on the ground in front of me, clapped her hands and retired into the shadows. I would ask Matapi to thank everyone. He would then give out our presents, in return. Money and salt for the chief, salt for the senior men and silver 'tickies' for the women. These would be placed in the bowls, after they had been emptied by the carriers for whom the meal was given. This would be accompanied by still more candalelling. After this, the 'audience' would be deemed to be over, and the chief and his men would join the messengers and carriers, round the fires, to exchange news and gossip well into the night. I would be brought my dinner, very conscious that all the women and children would still be squatting, watching me, absolutely enthralled. And so would end a real red-letter day in their lives.

On one of my trips, Matapi came to me and told me the women from the nearby village had not been stamping grain, as they were required to on the orders of Lewanika, for my boys. It was a large village, and so I assumed that a store of meal had been prepared beforehand. Time went on, and still there was no sign of the villagers. At last, the Chief and a few of his men arrived. After the customary period of waiting, he was asked if he had brought any food as a present. He replied that his people had refused to prepare food and he wished me to send my messengers to compel them to do so.

I said, 'No. I will not send my messengers. Neither they, nor any of my people, would eat food from a village that defied their Paramount Chief. If they tried to do so, the food would stick in their throats and kill them. They would go to sleep hungry, rather than touch anything from your village. Go back and tell your people to stay quiet this night. The sounds from your village would hurt our ears. And let everyone stay in their huts in the morning, as the sight of any of them would hurt our eyes.'

The Chief was in a terrible state, and I had the greatest difficulty preventing my messengers and carriers from going off and sacking the whole place. But I explained by saying, 'By whose orders are presents brought to us?' 'Morena O mu tunya', 'Our big Chief,' they said. Then I said, 'To whom is the insult?' 'To me or to Lewanika?' 'To Lewanika,' they replied. 'Then let Lewanika settle the matter'. That seemed to satisfy them. I then sent a runner to our resident magistrate, telling him what had happened and asking that action be left to Lewanika.

Later, I paid my usual visit to the Paramount Chief. He said, 'I have been shamed by my people and you, my friend, have been shamed too. The words you spoke were true, your people would have choked with food from that village. But it will not occur again.' A few days after this, I was awakened by the sound of a great many hands being clapped. Every man, woman and child from the erring village was outside, and remained there for an hour, sitting motionless and clapping. It seemed a new Chief had been appointed, and this was the public apology to me.

Natives are a most cheerful people, and they seldom are dispirited, unless they are sick, when their good humour swiftly deserts them. On the march, they always seemed to find something that warranted laughing at, as amusing episodes were recounted and then repeated down the line. When they sensed they were nearing the end of the day's march, one would invariably call out, 'Ki fa kaufi fera', 'It is but a short way now' in a special sing-song tone. All those near enough to hear would chant 'Yes, the way is short'. Then the first man would recite, in the same musical tone, the incidents they had all experienced on the way, and those in earshot would reply, 'Eh! yo, Eh! yo'. The pace would quicken and, finally, all the carriers would run into the chosen camp site, grinning from ear to ear and streaming perspiration.

With that familiar scene before my mind, I dragged my thoughts back to Livingstone in 1921 and to my new life. Maybe, in future, I would not be out on tour with Matapi and several scores of near-naked carriers, but my work would still involve me, every day, with the ever-cheerful and grinning Central Africans.

25

Crown Colony

⟫•⟪

I n 1924, the British South Africa Company's concession,
under the Royal Charter, for both Southern Rhodesia and
Northern Rhodesia ran out, and the territories were given the
status of full crown colony by Parliament in London. This made
a tremendous difference to the administration or government of
NR, as it now became the direct responsibility of the Colonial
Office. All the officials were transferred to the permanent staff in
the colonial service. To begin with, we older hands were not
altogether happy with this state of affairs. It may well have been
that we considered change, any change, as not being for the better.

We now had a Governor, as opposed to an Administrator, and
his powers and responsibilities were laid down by act of parliament
at Westminster. The most immediate change in the lives of senior
officials and department heads was in the expenditure of money.
Hitherto, we made our case out to the Administrator and, provided
he was convinced of our needs he could, and did, grant the funds
immediately. We still had direct access to the Governor on the same
basis but, if the expenditure was outside the annual estimate agreed
by Parliament, the request was referred to faceless civil servants in
London whom, we felt convinced, knew little of the background
of our needs and were not, necessarily, sympathetic to our cause.

There was another, not insignificant, factor. Previously we were
all, or almost all, career Northern Rhodesian men. By that, I mean
we had chosen to serve our full time in that particular territory.
Now, as members of the vast colonial service, we could be moved,
almost without our agreement, anywhere within the British
Empire. Soon after the change, officials began arriving whom we
looked upon as birds of passage, simply serving against their next
promotion, and move elsewhere. We tended to think, not without
justification in a few instances, that some were insufficiently

interested in the territories they were serving. In some cases, however, exactly the reverse was the situation, and we were to work with a number of very committed and professional colleagues. In some respects, we were to benefit materially – as with pensions – which now provided a much-appreciated security factor.

Interestingly, and perhaps surprisingly, Northern Rhodesia was to enjoy a much wider degree of self-government. Whilst Parliament, in London, supervised the actions of the Colonial Office itself, the colony was, in future, to pass its own laws within the framework of the Colonial Office procedures and disciplines. This self-government was to be executed by a legislative council which had, in fact, been in existence for some years, but which was moulded into a more formal and legally bound structure. It comprised a number of members who were locally elected, as are MPs at home, and others nominated by the crown. The latter consisted of the senior officials and comprised, as it were, the cabinet. They were known as the executive.

I was one of the originally nominated members, so found myself with the courtesy title of 'Honourable', which was used both inside and outside Legislative Council, or 'Legco' as we came to speak of it.

I remember our first session as a colony as difficult and, at times, something of a shambles. Everyone had to get used to a totally unfamiliar procedure, to debating every proposal, to the introduction of measures or bills, and to their defence against challenge from the opposition. We soon, however, began to master the new way of doing things, and to enter into the rough and tumble of debate.

For the most part, I enjoyed this new aspect of my life, but found it hard to dovetail in with all my work, especially my trips out to the territories, and with a steadily increasing load of legislative work.

Our first Governor was Sir Herbert Stanley, who was to exert a great influence on our actions in those early days and who was, undoubtedly, one of the ablest men in the whole colonial service. He was, in due course, to be promoted to be Governor of Ceylon and then of Southern Rhodesia. He taught me a great deal. A delightful man to work under and learn from, he was critical, but in a kindly way, and always appreciative of real effort. I was fortunate to get to know him well, early on, when he decided to make a tour of the areas in which European ranchers and farmers had settled, and asked me to accompany him. Travelling and living with him, watching the way he went about his interviews and handled deputations, was of great interest and advantage to me. In the evenings, usually in his coach on the special train, he would discuss the day's happenings and ask my advice on various points that had arisen. It was fortunate that, in the two years since my return, I had spent a lot of time amongst the settlers and had attended most of their meetings. This meant that I knew every one of them personally.

Soon after this trip, I was struck down with para-typhoid. I was in hospital, and in bed at Livingstone for some weeks, and was then sent south to Durban to recuperate by the sea.

On my return, I was fortunate enough to be promoted and placed in charge of all agricultural, veterinary and forestry work in NR together with native agricultural education. I was made a trustee of the Barotse National Trust, chairman of the European Settlement Board and a member of the Victoria Falls Conservancy Board. Three senior men were appointed as my deputies, Colonel Turnbull as Veterinary Officer, Mr Lewin Chief Agriculturist and Mr Stevenson Chief Conservator of Forests. These three now took on all technical administration, leaving me free for the formulation of policy and strategy, and for the increasing load of political work.

Gradually, 'Legco' became one of the principal amusements of the Livingstone wives. They used to sit in the public gallery, whenever we were discussing anything of interest. The whole place was packed when we debated a motion in favour of women's suffrage. Another occasion that aroused widespread concern was when, because of the trade slump resulting in reduced revenues, we had no alternative but to increase the duty on a bottle of spirits by 2/6, a considerable sum at that time. At the end of the debate the president, as usual, said, 'the question is that the bill be read a third time and passed. Those in favour say "aye"'. No 'ayes' were heard, just one long, sad groan which the President was obliged to take as assent. 'The "ayes" have it,' he announced with much reluctance, and with suitable sadness in his voice!

Whilst on the subject, I must recount an incident which, in many ways, was typical of the atmosphere and attitude prevalent in our enclosed society and tight-knit community at that time. Our son, Tony, was just four and had received, for his birthday, an admiral's uniform of which he was tremendously proud. My wife and I were to attend the official opening of the new session of Legislative Council, the equivalent of the state opening of Parliament. I was in my uniform of long white drill with pith helmet, medals and sword. Tony decided he would dress up, too. His governess, Miss Bromley, took him to stand on some steps where all the ceremonial was being enacted. When the contingent of troops, the Northern Rhodesia Rifles, was moving off, the commanding officer, Major Dickinson, could not resist giving the order 'eyes right' to the diminutive, four-year-old Admiral. Tony saluted in return. Such an irreverent incident helps to illustrate how we came to react to some of the more solemn occasions in our official calendar.

26

The Club

———◆◦◆———

T he Club, or to give it its full title, the United Services Club was, and had been from the earliest days in 1907, the centre of social life in Livingstone. Primarily, it was a club for men, although ladies were allowed in the grounds, where they often enjoyed tea after a round of golf or a game of tennis. In due course, a ladies' sitting room was added and, naturally, they were able to enjoy all the amenities at the frequent guest evenings and dances, held every two weeks.

Standing next to Government House in the middle of Livingstone, the building was of brick and in its own grounds. There was a large sweep of lawn with beds of roses and exotic annuals, which were set off against the background of bougainvillea creeper. A squad of native gardeners kept the grounds immaculate in those most inhospitable growing conditions. A broad terrace ran across the front of the building, which was reached up the usual flight of steps. These led to an equally deep verandah which, too, ran the whole length. Opening off the verandah, and part of it, was a large lounge with all the armchairs and sofas upholstered in cheerful, printed fabrics which would withstand the frequent and fierce laundering to which they were subjected. The lounge and verandah were, on guest nights, cleared of furniture and given over to dancing. When I returned in 1921, music was provided by the native band of the Northern Rhodesian police but, after a couple of years, an amateur dance band was put together by members, and I found myself playing the drums! It was an enthusiastic, if not hugely musical, group.

The walls of the lounge area were almost completely covered with a considerable collection of specimen game trophies, from vast elephant and rhino heads down to the smallest buck. Given by members and selected by the committee, so as to ensure that only the finest were hung, we were gazed upon, nightly, by a hundred or more glassy eyes as we sat relaxing or whirled, perspiring, to the limited repertoire of 1920s jazz and dance music. The floor, of highly polished African hardwood, was scattered with lion, leopard and silver-jackal skins. The whole area was sufficiently light, open and airy for it not to bear down upon one with the stuffiness usually associated with the trophy room of a London club.

Most of the bachelor members messed at the Club, which also had a billiard room, long bar, bridge and silence rooms, as well as a library. With so many of the members present for every meal, the finances were on a sound footing, and an energetic committee produced a programme of events which ensured the attendance of virtually all the members.

Guest nights were occasions when everyone always made a great effort. Dinner parties were held at bungalows or at the Club, and dancing began at 10 o'clock, continuing until midnight when, by convention, all entertainment ended. The proximity of the Club to Government House prompted Sir James Crauford Maxwell, the Governor, to tell me on one occasion that his favourite tune was 'Show Me the Way to Go Home' which, invariably, signalled that the evening was over, and that he and his wife then stood a chance of getting some sleep.

The biggest night of the year in Livingstone was, without question, New Year's Eve. An elaborate fancy-dress evening was laid on, and every member joined private dinner parties before heading for the Club. Dispensation was obtained from the Governor, so that dancing could continue into the small hours. We would then repair to one of our houses for a bacon and egg breakfast before driving down to the Falls, still all dressed up, to see the sun rise through the spray. It was an evening and a morning to remember.

In 1922, I suggested to the Club committee that some form of entertainment might be an added attraction to New Year's Eve, if it could be so conceived that it logically climaxed as the clocks struck midnight. Having put the suggestion forward, it was inevitable that I would be persuaded to take the project on, and so began my connection with eleven New Year's Eve entertainments.

I wrote the script and produced the whole affair, enthusiastically assisted by friends and fellow members. From the first little show, I established that we would review major events of the year in as satirical a manner as possible. We pulled legs unmercifully, and woe betide anyone who failed to take it all in good part.

The first 1922 party sticks in my mind particularly. I had recruited the Principal Medical Officer, Dr May, who was also one of my greatest friends, to help put the show together. He was a large, generous and endlessly cheerful Irishman, complete with monocle, the ideal partner for such a venture. We managed to muster up a number of topical sketches, but lacked the finale that would live up to our promise that we would herald in the new year in suitable style. Suddenly, as May and I thrashed about for ideas, we hit upon having his daughter Pat, who was then about five, dressed up as the 'spirit of 1923' and jump through a vast paper clock, just as the hands showed midnight and the gun fired from the barracks. It was an enormous success, and May was to help me run the evening, every year, from then on.

I also remember a rather different, but no less dramatic moment, a few years later. There had been a large fire at one of the stores in the centre of Livingstone, earlier in the year, and we decided to include this incident in our little entertainment. I had asked a couple of young men from the audit department, 'Sticky' Smart and his friend, to help me, and they readily agreed. The idea was to have a blaze going, just outside the Club, which would be visible to the audience. So that it would flare up, dramatically, at the exact moment in the script, I suggested to my two young helpers that they sprinkle a small cigarette tin of petrol on the unlit fire, so that a match would set it off with a roar.

They were determined to make New Year's Eve an occasion to remember in more ways than one. To this end they supported the bar enthusiastically from the beginning and, as the evening wore on, began to see me for a cautious old fogey. They were determined that a proper blaze should background our little sketch. A bucket of petrol should ensure that, they decided! It did! It also very nearly ensured the destruction of the Club, together with 'Sticky' and his pal. But all was well, fortunately, and the delighted pair declared later, 'Well, we got the effect you were after, didn't we'.

I was chairman of the Club when Sir James Crauford Maxwell arrived as the new Governor, a matter of a week or two before the year end. Not knowing his ways, I felt it prudent to go to him with his invitation and explain what usually happened on these occasions. Colonial life, at that time, was hedged about with a good deal of formality and rather obvious officialdom, and I did not want us all to 'step off on the wrong foot' with our new Governor. I explained the scene as it was likely to develop and, after a moment or two, he replied, 'in these circumstances, Smith, I gladly accept your invitation. I shall cease to be Governor from 10 o'clock until 1.00am, and hope that will put you all at ease.' It did, and we saw him laughing no less enthusiastically than the rest as we pulled the legs of everyone unmercifully.

If all this sounds somewhat trivial against the larger scheme of things, I can only plead once again, that we had to make the most of every opportunity we had, or could take. We worked hard, we certainly played hard and we needed, whenever possible, to keep our lives, metaphorically, on the move. Boredom, insecurity and domestic problems could easily have bogged us down into a morass of discontent and depression.

Associated with the Club, but run as separate entities, were the golf and tennis clubs. Sport, in all colonies at that time, and especially those with the hotter climates, was relentlessly pursued by just about everyone. It was not unusual for all eight hard courts to be occupied, throughout the afternoon and early evening, in temperatures of well over 100°. Wide-brimmed hats were invariably worn, by both sexes, and several pounds of weight could easily be lost through one session of tennis.

The golf club was, likewise, extremely well supported, and most of us members tried to get in at least three rounds every week, unless the rains prevented it. The course was very sporting, thanks mainly to 'Gordo' Gordon Smith, who was a plus-two golfer, and a great enthusiast for the game. Such was the reputation of the Livingstone Golf Club, that visitors presented a sufficient number of cups and prizes for a competition to be run most Saturday afternoons.

In 1925, the Prince of Wales paid a long official visit to Southern Africa, and spent some days in Livingstone and up-country. He was an enthusiastic golfer, and played several rounds on our course. He also made several visits to the Club, of which I was chairman at the time. A story, typical of many told of the future King Edward VIII, involved an unscheduled occasion when, at the last minute, he dropped in to the Club unannounced, and attended only by his long-suffering equerry, Admiral Sir Lionel Halsey. Later that evening, there was to be a large dance, at which he was to be the guest of honour, and the floor was receiving a last-minute extra polish. The usual floor-polishing drill was for a native servant to be pulled round the room, sitting on an empty grain sack, until the surface was deemed to be slippery enough for the dancing feet. But, this evening, in honour of the royal visit, a pair of polishing natives were in action. Just as they were getting going, in walked HRH. Quickly taking in the scene, he promptly suggested to the handful of members standing in the corner, that a race be organised between the polishers. This was, a few minutes later, in full swing when in walked the Governor, checking arrangements. He failed to see the competitors, and found himself deposited on the floor as they swept round, energetically trying to win the prize offered by the Prince, whose reputation for informality was given a boost.

On his last evening in Livingstone, a large and elaborate dance was given in the Prince's honour, in the grounds of Government House. The tennis court was laid with a floor and the netting was decorated with, literally, thousands of tropical flowers picked from all the private gardens round Livingstone.

Being a Saturday night, the dance was scheduled to finish at midnight and so, as this hour approached, Admiral Halsey suggested to HRH that he should start saying his goodbyes. 'But,' said the Prince, 'I'm having far too good a time to go home yet... Get the clocks put back an hour.' And they were! The authenticity of this charming illustration of Prince Edward's spontaneous enthusiasm is vouched for by my wife, with whom the Prince was dancing at the time! Ever afterwards, she could smile at the fashionable quip, 'I've danced with a man, who's danced with a girl, who's danced with the Prince of Wales'.

27

Morena, Noka E Eli
(Chief, the River Has Gone)

—————➤•◄—————

Matapi was at the station to meet me on my return in 1921, and I was glad to have him with me again, as he knew my ways. He was the senior messenger of the department, and felt important as having always been with me in earlier days. Matapi accompanied me on all my trips but one journey, in particular, caused him the greatest astonishment.

I was going to Fort Jameson, the post to the north east of the Nyasaland border, the original point from which Northern Rhodesia was discovered and opened up by the Portuguese and by Dr Livingstone and other explorers in the mid-1800s.

Fort Jameson is, today, but a few hours from Livingstone by plane, being about 920 miles away as the crow flies. But in the 1920s it was a ten day journey. We went, by train, through Bulawayo and Salisbury in Southern Rhodesia, to Beira on the coast in Portuguese East Africa. That took four days. Then there was an enforced break of two days before catching a train to Zomba in Nyasaland, which was a 36-hour leg, then two days by car along a so-called road to Fort Jameson itself. There is a true story of this road, just an earth track. Not long after I drove along it, a European bought some trucks and contracted to take our mails and supplies through from Zomba to Fort Jameson. He employed native drivers whom he trained. One day, a lorry on this run came round a bend in the usual reckless fashion of native drivers, bang into the hind quarters of a very large, bull elephant. The driver jumped for it and shinned up the nearest tree, whilst the elephant turned and stamped all over the lorry, hurling the bits, and the mails, in every direction with its trunk. History does not relate how long a walk home lay before the driver!

I took Matapi and Jackson with me on this trip. Neither had been further south than the Victoria Falls, seven miles from Livingstone, and thought Bulawayo must be the largest place in the world, but Beira took their breath away. They saw the sea for the first time, and just stood on the balcony, outside my hotel room, and stared and stared. I watched them carefully, but tactfully. At last, Matapi drew his eyes away and, pale with excitement, asked me how wide was this 'river'. I said, 'You know how far we have come in the train and the car?' 'Yes,' replied Matapi, 'it is a great journey and would have taken us many weeks had we walked'. I then explained that the journey, although long, was nothing compared with the distance this 'river' stretched. 'Mawei! mawei! mawei!', 'Unbelievable! unbelievable! unbelievable!' gasped Matapi and Jackson.

There was a Union Castle liner at anchor in the bay. 'What is that?' they asked, and neither could believe that it was a boat. The only one they had seen, other than the *Naliquanda* and all sorts of dugouts, was the Administrator's launch on the Zambezi. Fortunately, she sailed away a little later, and was watched by my incredulous boys until she was out of sight.

It was all too much for Matapi. He went to the beach and sat there open-mouthed.

The next morning, I was awakened by an urgent knocking on my door. Both natives rushed to my bedside, and Matapi said, 'Morena, noka e eli', 'Chief, the river has gone'. I got up and, as I thought, saw that the tide was out. 'It's all right, it will come again,' I said. 'But where has it gone?' I tried to describe the action of the tide but, not surprisingly, neither could grasp it, and both were convinced that a major catastrophe had occurred.

Matapi spent the morning watching the return of the tide, in a state of complete stupefaction. He had, of course, known the Zambezi rise and fall all his life, but the explanation for that was obvious. I then tried to explain the relationship between the tides and the moon, but Matapi pointed out, with attractive logic, that the moon went away each month and could not possibly pull the water if it wasn't there. I had to give up.

This journey, of course, gave Matapi terrific self-importance. Now he was a man of the world, had seen strange and wonderful places and things, had been where the land ended and a river, which stretched forever, began, where waters advanced and receded each day.

On our return to Livingstone, Matapi couldn't wait to tell all the other messengers of his travels, and of all he had seen and experienced. They dare not tell him, to his face, that he was a liar, but they made it clear that they believed him to have been dreaming.

Matapi now had a credibility problem, and felt his authority to be in jeopardy. So he paraded the messengers outside my office and asked for confirmation, from me, that he had been telling the truth. I didn't, of course, let him down, but the barely concealed smiles on the faces of our audience, which persisted during my explanation, conveyed just how much, or just how little, we were both believed.

The stories of the 'river that never ends' and of the 'water that disappears' will follow Matapi to the end of his days, and will be told and retold around the fires, evening after evening. The smiles and shakes of the head will continue, but, nevertheless, his considerable reputation had been greatly enhanced in the eyes of a people for whom magic is still an ever-present possibility.

28

Mining, Benefits and Problems

━━━➤●◄━━━

T he existence of copper, in this part of Central Africa, was known from the 1880s by several European governments, which were increasingly interested in the exploitation of mineral resources, but which were reluctant to commit taxpayers' money to such chancy ventures. It was against this background that Cecil Rhodes and a score of professional mining prospectors and engineers, began what was to become, 50 or so years later, an industry of world-wide significance. But it was a rough and thorny path they trod.

It was in 1902 that copper claims, with names that are today known throughout the world, were first pegged. William Collier shot an antelope, which fell on a copper-stained rock. The next day, he shot a rietbok and found another outcrop. Shortly after that, he was taken to a third outcrop, not far distant. And so were founded Roan Antelope, Rietbok and Bwana Mkubwa copper mines.

The coming of the railway in 1906 – the 300-mile stretch from Kalomo to Broken Hill was laid in 277 days – led to the opening of the famous Broken Hill workings. Mining in Northern Rhodesia was now beginning to be established, although shipments did not start reaching the world markets for five or six years, and only 24 white miners were actually involved. A worthwhile little boom was under way, but it was short-lived and, by the early 1920s, only Broken Hill was still producing profitably.

This brief history of copper mining needs to be digested against the awesome fact that the area being prospected between the turn of the century and the 1930s was the size of England, with scant mapping and no roads.

The years 1922-25 were to see a new, and much more scientific, approach to the mining possibilities of the colony. The rapidly expanding Anglo-American Corporation entered the scene, as did Rhodesian Selection Trust, and these two giant companies effectually controlled the mining activities in this area for the next 40 years, until independence in 1964.

Health was a continuous hazard. A well-founded, if sour, joke had the railway ticket clerks in Cape Town advise new recruits for the mines, 'don't bother to buy a return, you won't be there to use it!' It was not until the 1930s that rampant malaria began to be brought under control, and the appalling death-rate for blacks and whites alike declined.

In late 1929 came the Great Depression, which started in the USA and spread across the world. Rhodesian mining suffered accordingly, and activity slumped dramatically. The native labour force was reduced from 22,000 to 7000 and the white from 3300 to less than 1000.

Very slowly and cautiously, from 1933 onwards, the industry clawed its way back into full production and profit until, by 1946 at the end of World War II, the copperbelt was one of the world's major producing areas.

Perhaps I can now consider some rather more human aspects of the development of mining in this part of Central Africa.

When work began on new railway tracks, but before it had gone very far, huge quantities of mining equipment began to arrive at the railhead. Some years previously, one of our veterinary officers, Hornby, had discovered that antimony (sodium) tartrate, if injected into the veins of cattle and oxen, protected them for varying lengths of time from trypanosomiasis. A Dutchman, who figures large in so many NR stories, 'Wingy' Werner, knew of this treatment and bid for, and was granted, the contract for hauling mining gear from the railhead to the new, bustling mining areas themselves. He bought a number of wagons and hundreds of oxen, and acquired a squad of drivers so that he could keep on the road continuously.

He and his 'crazy' plan were written off by all; his partner bought himself out of the business and 'Wingy' soldiered on alone. And, alone, he made a fortune, thanks largely to Hornby. He even cut a road through for his wagons, and took on the responsibility for seeing that the thousands of natives employed by the mining companies were fed and watered. He was a genuinely kind man and became known as the mining district's godfather.

As the railway progressed, 'Wingy' had a shorter and shorter haul to the mining areas but, until the rail link was completed, every single necessity of life, and all the goods and equipment, were ox-wagoned in by him.

At last the railway arrived at the mines, and progress accelerated. The need for skilled labour was enormous, and the 'raw' native, seduced from his village by stories of wealth and adventure, was in tremendous demand. He suddenly became a person of importance. Wages spiralled upwards, recruiting teams combed farther and farther afield to find labour, and more and more natives converged on the mining towns.

It must be said that, from the outset, the mining companies did what they could to see that native labour was well treated. They, however, were not the only companies involved. Contracts for roads, buildings and essential services were handed out and sub-contracted, sometimes over and over again. White labour from the south, not always of the most desirable type, converged on the mines. Even farmers sold up and headed towards the 'bright new future' as they saw it. The traffic on the railways increased many-fold and the old track began to suffer, especially in the rainy season, when wash-aways became more frequent even than before. It was at this time that I left Livingstone one Friday morning to go to Lusaka, where the train was due at 9.00am the next day. I arrived in the early hours of Tuesday, nearly three days late, the track having been washed away in several places.

To try and cope with the added traffic, the railway company decided to re-ballast the whole line, and contracts were handed out which, in turn, called for even more native labour. In some districts, scarcely a single able-bodied native remained in the village. Normal tribal and family life suffered in consequence.

Eventually, the first mine began to bring copper to the surface. Townships had been built, roads laid, electric light and water-borne sewage systems installed. Schools and churches followed. In a very few years, attractive land that had remained untouched since the dawn of time, was transformed into one vast industrial area.

Then came the Great Depression. Mining slowed, and then stopped altogether; Europeans and South Africans who had joined the 'rush' climbed aboard trains and headed away from the life of opportunity, hope and freedom; all were disillusioned and lost. Cars, furniture and expensive personal belongings, bought with the high wages of yesterday, could hardly be given away.

The Northern Rhodesian Government also suffered. The facilities for the new population had been provided: school teachers, local administration and the housing and offices to shelter them. The cost had been enormous, and the rest of the colony had to bear it.

The natives were quite simply stupefied. They had neither the experience, nor the education, to understand what had, so suddenly, pulled the rug from under their feet. From being essential to the whole community, with an importance they found to their liking they, suddenly, and for them inexplicably, became un-wanted. Some had the strength of character, and the courage, to return to their villages to pick up their lives where they had left off. But others, and especially the younger ones, had no desire to go back in time or place. They had developed a taste for this new life, had broken away from tribal conventions and routines, and desired, instead, the high wages and good, plentiful daily rations to which they had so rapidly become accustomed.

The mining companies, in times of prosperity and high profits, had treated their labour force well. Food, of a kind never before available, was provided for the natives and their families; accom-modation was modern and, by their standards, luxurious. Schooling was available, and the amenities of European life had begun to be 'the right' of all. It was Christmas Day, every day!

Slowly, as Europe and the USA dragged themselves back from the horrors of depression, work resumed on the copperbelt. But nothing is ever the same second time round and activity, now, was less feverish, and life less frenetic. Europeans and natives returned, but in fewer numbers. Ever-more-modern mining methods began to be introduced, but the labour force required for these was lower. Unemployment was still rife.

The harm done to the native culture by this headlong rush into mining, and the almost-as-dramatic retreat from it, could not be computed. And there can be no doubt that the riots which took place in the mid-1930s stemmed from the unrest of the times of which I have just written.

To provide a balanced view of the development of Northern Rhodesia in those years, one must examine the overall picture. The copperbelt provided income to the colony, by way of taxes and employment, and both were badly needed. Rightly, much of this was committed to the mining districts themselves, but insufficient importance was, I believe, attached to improving the lot of the native population outside these newly industrialised areas. I cannot, altogether, exclude myself from this criticism, although I did endeavour, with the Mazabuka project for instance, to see the industrialisation of Northern Rhodesia as an opportunity to step up the overall education of the native population for its general well-being. The real problem was that the impetus for change, which grew as the mines prospered, was not regenerated after the slump, when the copperbelt again began to contribute to the colony's coffers. But then, even greater industrialisation was the goal, and the agricultural development policy which I had so strenuously advocated was not resumed.

The mining boom, bust and revival was, nevertheless, responsible for much progress in Central Africa. But, socially, it did more harm than good. Plucked from their tribal and village backgrounds, many natives found themselves in a moral and emotional vacuum. For a time, they were able to swim along with their new-found and, in most respects, highly agreeable lifestyle. But what was to happen to them when, growing older, they were no longer the pampered heroes of the labour force? It is a problem being encountered, over and over again, throughout the emerging world.

As I have written elsewhere, despite the many difficulties and problems, I cannot but be convinced that the true future of Northern Rhodesia, if it is to prosper in a balanced fashion, lies in progress in agriculture and pastoral improvements. Such available funds as are generated by industrial progress and prosperity should, I believe, increasingly be spent towards these ends.

29

Agriculture, My Responsibility

The agricultural scene in Northern Rhodesia has to be considered under two headings: the native with his cattle and crops for his domestic requirements, and the European with his farm, run as a commercial operation.

The natives farmed only for their own requirements. They had for centuries herded cattle to answer their needs for milk and meat, and, within their village, grown a patch of mealie-meal which, freshly ground each day, constituted their main source of food. Their cattle represented their personal wealth, and provided the wherewithal for barter and exchange. Cattle were sold for cash, cash paid taxes and bought wives. It could, also, be used at stores to buy cottons for clothing and utensils for cooking.

The history of the European farmers probably starts with H.F. 'Inshlope' Walker. In 1902, 'Inshlope' – his native name referred his mop of white hair – acquired 8000 acres near Kalomo which was, at that time, the HQ of the administration of North Western Rhodesia. He paid £10 per 1000 acres!

A few years later, in 1905, a Dutchman named Josselin de Jong was appointed by that administration to encourage the development of agriculture. In 1910, he opened an office in Livingstone, now the capital of the amalgamated NR provinces, and proved an enthusiastic and popular addition to the small band of officials there. Soon, he set off on a 5200 mile, six-month tour to establish the state of agriculture on the European-owned farms throughout the territory. He also set up an experimental station at Chilanga, where a wide variety of crops were grown and studied, and liaised with the newly formed Farmers' Association at Kafue, although this relationship does not seem to have been an altogether happy one.

This was, effectively, the situation when I arrived in 1913, although I was principally concerned, at that time, with veterinary matters and my assignment with the bulls.

With de Jong restlessly driving forward a positive agricultural policy, the whole scene slowly became considerably rosier so that, by 1921, he could write in his annual report of '...continuous progress and development in almost every direction'. Those last few years had been exceptional for most of the white farmers.

But, as so often, agriculture was set for another period in the doldrums. Because of surpluses, the price of maize dropped, whilst 1922 brought the worst drought ever recorded, with no rain in the first three 'wet' months of the year.

By that year, when I arrived with responsibility for all veterinary matters, cattle diseases stalked the land, agricultural staff numbers had been seriously reduced and the Farmer's Association was far from happy or cooperative.

As I have already explained, I was given an increased departmental budget and considerable support in implementing my plans. J.A.F. (Seamus) Morris, who was my number two at that time, and was to succeed me at my retirement, has written, 'In a very short time, John Smith managed to obtain decent conditions of service, housing instead of tents, transport and equipment. From then on, the department never looked back.'

In those first three years, my time was largely taken up with establishing the situation which Seamus Morris, my most loyal deputy and close friend, described. It was a long, uphill haul against, very often, the entrenched and conservative views of some of the ranching and farming community. The Governor's report for 1924-25 paints the background picture when it states, 'It cannot be said that, in the majority of districts of Northern Rhodesia, agriculture is yet upon a solid foundation. During past years, there has been a tendency to ignore the general principles of sound farming, and to enter upon a policy of planning large acreages of certain crops, with a view to considerable return. Climatic conditions have caused a complete failure of this policy, and the result is, in many cases, financial difficulty. The adoption of this policy, although condemned, is understood. The slump which followed the war was responsible for general depression in agriculture, as well as in other industries. It was felt by many that the return from big acreages of a crop such as cotton would, at the then prices, place them upon a sound financial basis.'

As soon as I had responsibility for all three departments, I set about getting agreement to, and support for, a project to which, over the past few years, I had given much time and energy. My ambition was to set up a major research and experimental station from which everyone could draw assistance, and which would be the hub of our expansion and proliferation programme. It would exceed, in scope and initiative, anything then available in Central or Southern Africa and would, I was confident, alter dramatically and positively the whole agricultural scene in Northern Rhodesia.

Funds were extremely limited in the middle 1920s, due to the reduction in tax revenues, and so, although I progressed all the planning and costings, I had to contain my soul in patience until the establishment of the colonial development fund in 1927. I immediately submitted my project, and asked for the huge sum of £100,000 (*about £4 million today*). To my, and everyone else's, amazement it was granted, and I lost no time implementing the plan.

I had earmarked a site at Mazabuka, and we started on the 17,000 acres as soon as the money began coming through. My first action was to stand on the highest point of the land, with a surveyor and planner, and point out to them where I wanted all the different departments and activities situated. No water was available but, as we anticipated, we struck unlimited supplies underground. We built miles of road, all lined with trees; 22 houses and a large laboratory; created cattle houses, dairies, and all supporting buildings; installed electric light from generators. In fact, we made a veritable township.

The whole project was pushed through with great speed and, only two years from the moment that I pointed out what I wanted from that hilltop, the station was operational, crops were already growing and cattle were breeding.

Mazabuka was all that I had dreamed it should be. It was of the latest design for experimental and research depots, and the equipment was the most up-to-date available. I was allowed to employ 11 qualified staff, immediately rising to 19 for the opening, and rising by a further 10 to 29 by 1931.

I have to admit I was pleased, and not a little proud, as I stood with the Governor at the door to the main laboratory which he ceremoniously unlocked, and when we both signed our names in the new and, I confess, rather elaborate visitor's book which I had ordered from London.

As soon as Mazabuka was fully operational, I arranged for pedigree cattle and sheep of several breeds to be bought in the UK and shipped out. I was particularly anxious to study their behaviour, so that we could start a programme of improving the native herds, and so help stabilise the market price which would, in turn, lead to better stock control generally. At the same time, a programme of pasture improvement was initiated which had parallel aims. The Mazabuka project was as comprehensive as I could devise.

On a lighter note, I thought it would be amusing to arrange for our family names to be perpetuated through these research activities. I therefore directed that the first bull calf born at Mazabuka to a shorthorn, my favourite breed, should be named 'Tony of Mazabuka', and the first heifer, 'Diana of Mazabuka'. I also instructed that, in due course, these two were to be mated, so that our family might always be connected with Northern Rhodesia through the pedigree cattle stud book!

For three years this Mazabuka station made great progress, and the benefits from its early, and short time-span work, were already feeding through to the sceptical farming community. But – 'the best laid schemes o' mice an' men' – 1931 saw the Great Depression beginning to hit Northern Rhodesia. The mines closed, taxes were raised, all non-essential operations were curtailed, and staff retrenchments cut deeper and deeper. The Mazabuka staff complement was reduced from 29 to 21 that year and, 12 months later, lower still to 11.

It was at this juncture that I found myself having to retire. The Governor's report for 1932-33 noted, 'It is a matter of regret that the close of his (John Smith's) service should have seen the temporary curtailment of an organisation which owed so much to his energy and foresight.'

Following my description of the freedom I was allowed in setting up and running the Mazabuka station, I felt it might be instructive to see just how our administrative procedures differed from those in the UK, despite our being answerable to the Colonial Office in London.

A brief story of the foot-and-mouth disease outbreak in 1925 – possibly the most alarming and serious situation in my professional career – will make my point.

One day, we received a telegram notifying us that foot-and-mouth had broken out in Southern Rhodesia. This disease spreads with extraordinary speed, and has to be treated without delay and with decisiveness. It could, otherwise, result in the elimination of every beast in the whole territory.

I saw the Governor immediately, and told him we had no alternative but to prohibit the importation and transportation of all stock of every description and, additionally, all associated agricultural products. I have to admit I did not, at first, appreciate what such a prohibition order meant, or what a long list of 'associated products' would be affected. Take straw for instance: how many things are packed in straw? It seemed to me, as time passed, that practically nothing was not packed in it, including whisky!

The Governor accepted my advice and we closed down: then the fun began. Great secrecy was essential and, additionally, we had to check the legality of everything we said and did, all this with an administrative staff of just four men.

The police were alerted to patrol our borders, and the railway informed that they would have their wagons searched as they entered Northern Rhodesia.

Having stayed up all night making these arrangements, I fixed for a special train to be at my disposal, and set off up north to meet as many of the settlers and ranchers as possible, to explain our actions and give them what assurances I could.

Travelling from centre to centre, I made arrangements for thousands of cattle to be brought to trucking points along the line, so that supplies for the Congo and Northern Rhodesia were assured. Prices rose, as we knew they would but, happily, by not too large an amount.

I returned to Livingstone to meet the full blast from my actions. The Belgian Congo administration had reported to Brussels and our Ambassador was called in. He relayed the complaints to the Foreign Office in London, who passed them to the Colonial Office. A deluge of telegrams flooded into Livingstone. Everyone protested, but we stuck to our guns. After about two months of mounting pressure, I suggested to Sir James Crauford Maxwell that the Colonial Office be asked to call together a panel of experts in the UK to examine all the information we had provided, and give an opinion as to whether what I had advised and executed was correct. I felt I must do that. The Governor was acting on my sole assessment and judgement, and experts from neighbouring territories were protesting, loudly, that we were being unnecessarily restrictive, as our measures had the effect of stopping practically all trade from outside Northern Rhodesia.

The Governor agreed to my suggestion, and action was immediately taken in London. I was most anxious. I knew I was right, but there were those who, many thousands of miles away and without an understanding of local conditions, might suggest relaxations that I had felt were not justified.

Eventually, the Governor sent for me and, passing the decoded cable over, said, 'There's your answer'. The action I had taken was whole-heartedly supported. 'Well, Smith?' asked HE. 'I don't mind admitting, Sir, that a whole load is off my mind'. 'And I don't mind admitting the same,' he said. I have explained this episode in some detail because it illustrates the responsibility which colonial officers have, at times, to assume. In England, this would have been a cabinet matter, and even ministers do not have the powers that an official, through his Governor, has in the colonies. The act of parliament under which I was conducting these restrictions specified certain actions which might be taken, but then continued... 'and he may take such other steps as he may deem necessary'. As my lawyer friend, Gordon Smith said, 'It would take a damned clever lawyer to discover a way round that clause'.

I want to end this brief description of the agricultural scene with a very few words on the deeply-held belief that guided my strategic thinking throughout my time in Central Africa. Northern Rhodesia's social and economic advancement must be based on a sound agricultural policy, and such a policy should not be introduced until its essentials have been thoroughly tested. Hence the importance I always attached to the Mazabuka station.

The territory came to depend too heavily on revenue from the copper mines. These can only, at any one time, employ a fraction of the native population. If the country is to remain settled, and is to progress in social, as well as economic terms, its people must be taught fundamental pastoral and agricultural knowledge and how, properly, to use it. Research, education, sympathetic supervision and a balanced programme of agricultural resources is the formula. Only thus will they be able to provide a continually better and more varied diet for themselves, and crops for barter and sale, on a sound rotational basis, and in world markets.

30

A Momentous Decision

⟽•◦•⟾

As 1932 wore on, my wife and I had to make a momentous decision. Ought we to return to England to live there permanently?

I was due for leave early the next year, and we had already planned for Tony, who was getting on for eight, to stay behind in England when we returned in the spring. The climate in Livingstone was not suitable for children over the age of eight, and no proper education was available to him. Diana had already been in England at school, for five years, living with my brother and his wife at their home in Surrey. We had seen Diana only once in the whole of that time. Were we all to have to endure yet another separation, with both our children growing up thousands of miles away from us, for almost the whole of their youth?

I was pensionable from April 1933 but, because I would be going 10 years early, I would receive only the very minimum amount. If, however, I chose to serve my full term to age 60, I could retire on a substantial pension as, with luck, I would have been promoted into a more senior position in a larger colony, but still in Central Africa. There is irony in the fact that, whilst on my retirement leave in England, I was offered a very senior and well-paid post in Kenya.

Although we talked the alternatives over and over, and agonised about what we should do for the best, Beryl and I knew, in our hearts, that we would reach only one conclusion. It has to be remembered that the only way of travelling between England and Northern Rhodesia was by a sea voyage of 21 days, followed by a train journey of nearly five. Leave only came round every 30 months, and the salaries of that time, together with the cost of travelling, did not really allow even for the wife to 'pop back' to England between leaves.

In September 1932, I resigned from the Colonial Service.

Beryl, with Tony, left for England in October, feeling a double thrill at the prospect of seeing Diana again and at knowing that the days of family separation were over. She was, I know, sad at leaving Livingstone. She had been extremely popular at HQ and at all the out-stations she had visited with me, and she had entered fully into colonial life since her arrival 11 years earlier. But that feeling of sadness evaporated at the prospect of being reunited, permanently, with her now 13-year-old daughter. Virtually the whole of Livingstone turned out to wave Beryl and Tony on their way.

I then settled down to three depressing months, alone in our comfortable house, where the four of us had known so many happy times. When it got to mid-December, I crated up all our personal belongings into two huge packing cases, which I had made from dark, African mahogany planking. I intended to have these used to make a dining table back in England but, somehow, that timber vanished into thin air once we got home! Everything else was to be auctioned a few days later.

I moved into the Club for the last couple of weeks, and my friends and staff made sure that I had no time or occasion to mope or be miserable. I was entertained without ceasing for weeks on end, was showered with leaving presents and mementoes, and overwhelmed by the kindness and generosity shown to me.

I was due to depart, officially, on 2nd January, but I funked having to face the final New Year's Eve at the Club and the Governor, Sir Ronald Storrs, understandingly allowed me to leave three days early.

December 30th eventually arrived. My gear was taken to be loaded onto the train, and I was driven by friends to the station. There a vast gathering, or so it appeared to me, was waiting on the platform and beside the track. All my department, all my friends and the whole crowd of those with whom I had worked and dealt over the almost 20 years since my first arrival, seemed to be there. My hand was shaken until it ached; my cheeks were kissed until they glowed. Taking a deep breath, to steady my emotions and strengthen my faltering steps, I climbed up to the carriage's open platform. Matapi saluted and my household boys, all of them, stood beside the steps with looks of bewilderment and dejection on their usually smiling faces.

Suddenly the guard blew his whistle, jarring into me the final, sickening realisation of what was happening. The hundreds of faces swam, the waving hands blurred. Farewells rang in my ears as, with its usual violent jerk, the train began to move, carrying me away from Africa. I kept on waving, as did they, until all the figures, black merged with white, were out of sight.

I stayed on the platform of my carriage as we passed Maramba, my first home in Africa 20 years earlier, and then crossed the Victoria Falls bridge into Southern Rhodesia. I stood, clutching the railings as the train bucked and rattled over the uneven track, and watched as the 'smoke that thunders' slowly passed from sight and sound.

As the train began to gather speed, I made for my coupe, suddenly conscious that my cheeks were damp with tears.

Epilogue

As the summer of 1964 gave way to autumn, my father's health began to falter until, at Brookwood on 5th November, he died. He was 81.

Had he been aware of it, I feel sure my father would have been amused at dying on Guy Fawkes' Day; it was not inappropriate. He had, on rather too many occasions perhaps, 'lit the blue touch-paper' but, almost invariably, had not then heeded the instructions to 'stand well clear'.

Reading and re-reading the almost 1000 pages of letters and notes, so neatly written that I missed not a single word, I have come to the uncomfortable realisation that, probably, I now understand my father better than I ever did during those 39 years we had together: uncomfortable and a little guilty. But then, for 32 of those he was retired with, as he saw them, his main achievements behind him.

In his field as an agriculturalist and animal husbandrist, and as a veterinary educationalist, John Smith's name was held in high regard, both in Africa and in the UK. He was profoundly knowledgeable, widely experienced and refreshingly innovative. He exercised a balanced judgement and remained calm. He always sought the straight-forward solution, and tackled problems from the practical, rather than the theoretical, viewpoint. Whilst my father enjoyed his early and later life in Britain, there is no question that Africa, once it had him in its grip, never let go. It was in Africa that he was best able to show his true metal and exercise his considerable skills. His vision was of a Northern Rhodesia, proud and prosperous as an agricultural country, and of Africans confident in their success as farmers and breeders of cattle.

But what of that Africa to which John Smith devoted so much energy, and which he loved so deeply? It is but 30 years since Northern Rhodesia grew, rather precipitately it must be said, into manhood to stand four-square on its own as Zambia. Ambitiously pushing the clock-hands of time against their natural pace, this former colony yearns for wider recognition. In the meanwhile, it is being rediscovered as a considerable tourist attraction.

What would John Smith have made of it all? Rather more to the point, what would Matapi, Jake, Sifue, Lewanika, Masange and all the others have made of it? We can never know. Yet, we can guess that their mouths would have dropped open as did Matapi's when, disbelieving, he watched the 'river with no end' ebb slowly away from him.

In December 1938, my father finished the first part of the book I had badgered him about. The letter he wrote to me then contains the words, 'I tried to treat Africa well. It did well for me'.

He succeeded.

John Smith, in Northern Rhodesia and in Britain, played a significant part in laying the foundations of a soundly-based agricultural policy; in educating the African population to a greater understanding of animal husbandry and veterinary hygiene; in reducing the devastation caused by cattle and horse diseases. But – much more than that – he conducted himself, with all those Africans amongst whom he lived and worked, in such a manner that, together, they moved forward to greater mutual understanding, respect and personal regard.

That was his achievement. It was, by any measure, considerable.

At Lealui in 1916 and in London in 1936, John Smith bade farewell to Lewanika and to Yeta III. Knowing they would never see each other again, they used the special words for such an occasion: 'Saila Fo,' they said to each other.

Now let us say our farewell, 'Saila Fo, John Smith'.

Postscript

Livingstone
Zambia
February 1996

I had to come back, even if it meant breaking one of life's more sensible rules! And so, a week ago, I crossed the Victoria Falls bridge and stepped, again, onto Africa's hot, soft sand. Two hours later, I was standing at the very spot where, 64 years ago, I had clutched my mother's and my father's hand, as she and I bade farewell to the Falls, just days before we headed home to England for the last time.

Over the next few days I sought, and in every instance found, the answers to the long list of questions I had logged in my mind.

I found the Maramba camp, where my father had built the stockaded enclosure for the bulls, the hutted village for 200 Africans and the two-roomed house he used as his cramped office, laboratory, store and home. I found the Veterinary Department office, a tiny, shabby, single-storeyed building on whose burning verandah Matapi, and half-a-dozen other government messengers had stood patiently awaiting instructions.

I found the Susman Bros stores, 'Mopane' Clark's Zambezi Trading Company, the Livingstone Hotel, with its five oven-hot bedrooms almost on the street. I stood where once were the manicured lawns and beds of English roses, in front of Government House and the Club.

Then, exploring further, I found St Andrew's Church where, in 1913, my father sang in the choir, stewing in suit, collar and tie, and where my family had worshipped every week. I stood at the font in which I had been christened by Padre Cooke, and beside the altar where Tinker, our smooth-haired terrier, sat patiently throughout the services, waiting to be taken home!

I wandered through Barotse Centre, the once beautifully laid-out and flower-bedded park to which, almost every day, my sister

297

and I were taken, by our governess, to play with the children of other officials. In a temperature of 92°, I walked down the long avenue of huge trees to the barracks and the parade ground where I had watched, wide-eyed, as the Northern Rhodesia Rifles marched past and, with band instruments flashing in the fierce sunlight, dazzled children and adults alike with their ceremonial. Alas, the parade ground and proud memorial are now host to a million weeds and grasses. Then to the golf club, where I saw my godfather's name on the challenge cup honours board, against the years 1913 to 1929. Dick Gordon Smith had been an outstanding golfer, as well as a widely respected lawyer.

On the Mosi-oa-Tunya road, along which now stand government offices, banks and stores, but which, in the early years of our story, was just a dirt track leading to the Falls, I gazed up at the cinema. There, every Saturday afternoon in the 1930s, an old, scratched and grainy 'flick' would be jerkily projected, whilst several Africans walked, continuously, up and down the aisles, dragging huge blocks of ice in what must have been a pretty vain attempt to lower the temperature!

Just minutes later, I stood at the spot where, in December 1914, the Transport Officer, hardly believing his eyes, saw Champagne, exhausted and caked in mud, gallantly carrying the unconscious and half-dead John Smith back to base.

I cruised the Zambezi on a pleasure steamer with a bar, rather than in a dugout with a couple of paddlers, watching the sun set over Zimbabwe, as a dozen hippos played at the river's edge. I even saw a crocodile raise its hideous snout above the surface!

Finally, I found where we had lived. The big tree, from which a 20-foot python had uncoiled itself as my father and I walked beneath its boughs, stood 60 years taller. Memories crowded in, as the African owner's wife proudly posed for me with her four children, puzzled that I lingered staring into the past.

Then, last night, with a full moon flooding down from a cloudless sky, I went again to the Falls and stood, spellbound, as the lunar rainbow, seen nowhere else on earth, gracefully arched the whole scene. The cascading waters sparkled, as if some giant hand was pouring liquid star-dust over the black rocks, and the spray fell, as it had for millions of years, warm and soaking, yet strangely acceptable. The African night sounds amplified as the moon rose. The second hand of my watch, ticking away my trip of nostalgia, was easily read, and the hippos smashed their way through the bush at the Zambezi's edge to leave huge pad marks for us to marvel at next morning.

Suddenly, it was time to leave. Once more I walked to the Falls, pausing to read the words 'Nurse M.G.A. Beaufort, died on active service' on the 1914-18 war memorial which stands exactly where, before the war, my father had picnicked with Judge Beaufort's daughter, one of his Livingstone girl-friends. No wonder he never mentioned her name again.

Beside the Eastern Cataract, I stood saying my farewell. The sun blazed down, the temperature pushed towards 100°, and the falls, swollen with rain from the previous week, looked more magnificent and awesome than I ever remembered.

Standing there, I rehearsed, for the umpteenth time, my reasons for editing my father's letters and writings into this book.

There were three. First, I wanted to record what an ordinary Englishman experienced and achieved, deep in a remote African colony, 50 years before that continent changed more dramatically than anyone believed possible. I wanted to publish a piece of history, albeit a modest and local one, but one which might help the student of tomorrow to complete the jigsaw that is the story of Central Africa.

Next, I sought to make a tiny, but relevant, contribution to the debate which questions the merits and motives of Britain's colonial rule. It is now fashionable, often without sufficient thought or understanding, to denigrate the whole imperialist era, the hundred or so years prior to most of our former possessions achieving independence. Two experienced observers, Sir Ralph Furse and Vernon Brelsford, have written, 'The Colonial Service, with its direct human contacts, calls for patience and good manners, for courage and decision, foresight, a sense of humour and imaginative sympathy' and 'In Africa, the colonial era lasted only about 70 years, a brief episode, but one during which the Colonial Service established law and order, developed health, education, agriculture and economic services over vast areas, from scratch and on financial shoestrings'.

My third reason was personal. I believed my sister and I had never fully appreciated how much our parents had given up when, long before they needed to, they had retired so that both of us could be properly educated from a family home in England. My father, in 1932, was a successful colonial servant, held in high personal and professional regard who could, reasonably, have expected to be in line for further promotion. My mother, too, enjoyed the life and was happy with her lot. But, unselfishly, they put their children first. Perhaps their story will give proper recognition to that devotion.

My father, in that Christmas letter to me, wrote, 'I hope you will always remember those natives whom you knew, and who looked after you so well'.

Behind all the smiling Africans, with their broad grins and infectious laughter, waving me goodbye, I sensed Matapi, Sufu, Jake, Masange and all the others waving too, and smiling their approval.

I would remember them, always.

Index

Entries under Smith, John have been confined to those sub-headings which cannot be readily found under other entries. His name in other entries has been abbreviated to J.S.

barges 58, 183-4, 189, 243-4

Barotse, National Trust 270

Barotseland native reserve 38, 55-6, 83-4, 145, 158, 176-7, 180 *see also* Maraman's village, Mongu, Sesheke
   British control 245
   cattle dying 213, 222
   lepers 262
   Lewanika rule 69, 84 *see also* Lewanika
   Livingstone journey 150
   native
      Commissioner 88
      police 143
   protectorate 243
   quarantine line 214, 216, 218
   telegraph line 178, 193
   tribes 29, 55, 157, 236, 240, 242, 245

Basuto Evangelist Mission 15

Beaufort, Duke of 11

Beaufort, Judge 37, 247-8, 299
   and Lady 37, 200, 209-10, 225, 229-30

Beaufort, Miss 206, 210, 227, 235, 237, 299

Bechuanaland 24
   kitchen boy 131

Bechuanas 158

Beesley general store 25

Beira 277-8

Belgian Congo 3, 31, 206, 220-1, 243, 289-90

Belgium, Great War battlefields 251-2

Bellis (District Officer) 228

Berlin Conference (1884-5) 29

Berringer, Mr (Native Commissioner) 176

Berringer, Mrs 233

Bindo Wina's village, Zambezi river 181

Jackson (personal boy) 257, 260, 278

Jake (garden boy) 258-9

Jalland, Mr and Mrs 'Dinkie' 210, 258

James, Captain and Mrs 133

Jameson, Sir Starr (Dr Jim) 13, 30, 60, 232-3

Johannesburg 18

Jones 213-14, 217, 223, 225

Kachekabwe rapids 76, 78

Kafue
    Farmers' Association 212, 226-27, 285-86
    river 29, 114-15

Kalamhora's Village (Zambezi) 61-6

Kali rapids 190

Kaliangula 103, 105-6, 108, 110

Kalomo, North Western Rhodesia 23, 225, 285

Kasai River 66, 68, 100

Kasama 208

Katima Mulilo 75, 83, 190

Katombora 143, 172, 193-6, 247

Kenley 8

Kenya 30, 292

Key, Sir John and Lady 60

Kimberley 20-1

King George V and Queen Mary, photograph 70

King's African Rifles 50

Lake Tanganyika 235

Lancashire County Council 6

Lane, Mr (veterinary boss) 88, 200, 202-3, 206, 234
Barotseland 214-15, 221-2, 224, 226-7, 229, 234, 236
and Mrs 207, 210-2, 215, 229, 231

Lazard, Mrs 224

Lealui (Lewanika's state capital) 169-71, 236, 242-4, 296

Leashimba (Litia's Prime Minister) 133, 145-6

Lekorongoma, village 159

leopard 239-40

Lewanika (Paramount Chief of all Barotseland) 29, 55, 58, 68-9, 71, 80-1, 83-4, 110, 119-20, 122-3, 131, 136, 146-7, 158, 168
brother 244-5
cattle 176, 213-14, 235
Champagne (horse) 58, 169, 175
compass 244
death (1916) 236-7, 241-5
dugout canoes 183, 240
farewell 243-6
Germans crossing 176
gifts 179-80
indunas 169-71
inner council 158
orders to village women 266-7
palace 171
Prime Minister (Sopi) 172-4
questions about the war 173
sisters (Moquai) 185
state barge 183
state visit 169-76
territory 163, 222
unofficial visit 178

Lewin, Mr (Chief Agriculturist) 270

Likopi, Barotseland 176-7

lions and ponies 99, 142-51, 163, 264

Litia (son of King of Barotse tribe) 55, 69-72, 74-5, 79-81, 83-87, 89-90, 110, 121-4, 127, 157-8, 172, 190, 242
cattle disease 236
eye trouble 147

Queensway 24-5
recall to 143
St Andrew's Church 58, 297
supplies for Maramba camp 34-5
telegraph line 191
United Services Club 24-5, 38, 50, 196, 233, 272-6, 293, 297
veterinary
    department 25, 191, 193, 202, 215
    officers 44, 142, 150, 181
    services, J.S. head of 193, 202, 253

Livingstone, Dr David 28, 72, 83, 100-1, 106, 277

Livingstone Island 32

Livingstone Mail 234

Livingstone/Cape train 147

Livingstone/Sesheke 89

Loanja river 153-6

Lobengula 13, 81, 158
    Chief (Zulu) 22, 83
    Impis 157

Lobengula/Lewanaika story 83

Lochner, Frank E. 29

London 11
    Colonial Office 202, 253, 269, 289-90
    Secretary of State, special adviser 10
    Roadcar Omnibus Company 6
    War Office 214

Loveday Committee on Veterinary Education 9

Lower Machile River 126-7

Lozi tribe 29

Lubassi (son of Lewanika) 186-7

Lumbi (stream running into Zambezi) 161

Lusaka (now capital of Zambia) 47-9, 52, 233-4, 282

Lusitania, sinking 218

Luton 6-7

Index

Wallace, Sir Lawrence (Governor) 24, 42, 44, 202-3, 208, 213-14, 216, 219-23, 225-9, 234, 237

Walmer Castle 18

Wardell, Mr 15, 17

Wardroper (new clerk) 216, 222, 226

Warrington (Montu Native Department) 168

Welencky, Sir Roy 30

Werner, 'Wingy' 281-2

Wigan 3, 7, 13-14, 33, 36, 122
    family 247
    Smith's Progress Works 3, 180

Woods, Mr (assistant to J.S.) 21, 208

Woods, Mr (brother) 31

Woods, Mr (college examiner) 13, 191

Wooldridge, Dr W.R. 11

World War I 3

Yeta III 172, 243, 296 *see also* Litia

Yule, Miss 11

Zambezi river 65, 88, 94, 99-101, 104-5, 153, 161-4
    Administrator's launch 278
    Arnot, M, burial 103
    Bagnall Smith, Tony, cruise 298
    banks 79, 159
    birds 112
    crocodiles 42, 89
    dugout canoes 31-3, 56, 74-8, 253
    fish 53
    government stations 261-2 *see also* Mongu, Sefula
    hippo shooting 136-7, 147-50, 181, 192
    island 32, 81
    letter written on 238-41
    mail 66, 100